# ONCE A HUSSAR

# ONCE A HUSSAR

## A MEMOIR OF BATTLE, CAPTURE, AND ESCAPE IN WORLD WAR II

## RAY ELLIS

Skyhorse Publishing

First published in Great Britain in 2013 by Pen & Sword Military, an imprint of Pen & Sword Books Ltd

Skyhorse Publishing books may be purchased in bulk at special discounts for sales promotion, corporate gifts, fund-raising, or educational purposes. Special editions can also be created to specifications. For details, contact the Special Sales Department, Skyhorse Publishing, 307 West 36th Street, 11th Floor, New York, NY 10018 or info@skyhorsepublishing.com.

Skyhorse® and Skyhorse Publishing® are registered trademarks of Skyhorse Publishing, Inc.®, a Delaware corporation.

Visit our website at www.skyhorsepublishing.com.

Typeset in 11pt Ehrhardt by Mac Style, Beverley, E. Yorkshire, United Kingdom

10 9 8 7 6 5 4 3 2 1

Library of Congress Cataloging-in-Publication Data is available on file.

Jacket design by Jon Wilkinson

Print ISBN: 978-1-62873-729-5
Ebook ISBN: 978-1-62914-081-0

Printed in the United States of America

# Contents

*This book is dedicated
To those of my comrades
Who grew not old.*

## Chapter 1

# In the Beginning

My father survived the horrors of the First World War, where he served in the Royal Garrison Artillery, and returned home from France in 1919, which was very fortunate for me because I was born in 1920.

My early years were spent in a troubled world that was still reeling from the shock of the recent conflict. The people of Britain were desperate to forget the miseries of the war years whilst they struggled to cope with the problems of a changing way of life. These were the days of silly fashions and exaggerated gestures, when it was considered smart to dance the Charleston and for women to smoke cigarettes in long holders. Motor cars were now a common sight on the streets and almost every city had tramcars and motor buses, which made travel a great deal easier than it had ever been. Although people still worked long hours, holidays beside the sea were becoming popular during the summer months, but in spite of such changes there was still a great deal of poverty and unemployment as the country was going through a period of depression, and dole queues were a common sight. Some people were desperately poor and had to subsist with the aid of food tickets issued to the needy by the Board of Guardians.

The large majority of homes were without electricity and although many houses had gas lighting some still had to make do with paraffin lamps or candles as a means of illumination. Radio and television were things for the future and for me, as for many other children of my age, a visit to the cinema to watch a black and white silent film was a rare treat. I do not recall having many toys – they were things to dream about – but to compensate I did have the vital element of freedom, which enabled me to wander the countryside around our home without fear of molestation.

My formal education commenced when I was five years of age, but for me school was not a very happy place, largely because my temperament was not at all suited to the conditions imposed by mass education. It would be surprising if any of my teachers remembered me with any degree of warmth because I was far from the ideal pupil. It was not that I was cheeky or disobedient – my upbringing made such behaviour unthinkable. At all times I was very polite and I really did try hard to please my teachers but, alas, with little success. They said that I had a good brain but was far too lazy to use it to any advantage. The teachers always complained I was too easily distracted and spent far too much time daydreaming. The latter was certainly true.

The truth of the matter was that I was bored to distraction for most of the time. There was too much 'chalk and talk' and little opportunity to use one's own initiative, hardly any visual aids to the teaching and no individual attention whatsoever. Everything was served up in huge chunks of knowledge, delivered in long, tedious oral lessons which droned on and on and on, and I would quietly slip away from it all, becoming lost in my own thoughts. Often, at the end of a lesson, a furious and frustrated teacher would discover that I hadn't heard a word that had been said. I must have been a very trying pupil!

In spite of my unco-operative attitude and lack of industry, I quickly learned to read. This was one of the greatest blessings of my life and my everlasting thanks go out to those underpaid spinsters who gave me this skill. (There were no married women teachers in those days.) Reading opened the door to a whole new world and I took full advantage of this wonderful gift, reading almost everything that came to hand. I loved reading and consumed books with an insatiable appetite.

In many ways I had a good home, and compared with many of my schoolfellows I was showered with the good things of life. There was always an abundance of wholesome food, all my physical needs were well catered for and there were books that fed my imagination with a host of fascinating ideas that found an outlet in my play. Tales of Robin Hood, Coral Island, Treasure Island, stories from the Great War and history, sea yarns, tales of the outback or the prairies, cowboys and Indians: these were the stuff of which dreams were made. The heroes were always men of courage and integrity, there was no dallying with half-measures, no making of excuses for those of evil intent, and cowards were not to be tolerated under any circumstances. Things were black or they were white; men were either goodies or they were baddies – and the goodies always won, or they died with their faces towards the enemy, steadfast to the end.

I often feel sorry for the children of today, surrounded as they are by expensive toys, radios, televisions, computers, electrical robots of various kinds and numerous plastic articles that carry the name 'toys' but are really just useless lumps of synthetic material. It is sad to see healthy children, bursting with energy, trapped in stuffy, overheated rooms. They have their eyes glued to television screens, while outside the sun shines on empty woods and fields and birds fly unheard and unseen by a generation of children who have lost the freedom that we enjoyed so much when I was young.

During those early years I spent some of my happiest hours with my two older brothers in a hut which father had built for us in the garden. It was constructed from sheets of corrugated iron, nailed to a framework of timbers. In the hut was a slow combustion stove that stood on a stone slab, and there was a long stovepipe chimney that went up through the roof. This hut was the focal point of all our games. Sometimes it was a dugout on the Western Front, from which we would sally forth with bayonets fixed to charge the German enemy across the mud of Flanders. On other days, with smoke pouring from the chimney, it became the engine room, or the bridge, or both, of a destroyer battling against the stormy winds of the North Atlantic. On cold, winter days it was often a trapper's hut or an outpost of the Royal Canadian Mounted Police in the frozen Yukon. In summer it could easily become a covered wagon from which we fought off hordes of savage, painted, screaming Red Indians.

It was in this way that I played my way through my boyhood days. I was brought up to know where my duties lay. First to serve God by trying to be good. Then to be fiercely patriotic and to serve the King by being brave. I was to emulate the spotless knight, the unsullied hero, the faithful comrade and the soldier who went unfalteringly into battle. All this was rather a tall order for a thin and rather timid little boy who was afraid of the dark and who wouldn't have dared say 'Boo' to a goose.

Most of our games revolved around fighting and killing. The influence of the Great War was still very strong, and death in battle was an accepted part of our play. We would throw up our arms and crash to the ground feigning death from machine-gun bullets, shrapnel or shell splinters. When I became a soldier many years later, no one had to teach me rifle drill: I had become familiar with that long before I was ten years old. I shall never know how many years of my childhood I spent marching up and down our garden path with an air rifle on my shoulder. Being the youngest brother meant that I was always the most junior rank in whatever game we were playing. George and Rupert, my two brothers, could be captains or colonels, even generals if they so wished, but I was always the poor old private soldier flogging up and down the garden path on sentry go. A fitting augury for what was to follow!

During my teenage years my brother Rupert was transferred to another branch of the company which employed him and this meant that he had to leave home and go to live in Northampton. I well recall the great sense of loss I felt when he went away and the eagerness with which I greeted his return each weekend. Almost every weekend for three or four years he came home on Saturday evening in order to spend Sunday with us and in all that time I don't think I ever missed being at the Midland station in Nottingham to meet his train which arrived at eleven o'clock.

How well I remember the excitement of waiting on the old station platform with the powerful engines wheezing and puffing as the trains came and went in a flurry of noise and smoke and steam. There was something very special about a railway station in the days of the steam locomotives; it had its own exciting sounds and smells and a uniquely exciting magic that made it very special. This glamour was to disappear along with the magnificent, fire-eating locomotives that hauled the trains and dominated the whole scene with their majestic presence. I used to love standing there amid all the smoke and bustle watching the minutes tick by on the old station clock as I waited for the train to arrive. We became quite good friends, that clock and I. Forty years later, when the Midland station was refurbished, an enthusiast who lived in the village of Thurgarton purchased this same clock and had it mounted at the side of his house overlooking the road. Nowadays, whenever I pass that way, I always give my old friend an affectionate wave and I am sure it nods to me in return as it keeps ticking on and keeping perfect time.

Towards the end of 1937 my eldest brother George married Barbara Collins in St Mary's Church in Arnold and it was a very happy occasion. I don't think George had ever had another girlfriend and I am pretty certain that he was the only boy she had ever considered, and so their marriage seemed to be as natural as the sunrise. They went to live in a house called Meadowside, which was situated on Spring Lane. Fortunately it was only about half an hour's walk across the fields from home. I say 'fortunately' because George and I, as well as being brothers, were also close friends and we spent a considerable amount of time in each other's company. Barbara and I were also on close terms and I was always sure of a warm welcome whenever I visited them. That was a good thing because I seem to remember that hardly a day passed without us making some form of contact.

In common with most young men I was attracted towards the opposite sex, and I became infatuated with a very pretty girl named Sylvia. I managed to make her acquaintance, but I was far too shy to make my feelings known to her. However, it chanced that we used the same bus into town and so we became travelling companions, and as time passed we became close friends. She was a very attractive young lady, very sweet and kind and with a delightful sense of humour. There were several other girl friends of course, but Sylvia was the special girl of my teenage years. Later on, during the war, she wrote to me regularly for almost three years and her letters brightened many an unhappy day for me.

A continual backdrop of international tension accompanied the years of my transition from boyhood to manhood. The growing strength of Germany under the Nazis was causing grave concern in some quarters and there was anxiety about the Italian Fascists under their bombastic leader Mussolini. It was during this period that I became accustomed to seeing pictures of hordes of fanatical Nazis waving banners of swastikas and screaming 'Sieg Heil, Sieg Heil' as Adolf Hitler passed by in his open car giving the Nazi salute. The face of Benito Mussolini was a familiar sight and the names of Ribbentrop, Count Ciano and Anthony Eden constantly claimed the headlines as more and more countries were invaded and annexed. There were sinister tales of things called concentration camps, where Jews and political prisoners were said to be kept in appalling conditions, often being tortured and put to death. The Rome/Berlin Axis loomed threateningly over Europe and it cast its shadow over all our lives.

With all this going on it gradually became apparent that we were heading towards another war. Not in this case a war to expand our Empire or to further the political ambitions of a king or leader, but a war to protect our country and our way of life from something that was fundamentally evil. New words were added to our vocabulary, words like Dictator, Totalitarian, Blitzkrieg, Panzer, Fuehrer, il Duce, and … Air Raid!

The thought of another war approaching must have filled my parents' generation with despair. They had already experienced the horrors of the Great War with its awesome casualties, and now, so soon afterwards, another conflagration could be seen rolling inexorably towards them. To make matters worse, the disarmament lobby had been holding sway to such an extent in the intervening years that all our defences had been cut to the bone. It became apparent to everybody that we were ill-prepared for any sort of conflict, and at the same time it was realised that the Axis Powers had formidable strength and were poised to strike against us. The Spanish Civil War had opened everyone's eyes to the horror of aerial bombardment on large centres of population, and there was the dreadful realisation of what could happen if planes dropped bombs containing poison gas as well as high explosives.

The political background to all this can, of course, be read elsewhere: the Polish Corridor, Neville Chamberlain's visit to Munich, Hitler's false promises, Stalin's war against Finland and his treaty with Hitler. All these political moves and countermoves were to affect the course of history and cost millions of lives, but my purpose here is merely to relate how they affected my own humble life at that time and how I reacted to the situation as I saw it.

It was in 1938 that we all began to waken to the idea that the country was in danger and every young man worth his salt wanted to play some part in its defence. It was a period when everyone seemed to be joining some organisation, such as the Auxiliary Fire Service (AFS) or the Air Raid Precautions (ARP). Some people became air raid wardens and others joined some branch of the armed forces. I first considered joining the Royal Navy, and then I had ideas about the Fleet Air Arm. I also toyed with the idea of going into the Royal Air Force and looked at lots of brochures and recruitment advertisements, but it was the Army that was always at the back of my mind when war was discussed. I could not see myself as anything but a soldier and so, without consulting anyone, I joined the Territorial Army.

It must be confessed that my knowledge of the British Army at that time was scant. I was very impressed with all the Guards Regiments, but I was more familiar with our local infantry regiment, the Sherwood Foresters, and it was with the full intention of joining their ranks that I set off for the drill hall in Nottingham on one fine evening in 1938. How strange it is that the very simplest of things can have far-reaching effects upon our lives. Although I was not aware of it at the time, the whole course of my life was to hinge on a decision I was to make that evening. It was a decision that I was to make very carelessly and nothing more than a simple noticeboard influenced my thinking.

This noticeboard was the first thing to catch my eye on my arrival at the drill hall. On it was a colourful sign that read: 'SOUTH NOTTS. HUSSARS'. The truth was that I had never ever thought of myself as anything but an infantry soldier, but now, suddenly, a new possibility had emerged. I could be a Hussar! It sounded very glamorous and I could see myself on horseback, wearing a colourful uniform and wielding a sabre as I charged into battle. The fact that I did not know how to ride a horse did not immediately occur to me. It did not seem to concern them very much at the drill hall either, for when I went inside and asked if I could join their ranks they raised no objections at all!

After giving some details to a sergeant I was taken, in company with another young fellow, to meet an officer, in front of whom I swore an oath of allegiance to King George VI and promised to protect him against all his enemies (rather a tall order, I thought). The officer who was conducting this ceremony winked at me whilst I was repeating the oath and, thinking that he was making light of the whole affair, I winked back. It was only later that I discovered that this officer had a nervous tic that caused him to wink from time to time. I have no recollection of any medical examination but this must have taken place at some later stage. All I remember is putting my signature on a couple of documents and discovering that I had become a Hussar. I was now a soldier in the Territorial Army and I was eighteen years of age.

It soon became apparent why my lack of equestrian skill had not troubled anybody: there were no horses to ride. The modern army was mechanised, they said. It was explained to me that the regiment was proud to keep its Hussar name even though it was no longer a horsed cavalry unit. It was now part of the Royal Regiment of Artillery and was equipped with two batteries of guns. The full title was the 107th Regiment, South Notts. Hussars Yeomanry, Royal Horse Artillery. The regimental badge was a silver acorn with four oak leaves, signifying our proximity to Sherwood Forest, and the regimental colours were red, yellow and blue. The two batteries were numbered 425 and 426, and I found myself in 425 Battery, which was equipped with 18-pounder guns. The other battery had 4.5 howitzers.

That evening I was introduced to the 18-pounder gun by a sergeant; he reeled off the names of all its component parts with bewildering rapidity, and I forgot them again with the same turn of speed. Then it was time to start with my first gun drill. The other recruit who had joined with me was trying hard to be smart and soldierly, just as I was, but we both tried a bit too hard and finished up stamping on each other's feet. That was the start of a long friendship that only ended when he was killed by shellfire in the Western Desert south of Tobruk. His name was Fred Lamb and when the session finished that evening we made our way to a nearby pub to drink our first pint together. It was to be the first of many. Fred was an exceedingly nice fellow, always quiet and reliable, and he was to prove himself to be a true friend.

When I arrived home that evening and announced that I had joined the 'Gunners', there was some consternation in the family. They were worried and said that I was both stupid and headstrong to go rushing in without a moment's thought to join a combatant unit that could place me in the gravest personal danger in the event of war. How right they were, as I was discover to my cost in the years that followed, but at the time I was full of the glamour and excitement of being a soldier.

My memories of those final months of peace seem to contain little else than the preparation for war that was going on all around me. There was a sort of war fever that infected almost everybody; no one had any doubt that it was coming and it was almost as if people were hoping that it would start in order to get rid of the anxiety that accompanied the waiting.

I became involved with my duties as a soldier in the Territorial Army, attending drills in the evenings and also, very often, at the weekends. I was issued with a uniform that comprised a service dress tunic with ball buttons, riding breeches and spurs, leather belt, peaked cap and a white lanyard that they said commemorated some battle honour. It was all very exciting; I was brim-full of patriotism and regimental pride and found every possible excuse to wear my uniform.

By this time my brother Rupert was working in the city of Sheffield. He had also joined the Territorial Army and was in a Sheffield unit of the Royal Army Ordnance Corps. This only left George, my eldest brother; of course he was married and therefore had greater responsibilities than Rupert and myself, but he also wanted to share in the excitement of the times. Everybody prevailed upon him to use discretion; they urged him to find some other form of national service or at least to select a non-combatant unit in which to serve, but instead he followed my example and joined the South Notts. Hussars.

Apart from the feverish preparations for war, everything else carried on as normal. I still spent some of my leisure time with my girlfriends, but more often I was with George during the evenings and weekends. We were the closest of friends as well as brothers, and we were now in the same regiment, the same battery and even the same troop, and consequently we spent a considerable amount of time together.

During the June of 1939 we went to firing camp at Redesdale, where there was an army gunnery range in the middle of the Cheviot Hills in Northumberland, just south of the border. My first sight of these hills was very daunting for it was about five o'clock on a cool, wet morning after a virtually sleepless night. The previous evening had been spent drinking with friends before reporting to the drill hall at ten o'clock. After assembling we had marched to Victoria station to climb aboard a specially chartered train that left just before midnight. We were all carrying bottles of beer in our packs.

And so the drinking continued for several hours until we all fell into a restless sleep, only to be awakened on our arrival at five o'clock in the morning. Staggering from the train desperately tired and with a fair-sized hangover, we had to climb onto open lorries for the journey from the station to the camp, where we arrived cold and wet and thoroughly miserable. My only thought was for sleep. I looked forward to a good, hot breakfast before climbing between my blankets for some much-needed rest and warmth.

Breakfast was neither good nor hot; it was a piece of stale pork pie with oily tea from a dixie that had been in store for a year and still bore traces of the thick grease with which it had been coated. We then had to make a start erecting bell tents in the pouring rain on a muddy field and by this time all our personal equipment was soaking wet. My head was throbbing as one by one the tents were erected and how I looked forward to the moment when they would be allocated. I fondly imagined rolling myself in a blanket and closing my weary eyes in sleep. It was eight o'clock before we finished and I found myself standing on parade listening to the orders of the day and then I realised to my horror that there was to be no sleep. The day was only just beginning and we were faced with hours of hard work: gun cleaning, marching and rifle drill and gun drill. I think that was the longest day of my life up to that period and it was just a taster of the things to come.

At the end of the first week we were to be granted a day's holiday and coaches were provided to take us either to Whitley Bay or to Newcastle, according to choice. I was really looking forward to this outing, but needless to say I was detailed for guard duty on the Saturday evening. So, whilst my friends were all clambering light-heartedly aboard the coaches, I was sitting rather dejectedly in my tent, polishing my equipment in preparation for the guard-mounting ceremony. It seemed that being on sentry duty had dogged me all my life, but I made the best of a bad job and turned out on parade with everything spick and span. I was chosen as first relief, which meant that I went on duty straight away and for the first time in my life I was a real sentry and I was carrying a real rifle on my shoulder.

I swear that no guardsman ever had a straighter back and my drill was impeccable as I paraded up and down the beat, stamping my feet and with my rifle swinging in precise arcs as I came down from the slope to the order arms position. A very proud soldier indeed. I noticed with pleasure that the regimental sergeant major was standing at the side of the orderly room watching me. He was a regular soldier with years of experience behind him and I could see that he was duly impressed. After a short time he marched smartly over until he was standing directly in front of me and I waited to hear his words of praise. He drew a deep breath and bellowed:

'Straighten yourself up, boy; you're a disgrace to the Regiment. Do you know what you look like?'

'No, sir,' I quavered.

'Then I had better enlighten you, you horrible little man. You don't look like a soldier at all. You look like a bag of shit tied up ugly!'

With these ungrammatical but colourful and well-chosen words, he made his way towards the sergeants' mess, leaving behind a sadder and a wiser young soldier.

In spite of these little incidents, I thoroughly enjoyed my first brush with army life. I loved the comradeship and the fun and the nights in the Redesdale Arms when we drank foaming pints of beer and walked back to camp singing our newly acquired repertoire of army songs. It was exciting to be out on the moors with a gun and a limber full of ammunition bouncing behind the gun-tower, and then there was the thrill of firing real shells and watching them explode on a distant hillside. It was a completely different world and a refreshing change from the humdrum of daily life – so much so that I have to admit that I looked forward to the coming war with growing excitement.

The fact that I was anticipating the outbreak of war with eagerness does not mean that I was of a warlike disposition, it merely reflects my innocence and ignorance at that time of the true horror of war. I find it strange to reflect that I had grown up amidst the aftermath of what had been the greatest carnage in the history of mankind and yet I still did not appreciate the devastation, the suffering, the misery and the disillusionment that followed in its wake. I never consciously thought of killing anybody, or for that matter, of anybody killing me: that part was all shrouded in a sort of mental mist; I knew it was there but I never brought it to the front of my mind. It was of course the adventure aspect that was the great appeal, a promised escape from the boredom, the monotony and the unrewarding grind of everyday life. I was not alone in this eagerness to throw off the restraints of civilian life; there must have been thousands of young men who thought the same, and the sad thing was that we were merely jumping out of the frying pan into a very hot fire.

As the days wore on I began to feel a growing awareness of the gravity of the situation. Together with my brother George, I attended lectures concerned with aspects of modern warfare that had come to light as a result of the Spanish Civil War. Many of these lectures dealt at length with the loss of life and the devastation that resulted from the aerial bombardment of open cities. We were also brought to realise that there was every likelihood of poison gas being used in such attacks. The thought of our loved ones being subject to heavy bombardment, or of them being blinded or choked to death in a cloud of poison gas, caused us to take a fresh look at the situation. We began to realise that our country was under real threat from a powerful enemy and we wondered if we would be strong enough to survive. Our conversations became more serious as for the first time we contemplated the possibility of defeat. We drank our pints of beer together but we were often in a sober frame of mind as we found ourselves imagining what life would be like for our families under the Nazi yoke. We contemplated the possibility of German stormtroops swaggering through our towns and cities if the Gestapo and the SS took over the running of our country.

Events moved inexorably towards the inevitable: Danzig, the Polish Corridor, Hitler, Chamberlain, threats and counter-threats. There seemed to be no way of stopping this headlong rush into war. The newspapers were full of reports, the BBC was issuing hourly bulletins on the general situation and we knew that it was only a matter of time before somebody declared war. It was little surprise to me therefore when one afternoon I was called to the phone to hear my mother telling me that my call-up papers had arrived: the Territorial Army was being mobilised and I was to report for duty immediately. I said goodbye to my colleagues at work and left, never to return.

At home, when I arrived there, I found my mother in tears and my father in a state of real agitation – a situation no doubt that was being duplicated all over the country. I climbed into my uniform, kissed them goodbye and went off to join my regiment. I was walking away not only from home and parents, but also from a way of life that was gone for ever. I was leaving behind my youth and entering a world that was different from anything I had ever previously known.

Considering the fact that we had been expecting and preparing for war for such a long time it is difficult to understand why there was such an absurd lack of organisation when we were finally mobilised. One would have thought that all the finer details would have been worked out and rehearsed in advance and that we, as part of the armed forces and partially trained, would have known exactly what to do and where to go in the event of an emergency. Nothing could have been further from the truth!

Having collected my uniform and small kit from home, I made my way to the drill hall in Nottingham to find everything in a state of confusion. After milling about for some time in a welter of bodies and equipment, I discovered that battery headquarters had been established in a nearby factory known as Hollin's Mills. Here it was the same story of utter confusion and disorder, but I did manage to acquire two blankets, a ground-sheet, a rifle and sundry other articles. Unfortunately there were no kit bags available so I made a pile of my equipment by the side of a wall and waited in vain for something positive to happen. Eventually a small group of us decided that the best thing we could do under the circumstances was to go in search of refreshment. So, together with Harry Day, Bob Foulds, Bob Paulson and Patrick Bland, I found myself in a pub called The Peacock, and here we spent the remainder of the evening in good fellowship.

When we returned to Hollin's Mills at about eleven o'clock there was a complete transformation: everything was quiet and still. Bob Paulson and I were both in 'B' Troop, but 'B' Troop had disappeared and no one knew where they had gone. All that we could discover was that they had marched off in the direction of Lenton Boulevard. We both gathered our kit into our arms and then, with all our worldly belongings clutched before us, we set off into the night to find some place to sleep. As we lurched along the road a squad of marching men overtook us. We did not recognise any of them, but we realised that they were from our own regiment. With a feeling of relief we marched behind them until they stopped near a small chapel and filed inside. We followed, to see them spreading their blankets on the floor and settling down for the night and it was only a matter of minutes before we too were rolled in our blankets and fast asleep.

Our rest was to be short-lived. I remember being awakened by a heavy boot against my backside. It was a sergeant major, who informed us that this billet was for a troop in 426 Battery. We pointed out that we were all in the same regiment and we were all about to serve in the same war, but he was not impressed. As far as he was concerned, being in 425 Battery was akin to being a Panzergrenadier and he kicked us out into the street. I cannot remember how we came to find our own billet, but I do have a strong memory of dragging about the streets for hours before we eventually found our way into the Western Tennis Club on Derby Road, not far from Wollaton Park Gates. The troop was there, all sound asleep and every bed space on the floor occupied. Bob and I found a room containing a billiard table, and on this very hard but welcome surface we rolled ourselves fully clothed into our blankets and once again fell fast asleep.

We remained in Nottingham for a few weeks and it was possible to return home frequently, but we did not properly appreciate this privilege because it seemed a very natural thing to do. We were all very inexperienced in army life and there were several incidents that occurred during this period that reflected our lack of proper military training.

I was on sentry duty one morning outside the main entrance to the drill hall when a major from the regular army alighted from a staff car and entered the building. As he passed I smartly saluted with a 'butt salute' and he stopped dead in his tracks.

'That was an incorrect salute, sentry,' he snapped. 'An officer of my rank is entitled to a Present Arms.'

'No, Sir,' I corrected him. 'You are only entitled to a Butt Salute – Sorry.'

He slowly turned a brilliant shade of purple, snorted in anguished despair and made his way into the drill hall, shaking his head as he went.

Whilst still on this same guard duty I had to escort a prisoner who was under close arrest from the cell where he was held to a nearby toilet. On the way it was necessary for me to unlock a door and I had trouble in finding the correct key. Turning to the prisoner, I handed him my rifle, saying, 'Here, hold this a minute whilst I sort out the keys.'

'Sure, mate,' he replied and he waited until I had opened the door before handing the rifle back to me. I never did find out what crime he had committed but it must have been something serious for him to be held under close arrest.

On occasions we were marched into Wollaton Park, where an officer would shout 'Gas Alert!' or 'Take Cover!', at which we would quickly don our gas masks or dive into the nearest ditch. It was noticeable that the officer himself never did any diving into wet ditches full of nettles and brambles. Also during this period we went on several long route marches wearing full kit and, of course, army boots, to which we were not accustomed. On these marches we were always led by an officer who wore comfortable shoes and carried no equipment at all. Every few miles we would be met by a car carrying a different officer and after an exchange of pleasantries they changed places. This exchanging of officers would go on until we arrived back exhausted and with sore, chafed and aching feet. They told us that this was necessary to toughen us up for future active service. It occurred to me at the time that it was rather strange that the officers were not apparently in need of any such toughening up, but as yet I was not experienced in the ways of the British Army.

During the evenings after duty we used to go across the road to a pub called the Rose and Crown and there I became friendly with a girl. One evening when I was on guard duty she came across to keep me company at my solitary post beside the entrance to the billet. There was (and still is, I believe) a fairly wide stream at that place and a bridge over which the road passed to gain entrance to the tennis club where we were billeted. My post was on the bridge itself. After a while we decided that it might be a good idea to find a quiet little corner underneath the bridge and so we crept down the bank together in the gathering darkness and passed the time most delightfully.

Unfortunately, the orderly officer, making his rounds, discovered that there was no sentry on duty and after searching around for a while he shouted, 'Sentry, where are you?'

'I'm here, sir,' I replied, scrambling back up the bank with the girl in tow.

He shone his torch over me and then queried, 'I say, sentry, where is your rifle?' By this time I was searching feverishly along the wall of the bridge for the damned thing but could not find it.

'I don't know, sir, I put it down here somewhere,' I replied, still scrambling around in the dark. Fortunately for me the officer was just as inexperienced as I was myself and so he merely said, 'I say, sentry, I don't think it's a good thing to lose your rifle whilst you are on guard duty.' This must have been the understatement of the year! He left me to continue my vigil; the girl had disappeared and I don't think I ever saw her again.

I mention these incidents because, though trivial in themselves, they do reflect in a very simple way the state of unreadiness of the country as a whole at the time when the political manoeuvring came to an end and war was finally declared. On the same evening of the declaration of war the air raid sirens were sounded and we all dashed outside and started digging trenches, but it was only a practice.

The short period that we remained in Nottingham was something like a holiday. Almost every evening I was able to return home and strut about in uniform with buttons and badges shining, winged riding breeches and puttees, and gleaming spurs which clinked and jangled as I walked proudly around the town. I was a real homespun hero who had never fired a shot in anger but I enjoyed every minute of it. Sadly it did not last very long. After ten days volunteers were required to form an advance party as the regiment was under orders to move.

Still being young and very keen I volunteered and we set off early one morning in a motley collection of vehicles. There were private cars and commercial vehicles that still bore the names of the firms from which they had been commandeered; there were also some very antiquated lorries that had been in store since the previous war. I travelled in one of the latter and it was quite an experience. The driver was protected from the weather by a canvas screen and I seem to recollect that the wheels had hard tyres. At the back there was no protection at all and we had a very bumpy and windy journey in a vehicle that had last seen service in 1918. Our destination turned out to be the village of Rillington in Yorkshire, not far from Malton.

The regiment marched through the city of Nottingham before leaving by train from Victoria station. The streets were lined with people and the band was playing as they made their way through the city. It must have been a stirring sight, but I had no part in this farewell parade because I was already in Yorkshire. I was pleased to see all my friends again when they arrived at the little station in Rillington. Our troop moved immediately to a place near the hamlet of West Knapton. Here was a stately hall in which the officers were billeted, and behind the main building there was a collection of buildings around a courtyard – stables, shed and barns. It was here, in a loft above the cowsheds, that we were to be housed and we quickly set about making ourselves as comfortable as possible.

The weather was dry and warm during our stay in Yorkshire and this was fortunate, for when it did rain the barn proved to have a leaky roof. The living conditions were really disgraceful; the whole troop was packed into this barn loft and when we laid our straw palliasses down there was not an inch of floor space uncovered. The entrance to the loft was by a ladder and through a trap door. Had there been a fire it would have been disastrous, as it took quite a long time for us all to go down the ladder one at a time. The whole building was built of wood and there were bales of straw stacked beneath us. I still shudder to recall how we all lay on our straw palliasses smoking cigarettes.

There were no proper facilities for washing and the sanitary arrangements were less than basic. Each morning the toilets were cleaned by loading them onto a handcart and wheeling them deep into an adjoining wood where they were just emptied under the trees. To be pitched into such conditions within a few days of leaving our comfortable homes was a shock for us all, but we accepted it without complaint, believing that this was a necessary part of wartime soldiering. We were not experienced enough to realise that it was all completely unnecessary.

The filthy conditions under which we were living quickly began to take their toll and several men developed impetigo, which is a contagious pustular disease of the skin. It is a most unpleasant thing to catch because the face becomes covered in a mass of horrible, scabby, running sores. In our situation it was made worse because in addition to the pain and discomfort, the unfortunate sufferers had to bear the obvious revulsion of their friends, who were compelled to live and sleep in close proximity to them.

The large majority of the young men who at that time filled the ranks of the South Notts. Hussars had joined just prior to the war. They had done so in a spirit of patriotism, eager to serve their country in its hour of need. They came from a wide variety of backgrounds and many of them were well spoken and extremely polite, and obviously came from good homes. It was to be proved in the days that followed that they were also men of the highest calibre and I am still proud to have been one of their number. As is typical of British soldiers, we tackled all our adversities with good humour and laughed our way through all our discomforts. There was a positive spin-off from these early days of bad conditions and hard living. It was in overcoming these hardships together that we began to forge the true steel of comradeship that was to see us through when the real test came.

We were now a part of the 1st Cavalry Division and also involved in something known as ADGB, which stood for Active Defence of Great Britain. How we were supposed to defend Great Britain I have no idea for we were equipped only with a large covered van bearing the name 'Weaver to Wearer' and 'B' Troop had but one ancient 18-pounder gun with a wooden bung in the muzzle. This gun bore on its shield in red paint the words FOR DRILL PURPOSES

ONLY. NOT TO BE FIRED. With this equipment we careered about the Yorkshire countryside pretending to come into action with four guns, though in fact three of the gun crews would just be standing in the space where their gun would normally have been sited.

The regiment did have more than one old gun. To the best of my belief we had four 18-pounder field guns and four howitzers. These guns had wooden wheels and were of the type used by the British Army during the final years of the First World War. The four guns of 425 Battery were kept at Rillington and were used for gun drill purposes only. We could not use them for field exercises because we had no proper gun-towing vehicles, and whenever the guns were moved they had to be manhandled with drag ropes. We did quite a lot of gun drill during this period, and by this time I had passed my Gun Laying Test and was entitled to wear the letter 'L' surrounded by laurel leaves on my left sleeve. The gun layer is the member of the gun team who sets the sights, adjusts the angle and elevation of the piece and actually fires the gun. Everyone else is concerned with loading the ammunition, or dragging the gun round to point in the direction indicated by the layer.

We were ordered to mount a guard under the archway that led into our little courtyard but by this time our rifles had been withdrawn, as there was obviously a shortage of weapons. Instead of rifles we each carried a piece of stick and we had to go through a ridiculous ceremony of mounting guard with sticks instead of rifles. It was even sillier than my boyhood days of playing 'sentry go' outside the shed in our garden. In those days I did at least carry an air rifle to challenge any marauding enemy; now, we had to mount a 24-hour guard outside a lonely cow shed carrying nothing more than a piece of stick.

They were long, lonely vigils that served no useful purpose. One day, whilst I was on guard, we were visited by a general who came to our little billet in company with the usual retinue, which this time included our own colonel and his second-in-command. The general inspected the guard, and as I happened to be on sentry duty at the time, he selected me as his target. To my horror he tapped me on the shoulder with his cane and said, 'Now, sentry, what exactly are you guarding?' I had never felt so foolish in my life as I did at that moment for I had no idea what I was supposed to be guarding. There was nothing to guard and I had to admit that I didn't know. He turned to the sergeant of the guard, who was very red in the face as he also failed to find a suitable reply. The orderly officer was the next to meet the general's quizzical eye, and with the same result. The situation was saved by the regimental sergeant major, who stepped smartly forward to say, 'It is a tradition of the regiment, Sir, always to mount a guard over the guns. Sir.'

The general turned his glance in the direction of our pitiful old, non-firing 18-pounder. He nodded in half-approval before saying to the colonel in a friendly and understanding voice, 'It may not be a good thing to have these men standing about unnecessarily, Colonel.' The colonel nodded in agreement but we still carried on with our guards after the general had left; nothing changed.

* * *

Considering the fact that the war had only just begun and as yet there was no rationing of food, our feeding arrangements were nothing short of appalling. There was no shortage; the weakness lay in the cooking and the general organisation. Our food was badly cooked in the first place, but to make matters worse, the cookhouse was several miles away in Rillington. There were no special storage containers or hot boxes in which to transfer the food, and it came to us in open dixies on the back of a fifteen-hundredweight truck. The result may be imagined: it was always cold and congealed and it was usually covered with dust. Moreover the diet hardly ever varied: porridge, bacon and beans for breakfast, bully beef* sandwiches at mid-day and greasy stew at night. Had we been in action or in difficult circumstances, such conditions would have been understandable, but we were in what was virtually peacetime Britain and there was no excuse for the neglect which sprang from the attitude that anything was good enough for the common soldier.

At the beginning of November I was granted seven days' leave and I was happy to pack my kit and get away from the leaking barn that had been my home for the previous five or six weeks. One of the difficulties we all had to overcome during those first days of the war was homesickness. No one ever admitted to such a thing – it would have been considered weak and unmanly to do so – and because of this it was something that everybody had to face in private. There was a popular song at that time which finished with the words: 'Ma, I miss your apple pie, but most of all I'm missing you.' We used to sing the words light-heartedly but there was a ring of truth in them that found its mark with us all.

I was certainly missing my mother and her apple pies. I was also missing my clean, comfortable bed, the table laid with a crisp, white cloth, the leaping fire in the grate, clean underwear, well cooked, wholesome food and a clean bathroom and toilet. In fact, all the comforts of home that I had previously taken for granted. The train could not carry me quickly enough in the direction of Nottingham, but in spite of my eagerness to return home, I did feel a tinge of regret about leaving my pals. Whilst I might have been loath to admit it at the time, I did actually enjoy being a soldier and living a corporate life in the company of men whom I had come to respect.

---

* Bully Beef was the soldiers' sobriquet for corned beef. It originated during the First World War when the main British food supply depot in France was in the town of Bouille.

Soon I was wallowing in comfort, being spoilt by my mother, eating the tastiest food imaginable and having a wonderful leave. I had girl friends that were not loath to be seen on the arm of a soldier. Sylvia was my favourite, whenever I could persuade her to meet me. There were nods of respect from the neighbours and serious man-to-man type conversations with men of my father's age who had served in the Great War. I loved waking in the morning in a warm, comfortable bed to find my mother standing there with a tray laden with bacon and eggs and sausage and toast and a steaming cup of coffee. Breakfast in bed, propped up by soft, white pillows, was a far cry from greasy beans in a barn festooned with cobwebs. I made a feast of it all and thoroughly enjoyed myself as the leaking barn and the filthy conditions slipped from my mind as if they had never been.

Unfortunately times like this pass all too quickly and the days slipped away with incredible speed. I was brought back to reality with a sudden shock when a letter arrived ordering me to return to my unit. It said that the regiment had moved and I was to report immediately to the town of Wragby in Lincolnshire. Having now sampled some aspects of army life, it was in a more sober frame of mind that I packed my kit on this occasion. It was much more of a tug to leave home than it had been in those heady days of late August, when leaving had seemed like the start of a great adventure. Now it was with a rather heavy heart that I said my goodbyes and made my way to the station to go in search of the town of Wragby.

It was a bright, crisp morning in early November when I made my way to the Midland station in Nottingham, where my old friend, the station clock, gave me a friendly wave as I boarded the train for Lincoln. It was an old-fashioned type of carriage with lots of small, unconnected compartments, one of which I had to myself. I was not in the happiest of moods as I watched the familiar old platform glide away. My two months of service had toughened me up a little, but I was still far from being a hardened soldier and I was dreadfully homesick sitting there all alone in the moving train thinking of the warmth and comfort I was leaving behind.

At Lincoln station I had to change trains and soon found myself behind a fussy little engine that rattled along the line at a fine old pace. I can clearly remember that there was a section of the line between Lincoln and Wragby where the track made a sweeping curve and it was possible to see the engine from the carriage where I was sitting. It was puffing out smoke and steam and appeared to be thoroughly enjoying itself, which was more than I could say for myself. I was just praying that there would not be another leaking barn at the end of the journey.

Wragby station was deserted and so I shouldered my pack and strode out in the direction of the village, where I quickly found members of the regiment going about their various tasks. I was informed that 'B' Troop was stationed not in Wragby but in a small hamlet rejoicing in the name of Holton cum Beckering. There was no transport available but I was directed to follow a narrow road that led in the direction of Market Rasen, and following these instructions I was soon deep into the Lincolnshire countryside. This narrow country road seemed to go on for ever; there were no houses and no traffic and not a soul did I meet, and the endless trudge along this lonely road did little to revive my flagging spirits. At last I arrived in Holton cum Beckering to find that it comprised nothing more than a church, a vicarage and a couple of farms with attendant cottages and it was surrounded by agricultural land that seemed to stretch into the mists in every direction.

There was no sign of anyone or of anything remotely connected with things military, and so I ventured into one of the farmyards to enquire into the whereabouts of the missing 'B' Troop. The farmer paused from his work long enough to point across a yard piled high with squelchy, stinking manure, to a barn door on the opposite side. He informed me that if I went into the barn and climbed some steps I would pass through a trapdoor and into a loft where the soldiers were billeted.

Thanking him for his trouble, I gingerly tiptoed around the edge of this noisome midden to enter the barn and climb the steps into the loft. Here I could see each man's kit on the wooden floor and I knew that I had arrived. There was very little light in the loft other than that which filtered up from the barn. I was soon able to find my own equipment which one of my colleagues had kindly laid out for me and I sat down on my blankets to survey our new abode. It was a typical barn with wooden beams and bare brick walls festooned with cobwebs. The air was filled with the smell of rotting manure and, apart from occasional animal noises emanating from the farm below, there was absolute silence.

This billet was far, far worse than the leaking barn in Yorkshire and compared with the luxuries I had so recently enjoyed whilst on leave, it was the epitome of squalor. I felt very sorry for myself sitting there all alone, miles from anywhere and far from home and then I realised that self-pity was pointless in this situation. I stopped indulging my miseries and set about making myself as comfortable as possible. I now realise that I had reached one of those times in life which mark a change of outlook, another stage in the progress towards maturity had been achieved and I came to terms that morning with the fact that being a soldier in wartime is no sinecure. It has little to do with posturing in fine uniforms and much to do with learning how to survive in adverse conditions.

That morning also brought another aspect of wartime service life into its true light. It came as I heard the sound of friendly voices and the noise of booted feet thumping up the wooden steps. Then came a sight I shall never forget as long as I live: it was Fred Lamb's friendly, smiling face as he climbed through into the loft. Suddenly the gloom was dispelled; there were Fred and George, Wag. Harris, Bob Paulson, Jim Hardy, Danny Lamb and all the other lads of 'B'

Troop crowding around, glad to see me back. They were all eagerly enquiring about my leave, demanding to know about the meals I had enjoyed, the films I had seen, my success with the fair sex and all the usual nonsense of such welcoming. They told of their journey down from Yorkshire, grumbled about the inefficiency of the army in general and our regiment in particular, and as they talked, the barn lost its drabness and became a cheerful and friendly place.

I warmed to the bond of friendship that we had forged, and for the first time I felt the protective custody of that special comradeship which was peculiar to those times and conditions. Although I did not appreciate the fact at the time, these men, and others like them, were to replace the securities of my previous life. It was in their company that in the future I would feel secure and at home.

Fortunately our stay in Holton cum Beckering was to be short-lived and we were very thankful for this because at the end of the day there was nothing at all to do. The nearest centre of life was in Wragby almost three miles away, and if most of the day had been spent route marching, then this was a lost cause. We did sometimes make the journey, but although we were young and fit it was something of a drag on the way back.

Our good fortune in moving so quickly was solely due to the efforts of a local lady named Dorcas Holmes, who was a typical countrywoman of the 'no nonsense' variety. Rank and position were of little consequence to her and the affairs of the village were her prime concern. When she learned of our situation she decided that this was not to be and she gave the colonel to understand that his billeting officers must do better, and at once! As a result we were moved to a new billet in the town of Wragby. It was an empty house down a track near the railway station and here we were glad to lay our blankets on the bare boards of its rooms even though we were packed in like sardines in a tin.

We were now into the middle of November and the weather was beginning to prepare for what was to be a very severe winter. Needless to say we had no form of heating in the house but the press of bodies generated sufficient warmth for most of the time. Our meals were served in a partly completed shop building on the Bardney Road, about three-quarters of a mile from the billet. We used to march to and from this crude dining room three times a day carrying our enamel mugs and plates with our 'eating irons' tucked into the pockets of our tunics.

The cooks seemed to have been chosen from the dirtiest and most illiterate men in the Battery and the food they produced was indescribably awful. I have a vivid recollection of a filthy man with a pair of greasy mittens on his hands, dipping his mug into a dixie of cooling mutton stew and of him pouring the congealing mess onto my enamel plate. He was followed by another equally grubby individual who slopped a ladle full of watery potatoes into this greasy mess that was to be my main meal of the day. We sat on forms at trestle tables set out on the concrete floor of the half-built shop that had neither windows nor doors. At the end of the meal we had to wash our plates in a dixie of filthy, greasy water that had to serve the whole troop. It was disgusting and quite unnecessary, but we accepted it as part of going to war.

Our hardships were alleviated to some extent by the good people of Wragby, who lost no time in making their welcome felt in a practical way. A canteen was opened to give us a place of refuge during the long, dark evenings. It was a joint effort by the folk of the local church and the Methodists and it was situated in a room behind the Methodist chapel. Here we could buy tea and toast and sandwiches quite cheaply and have the comfort of sitting in a warm, lighted room. We also used the two pubs in the town, the Turnor's Arms and the Adam & Eve, but money was scarce and we could not afford to spend much time drinking. We also began to meet the local people and I met one in particular who was to play a major part in my life during the next five years and beyond.

It was still my practice to attend church on Sunday whenever this was possible and so it was not surprising that one Sunday morning soon after our arrival in the village I found myself climbing the stairs to the balcony at Wragby Church. This was something of a novelty to me because I had never before attended a church that had a balcony. As the service began, the organ played and the vicar and the choir filed into the nave and they all took their places. This was another novelty because there were girls in the choir and this was something I had never seen before.

The first hymn was being sung when suddenly I stopped singing and fell in love! It was sudden and unexpected but absolutely definite, there was no doubt in my mind at all ... I was in love; I knew it immediately, in fact I had known it for as long as I could remember. It was new and startling and yet it had always been there and it wasn't new at all. It was as old as time.

One of the choir girls had looked up to the gallery; our eyes met and I recognised her immediately as the girl I had been dreaming about for years. She was absolutely beautiful – but it wasn't just her beauty, there was something else about her that made her special, something about her expression, something about her eyes, some magical bond, some instant recognition that flashed between us as if we had met somewhere before.

I was like a man transfixed; I heard not a word of the sermon, I forgot the prayers and ignored the responses. All I could do was to sit and gaze in wonder at the girl who had always been in my life as a wispy sort of dream; it was beyond my comprehension that she could actually be real. Any doubts I had about her real-life existence were quickly dispelled by the covert glances she was sending in my direction to show that she also was aware that something very special had just happened between us. (Writing these words over seventy years later those feelings have not changed.)

After the service she just disappeared. I could find no trace of her anywhere, so I made my way into the Turnor's Arms to spend a large proportion of my weekly wage of ten shillings on a decent meal. Later that afternoon, along with Bob Foulds, Charles Westlake and Danny Lamb, I was invited to the house of a wealthy local businessman named Alwyn Mawer. The Mawers had a very attractive daughter of about eighteen years, who had already caught the eye of almost every man in the battery. Her name was Fay and she was one of a small group of girls in the village who were about the same age.

When we arrived at the house we found that she had also invited several of her friends and to my delight my beautiful choir girl was amongst them. We were all introduced rather formally but in a friendly manner. There was a pleasant girl who went by the rather strange name of Trot, and a very friendly girl named Molly, who was with her younger sister. It was the younger sister who claimed my attention for it was she who had spent the morning peering up at me from her eye corners. I discovered that they called her Binkie. She was much younger than I had imagined and as we chatted together I learned that she was only fifteen and still attending Horncastle Grammar School. This did not make her any the less attractive to me; in fact as the evening wore on I became more and more infatuated but I did not arrange to meet her again on account of her youth.

The following Saturday afternoon I was lying on my blankets upstairs in the billet when there was a knock on the front door. The whole house went instantly quiet. People do not normally knock on the doors of billets. The sergeant major himself opened the door and we all heard a girl's voice saying, 'Good afternoon. Please may Ray Ellis come to tea today?'

There was a startled silence whilst the sergeant major recovered his wits, and then his voice thundered 'GUNNER ELLIS!'

I hurled myself down the stairs two at a time to hear him say, 'This young lady wants you to go to tea with her.' There was the hint of a sardonic gleam in his eye and I was at a loss for words. Such things just did not happen! As I stood speechless, he said, 'Well, put your tunic on, smarten yourself up and escort the young lady home.'

I was upstairs and back in less than five seconds, complete with tunic and a thumping heart and as I made my way to 'escort the young lady home', he grunted in his best sergeant major voice, 'And you may stay for tea.'

Binkie and I walked up the lane together arm in arm and I was the happiest soldier in the British Army ...

\* \* \*

It was during this period that we began to notice a marked change in our activities. It became apparent that we were preparing to go to war. All the men who were under nineteen years of age, or who were not physically fit in every way, were transferred to our second line regiment, 150 RHA.

Our guns were replaced, the new guns having pneumatic tyres in place of the old carriage wheels with their wooden spokes and metal tyres. The strange thing was that our previous guns had been Mark IV 18-pounders whilst the replacements, in spite of their more modern wheels, were of the same calibre but Mark 2s, a type of gun that had become obsolete during the previous war twenty years earlier. All the new guns were marked 'FOR DRILL PURPOSES ONLY' and each had a wooden bung in the muzzle. The wooden bungs were quickly removed, the signs were painted out and in the fashion of 1939 we were equipped and ready for war.

The regiment was also reinforced by a hundred militiamen, who were appalled by our living conditions. (They had previously been in barracks.) These men, together with a number of ex-regular reservists, quickly settled down and were readily accepted as part of the regiment. Some of them I was later to count amongst my best friends and I still remember them with affection. A new set of vehicles arrived – and what a bunch of old crocks they were, mainly civilian vehicles that had been taken over on the outbreak of war, but they did allow us to step up our training. We were now able to do drill orders with the guns and there were countless hours of gun drill, night schemes, long route marches, rifle drill and marching drill – and all the time the weather grew colder and colder.

Each Saturday morning we had to parade in the village square before climbing into the back of an open lorry that carried us into the city of Lincoln for our weekly bath. Then, having soaked in a good, hot bath for about fifteen minutes, we had to climb back onto the lorry for the freezing journey back to Wragby. It was a miracle that we didn't all catch pneumonia! In fact the bleak, bitterly cold weather, coupled with our miserable living conditions, did begin to take its toll in the form of an influenza epidemic that swept through the regiment. A large number of men became seriously ill and should have been sent to hospital, but an unsympathetic Medical Officer decided to keep them in a loft above Dove's garage, and this caused a great deal of unnecessary suffering. The higher echelons, however, considered this to be a splendid thing to do and the Medical Officer received a commendation.

At the back of our billet a flimsy wooden framework was erected and covered with hessian. On one side were the open toilets that had to be emptied each day, and on the other side was a wooden bench holding crude metal tins in which we had to wash and shave in cold water. The weather was now so cold that the water froze within moments of carrying it outside, with the result that washing and shaving became a nightmare. It was in these conditions that we were foolishly ordered to wash our fatigue uniforms and when we had done so they all froze stiff and solid. We had fun standing them up in the snow like soldiers on parade.

At the back of the house was a brick-built washhouse containing an old-fashioned copper that we put to very good use. Many a cold evening was spent toasting bread in front of the copper fire and we were able take it in turns to wash ourselves down in the hot water it provided. The weekly bath parade to Lincoln became a farce. We merely went into the public baths, smoked a cigarette and then climbed back into the lorry having not removed a stitch of clothing nor touched a drop of water.

I had enjoyed meeting Bunkie's family, who had made me feel very welcome on that first afternoon when I had been invited to tea. I discovered that she lived with her parents and her sister at Wrangham House, a large dwelling in the centre of Wragby. Her real name was Enid Bartholomew, but she was never called anything but Binkie, which was her pet name. Her father was a farmer, a quiet and friendly man, and her mother, who was an accomplished pianist and a talented artist, was also a kind and gracious lady who quickly put me at my ease. How good it was to be entertained in this lovely home. It was warm and spacious and everything about it reflected the good taste and the refinement that were immediately evident in the level of conversation. Sitting there in a comfortable chair in front of a large, blazing fire was blissful enough, but with the added warmth of this adorable girl smiling at me across the hearth, it was, I was certain, a foretaste of heaven.

Binkie and I often met in the company of our friends. There were some very pleasant evenings when we were the guests in various houses where we would chat together and very often gather around the piano and sing. (There were no televisions in those days!) People were very kind in this way and those evenings when we were allowed to share the warmth and comfort of their homes meant a great deal to us. When we met alone we had to be prepared to face the rigours of the weather. On these occasions she would come home from school and change out of her uniform, put on her swagger coat, all the rage at that time, and then we would go walking together in the darkness. It was delightful and fresh and very innocent, and we were very happy together in spite of the bitterly cold weather.

Our relationship bore very little resemblance to the modern equivalent but to my mind it was much more delicate and romantic. Although the little time we were able to share was usually spent shivering in the frosty air, we found delight in each other's company. Sometimes we would find a sheltered corner where I would kiss the snowflakes from her lips and vow to love her for ever – and that was the full extent of our endearments.

To a modern young person all this must sound rather trite, but these were other times. It was still the early days of the war and we had different standards – the age of the permissive society lay far in the future. We were happy with the simple moral principles of our age and our place in society. For me at any rate the short time that I was able to spend with this pretty and trusting girl was of great significance. These were the precious moments that I was to carry with me to brighten many a lonely vigil in the dark days that lay ahead and I still remember them with great warmth and affection.

One Sunday morning I decided to go absent without leave for a few hours in order to spend a little time at home. It was fairly easy because it was only about fifty miles distant. First I got a lift into Lincoln and then caught a train for Nottingham and I was home in time for lunch. I spent a pleasant afternoon and early evening with my family but then, without any warning, a thick fog descended and the buses stopped running. There was no way that I could get to the station in time to catch the last train and so I had to stay the night.

Early the next morning the fog had lifted and I was able to catch the first bus into Nottingham. When the Lincoln train pulled out of the station it was still pitch dark and the carriages were illuminated only by tiny blue lamps because of the blackout, a part of air raid precautions. During the journey two young men in civilian clothes eagerly questioned me; they were awaiting their call-up and were obviously very apprehensive about service life. They wanted to know about army discipline and about sergeant majors in particular. To be truthful, our own sergeant major was a very kindly man (it was he who had allowed me to escort Binkie home and to stay for tea), but this was not what they expected to hear and so I did not disappoint them. I was tired and it was cold and dark and I knew that I was in for trouble on my return to the unit and so I was just in the right mood to give a lurid account of army life.

After blackening the name of every sergeant major in the army, and expressing doubts about the legitimacy of their births, I turned to another soldier, who all this time had been sitting quietly in the other corner of the darkened compartment. 'Which regiment are you with, pal?' I asked, with the familiarity of one soldier to another. He turned his head sharply in my direction and replied, 'I am the regimental sergeant major of the King's Own Dragoon Guards!' There was absolute silence in the compartment for the remainder of the journey.

It was nine o'clock before I reached Wragby, where I was placed under open arrest for being absent without leave. Later in the day I was brought before the battery commander, who decided that I should pay for my sins by losing seven days' pay and being confined to barracks for fourteen days. Fair enough. I accepted this without rancour, although it was common knowledge that the officers were popping off home in their cars almost at will.

As we had no barracks in which I could be confined, it was decided that I should spend my evenings and nights for the next fortnight in a wooden shed belonging to Mr Thorne, who owned a firm that specialised in making beehives. This particular shed had been taken over to be used as a store and my punishment was to spend my leisure hours guarding the equipment it contained. In no way did I enjoy this curtailment of my leisure time, but there were compensations. The shed stood at the bottom of Jean Bradshaw's garden and Jean was one of Binkie's closest friends.

Each morning her mother allowed me the use of their bathroom to wash and shave, and in addition to this she cooked me a delicious breakfast of bacon and eggs. This shed is still in existence at the corner of Louth Road and Silver Street, and it serves as a constant reminder to me whenever I visit Wragby of the fourteen days I spent 'doing jankers'.

The first Christmas of the war was drawing near and everybody was hoping to be given leave during the festive period. Arrangements were made for as many men as possible to be given their embarkation leave at this time and so a few days before Christmas there was a general exodus as they all went off home in high spirits. A small party had to remain in Wragby to guard the guns and equipment, and I was one of the few unfortunate souls who were left behind. No one had given any thought to our welfare or to providing us with any special fare or entertainment and after watching my friends depart I found myself sitting alone in the empty house down by the railway.

It would have been a very miserable time without the kindness of the local people, who all went to a great deal of trouble to make sure that we had a happy Christmas. I was especially fortunate in being able to spend much of my free time with Binkie and her family and friends. By this time I was getting to know Binkie's family very well; Molly and I had become firm friends and I had grown quite fond of her. I also enjoyed sharing a pint of beer at the Adam & Eve with Binkie's father, who was a very pleasant companion, and I discovered that he was a practising Christian and closely involved with the life of the local church. Mrs Bartholomew had been watching me very closely from the outset, not surprisingly under the circumstances, but she must have been satisfied with what she saw because she showed me every kindness and we were on very good terms. With all this hospitality and affection, and with Binkie's eyes twinkling and shining in the Christmas lights, it was to be one of the happiest Christmases I had ever known.

Early in January I received my inoculations prior to going overseas and they caused me a little trouble. My arm swelled and turned a fiery red and I developed a high temperature and was feverish. It only lasted for a couple of days and was not serious but I remember the incident because of the rough kindness I received from my pals. They went to great lengths to shelter me from any hard work and at night they made sure that I was warm and they brought me mugs of hot tea and cocoa. It was just another instance of that wonderful spirit of comradeship remembered so well by all old wartime soldiers, but never again to be recaptured.

At last it was my turn to go on embarkation leave. A final taste of home life, and probably, the last moments ever to spend at home with my family, but this thought was kept right at the back of my mind and never allowed to surface. It was a time of bravado, a little bit of swaggering now and then, a lot of fun, plenty of good food, late nights and late rising, and a good deal of drinking and smoking. The days passed all too quickly and the time had to come when I found myself walking around the house and the garden and all the old familiar places, taking a last look at the things that had mattered in my life and wondering if I should ever see them again.

Saying goodbye is always difficult, but in time of war it is often a shattering experience that becomes a common occurrence. I said goodbye to Sylvia and another girl called Dorothy, both of whom promised to keep on writing to me. Then I recall a tearful kiss from my young sister, a sobbing hug from my mother, and a lot of false cheerfulness on my part and I was through the door and walking towards the bus stop with my father by my side.

Father always found it difficult to display his affection and in this situation he was unable to find words suitable to the occasion. We walked in silence for a short time and then he put his hand in his coat pocket and gave me a handful of nuts. It was a trivial thing, but one which has always remained in my mind ever since. I shall never know what he was trying to say – it was probably just a way of covering his emotions. It was certainly a strange thing to do, but I thanked him and pocketed the nuts as we waited for the bus to arrive. There was a firm handshake, a rough, bristly kiss and I was away; my home life became a thing of the past.

On the bus I saw a local girl named May Lindley. I went and sat beside her because although she had never been anything more than a school friend, we knew each other reasonably well. She enquired where I was going and when I told her that I was going back after embarkation leave she was astounded.

'Do you mean that you are going overseas and no one is going to the station to see you off?' she said, her eyes wide with disbelief. When I confessed that this was so she slowly shook her head saying, 'Then I will come and kiss you goodbye.' I suggested that she must be going somewhere herself and I explained that there was really no need for anyone to see me off, but she would have none of this.

'What I was going to do can wait,' she said. 'First I am going to the station with you.' So we went to the station together and that was how I came to take my leave of Nottingham: in the company of a very kind girl who kept her promise and kissed me goodbye as my old friend the station clock moved its minute hand in salute. The train drew away from the platform and I watched this friendly girl waving until she was swallowed up in the gathering darkness and my embarkation leave was over.

Shortly before our departure there was a regimental parade to Wragby Church. The small church was packed from wall to wall, and by the strangest of coincidences I found myself in the gallery in the very same seat I had occupied on my first visit. It was all very grand and sombre, as everybody knew that this was really a farewell service. It was to be the last time that I would be able to look down at Binkie in her cassock and surplice and mortarboard as she looked up at me from her eye corners, and it made me feel very sad.

After the service we marched past our Honorary Colonel, Sir Lancelot Rolleston, and although it was a foggy, frosty morning he took the salute wearing his service dress and without a greatcoat. Not bad, we thought, for a man of over ninety years. After the parade he addressed the regiment in stirring fashion, finishing with the oft-repeated words, 'Once a Hussar, always a Hussar!'

\* \* \*

We came under Movement Orders on 18 January 1940. The regiment paraded in the village square at Wragby during the late evening. There was a deep covering of frozen snow and a biting wind swept along the ranks of heavily laden men as they formed up in the darkness. I had been fortunate enough to escape the influenza epidemic of the previous weeks but now I had all the symptoms and I longed for a warm, comfortable bed. Instead, I stood with all the others, bowed beneath the weight of my equipment. We were in Field Service Marching Order with full kit, rifle, ammunition and kit bag.

All the last goodbyes had been said and all the farewell kisses exchanged when the order came to move and we marched to the station along the icy road, staggering under the weight of our loads and slipping from time to time on the glassy surface. All the good folk of Wragby had deserted their beds to watch our departure and as we passed the church I heard an old lady's voice in the darkness, 'God bless them. They don't know what lies in store for them.' They were prophetic words!

There was a cracking frost as we climbed aboard the train and tried to find the space to stack our kit. This was extremely difficult because so many men were packed into each compartment and there was not enough room for everything. It was a jumbled mass of rifles, kit bags, webbing equipment and cold, weary men.

In spite of the frosty weather and the lateness of the hour, the platform was full of well-wishers and of course Binkie was there amongst them. It was midnight when the engine, with spinning wheels and hissing steam and clouds of smoke, made the first effort to move its heavy load. Binkie gave me a forlorn wave as the wheels started to turn and then she was gone and I was not to see her lovely face again for five long years.

# Chapter 2

# In Sunny Palestine

Our first task after we had steamed away into the darkness was to get everything stowed away so that we had somewhere to sit in the congested compartment. This had no sooner been accomplished with some degree of success than someone pulled the communication cord. The train shuddered to a halt and we all finished up in a heap on the floor with everything on top of us once more. We later discovered that the RSM had loaded some equipment into a faulty coach that had been shunted off, and this equipment had to be recovered. After much bumping and clanging and shunting backwards and forwards, we resumed our journey through the night to arrive at Southampton the following morning.

By this time my dose of influenza was really taking hold and I was beginning to feel very much under the weather. It was bitterly cold and rations were in short supply, but at mid-day we were issued with a mug of hot tea and corned beef sandwiches. It was evening before we embarked on a cargo boat, which was to take us across the Channel. We were accommodated down in the hold, where we threw our blankets down on the steel plating, glad to be free of our heavy packs, and as the ship sailed we settled down to sleep.

We disembarked at Cherbourg early on what must have been the coldest morning in the history of the world. At least that was how it felt to me as I sneezed and coughed and shivered in the throes of a heavy cold. We were to spend the whole day standing on the quayside without any food or any protection from the weather, and all this time we were subject to an endless monotony of contradictory orders. At first it was a relief to hear the command 'Packs Off'. In order to remove our packs it was necessary to lie down on the ground before releasing the straps because the packs were too heavy to be just 'slipped off'. No sooner had we regained our feet than we heard the order 'Packs on' and so we struggled back into our harness again to stand bowed under the weight of all our equipment for about half an hour and then the whole pantomime was repeated. Sometimes we would march for about a hundred yards and then, an hour later,

march back to our original position. So it went on, all day long: 'Packs off' ...
'Packs on' ... until we were exhausted with the freezing temperature and the
weight we were carrying. We beat our hands and stamped our feet in a misery of
cold as the pitiless wind swept us with freezing sleet.

There was nothing to eat or drink as the long day passed, but at about six
o'clock in the evening, just after darkness had fallen, we were issued with our
first meal in twenty-four hours: it consisted of one tin per man of meat and
vegetables. We had to open the tins with our jack-knives and eat the contents
cold, straight from the tin. There was nothing to drink at all. The night was even
colder than the day had been and with no warm food in our stomachs we
huddled together to try to find some protection from the elements. The night
seemed endless. We learned later that we should have left Cherbourg
immediately after disembarkation but Traffic Control had forgotten to arrange
for the necessary rail transport to be assembled.

It was early the next morning before we entrained for what was to be an
unforgettable journey across France. The train on which we travelled was the
very last word in discomfort. The seats were wooden, there were no toilets and
no water, but more important than any of these deficiencies, there was no heat.
Once again we strove to find room for all our equipment and, rather hopelessly,
for a place to sit in some degree of comfort. The windows offered no view of the
countryside because they were thickly coated with ice and the atmosphere was
thick and fetid. We were all numb with the cold and by now I was coughing
almost incessantly and almost certainly running a temperature. During our wait
at Cherbourg, I had asked one of the officers if I could report sick (this is an
army term for seeing the doctor); his reply had been short and to the point: 'You
must be joking!'

The journey through France lasted for two days and three nights, and it was
a misery in every respect. The train had faulty brakes, which meant that each
time it stopped, which happened every half an hour or so, all the carriages jerked
violently and our equipment was flung in all directions. After a time we just left
everything where it landed and lay amongst the tangled mess, too weary and
despondent to move. I have only a vague memory of the final stages of that
miserable journey because I became rather ill, coughing continually until I burst
a capillary in my throat, which was very painful. There was no hot food of any
kind but I do recall an occasional mug of hot tea being issued. Calls of nature
had to be answered in the snow-covered French countryside during one of the
innumerable halts that were made as we progressed on our journey south.

When we reached our destination, which turned out to be Marseilles, it was
just a repetition of the fiasco we had endured at Cherbourg. After an
interminably long wait we started to embark on a ship, but after half the men
were aboard someone had a change of mind and we all had to clamber off again.
It was finally decided that we should sail on the troopship *Devonshire* as part of

a convoy en route for Port 'Q', but I knew little of this at the time because by now I was too ill to walk. I was lying on a stretcher, covered with a blanket, and waiting to be carried aboard. I have a vivid recollection of lying there on the dockside and looking at a huge waterfall that had become frozen solid. It was a wonderful sight and it clearly illustrated the severity of that winter when such a thing could happen in the south of France. It occurred to me at the time that whilst I had often contemplated the likelihood of my returning from the war on a stretcher, it had never crossed my mind that I would make my way there in such a manner.

After several hours of waiting I was carried aboard the ship and placed in a gangway outside the sick bay in company with other stretcher cases. We lay there unattended for many hours until we knew by sound and movement that the ship had sailed. Eventually a medical officer appeared and announced that the sick bay was full. After giving us a cursory examination, he told us that there was no possibility of us getting any attention and ordered us to report back to our units. That was the situation and we had no option but to climb from our stretchers, collect our equipment and crawl away in search of our comrades.

It was a large troopship and it took me a long time to track them down to Number Three Lower Troop Deck, where everyone was fast asleep in their hammocks because by now it was late at night. I found Bob Paulson, who told me that whilst I had been lying outside the sick bay they had all been issued with a hot meal. I was too sick to care and I just dropped my kit on the floor, rolled myself in my blankets and went to sleep.

On the night of sailing I had been unable to find any spare hooks for my hammock; every space had been taken and I never did find anywhere to sling my hammock. Instead I slept on our mess table with a forest of swinging hammocks above my head. The food on board the SS *Devonshire* was excellent in both quality and quantity, and as we sailed across the Mediterranean Sea the weather grew progressively warmer until we were able to sit on deck in comparatively warm sunshine. Under such conditions I quickly began to recover from my illness.

It was during the voyage that we discovered the identity of the mysterious Port 'Q'. We heard it not from our own sources but from a German radio station. It was obvious that the Germans knew exactly who we were, where we were and our port of destination. They informed us that we were in transit for Haifa in Palestine. All this was very disconcerting and we hoped that they didn't have any U-boats operating in the vicinity of our route.

The Germans were quite correct in their intelligence, for we did dock at Haifa on a bright, sunny morning. We marched off the boat, a much smarter body of men than the cold, weary souls who had dragged themselves aboard at Marseilles. The band was arranged on the quayside playing stirring marches as we left the ship and I remember that they were playing a march called 'On the Quarter-Deck' as I marched down the gangplank into Palestine.

We were taken by lorry to a camp at a place called Sarafand, and on the journey I marvelled as all the biblical pictures that I had known from my childhood came to life. We saw Mount Carmel, and palm trees, and houses with flat roofs; there were Arabs astride small donkeys as their veiled wives walked behind them. We passed orange groves and lemon trees and grapefruit in abundance and the air was filled with the sweet scent of a lush countryside. Above this fertile plain a warm sun shone benignly from a cloudless, blue sky and I had no difficulty in understanding why it had once been referred to as 'a land flowing with milk and honey'. As the lorry made its way towards Sarafand I had a strong feeling that I was going to enjoy soldiering in the Holy Land.

My knowledge of the politics of the Middle East was, to say the least, scanty and for me the country we knew as Palestine was significant only as the part of the world where Jesus had lived nearly two thousand years before. I knew that it was a British Protectorate under the auspices of the League of Nations, but I was not at all sure what a Protectorate was. It is a certainty that most of my friends shared my ignorance in the field of world affairs and as we made our way towards Sarafand we were far more interested in the general scenery than in the fermenting political situation. None of us had any preconceived ideas concerning the rights or otherwise of Jews or Palestinian Arabs.

We only stayed in the camp at Sarafand for a short period and nothing of any significance happened during that time. We were under canvas and also in quarantine because of a meningitis scare. Three of our men went down with this very dangerous disease, but they were all fortunate enough to recover and there was no general epidemic. I later discovered that Binkie became seriously ill with the same disease some time after our departure from Wragby and was seriously ill for many months. I wondered if their infection had a common source.

Our guns and most of our equipment were still en route from England and so there was little for us to do but lie in our small bivouac tents and swat flies. There were millions of flies, and as they were a potential health hazard we were encouraged to kill them. Anyone presenting himself at the camp cinema with a cigarette tin full of dead flies was given a free ticket, but this was of little use to us because being in quarantine we were forbidden to use the cinema. The canteen was also out of bounds. I was pleased to be able to fall back on my love of reading. It was during our stay in Sarafand that I read *The Forsyte Saga*, but even this literary masterpiece failed to completely kill my boredom and so once again I became a volunteer. This time it was to join the advance party, which was detailed to go and prepare a new camp for us at a place called Gedera.

The conditions at Gedera when we arrived were anything but pleasant. There had been a considerable amount of rain during the previous week and the land on which we were to build the new camp was wet and muddy. During the day we sweated as we pitched tent after tent in long, straight rows, and one day I had the misfortune, when swinging a large mallet, to miss the tent peg and hit my leg. It caused me a great deal of pain.

After nightfall we had to stand guard, sometimes at the camp entrance but more often as 'prowler' guards, when we wandered about in the dark trying to remember the password that was changed every day. There was only a small group of us in the advance party so we were on guard every night. Prowler guards always went in pairs for reasons of safety, and this made the duty far more pleasant because it killed the loneliness. Now, for the first time, guard duty had a real purpose: there was an element of danger.

One night when Fred Lamb and I were on duty together we saw a shadowy figure approaching the tent lines. Fred leapt forward, his rifle thrust menacingly before him as he shouted, 'Halt! Give the password.' The figure halted and threw up his hands, and we marched him to the guard tent. Our prisoner was a local Arab, who was employed on the site, but he did not understand a word of English; Fred's rifle had put him in fear of his life and he was trembling with fright. I remember thinking that it was an incongruous situation because Fred, beneath his steel helmet and threatening rifle, was one of the kindest men I had ever known.

When the main body of troops finally arrived, the tent lines were given names; not surprisingly, they all had a flavour of Nottingham about them. There was Long Row, Clumber Street, Derby Road and many more local street names. Many years later I learned that this camp remained in use throughout the war and the lines never lost their original names. During this period we had no guns. Apparently a mistake had been made at the docks, either in England or in France, and our guns, instead of being despatched to Haifa in Palestine, had been sent in error to the United States of America. This meant that as an artillery unit we were pretty well useless.

One of the things I quickly learned during those early days was the fact that the English were not universally popular, as I had been brought up to believe. The sad truth was that we soldiers were looked upon by many as the representatives of an imperial power, and for this we were hated. This was brought to my notice very forcibly one afternoon when I politely bade a Jewish lady 'Good afternoon' and she replied by spitting in my face. The Arabs seemed friendly enough whenever we met them but the Jews were often very hostile. At the time I found this difficult to understand because to the best of my knowledge it was the Germans who were treating them so cruelly and we were at war with the Germans. It was rather puzzling to my young mind.

There were continual riots and we were warned to be on our guard against acts of terrorism. Without guns it was not possible for us to continue our normal artillery training and we had to fill our time in other ways. This usually meant marching through all the towns in the district in a show of force. It was hot work marching along the dusty roads and we soon evolved a pattern of behaviour. Whenever we arrived at the outskirts of a village or a small town the band would strike up and we would march smartly through the streets until we had passed through and into the countryside again. Then, in a more relaxed manner, we would march 'at ease' as we made our way towards the next settlement.

I quite enjoyed those route marches in the bright sunshine; the weather was warm and by this time we were well accustomed to marching long distances and so we experienced no physical discomfort. Oranges were in plentiful supply and we just helped ourselves from the trees. An orange eaten freshly picked whilst still warm from the sun's rays has a flavour all of its own, quite different from the taste we know in England.

The onset of war had disrupted the export market and so there was a glut of oranges in Palestine, and for this reason no one objected to us taking them. Those big, juicy Jaffas were absolutely delicious. The mimosa was in flower at the time and some of the roads were lined with hedges of this bright and attractive plant. The cascades of brilliant yellow florets were a source of great delight to me and many a dusty mile was freshened by their brilliance.

At last our guns arrived in Palestine and I was amongst the party detailed to collect them from the docks at Haifa. I remember setting off very early on a bright, sunny morning in the back of a thirty-hundredweight truck and thoroughly enjoying a huge sandwich of hard-boiled eggs which the cookhouse had provided for my breakfast. All went well until the return journey, when something went wrong with the towing gear on one of the trucks and the gun it was towing had to be unlimbered and left behind. The officer in charge of the party ordered me to remain and guard the gun. This incident had occurred in the middle of a small town and I felt very uneasy as the rest of the convoy moved away, leaving me unarmed and all alone.

Soon a hostile crowd began to gather and I realised that I had been left with no arms with which to defend myself in case of trouble. The gun had no ammunition – and in any case an 18-pounder field gun, even with ammunition, would be of little use in such a situation. The people in the growing crowd were scowling and muttering and pointing at the gun, whilst I stood there doing my best to look calm and unafraid. They were obviously curious because a field gun in the middle of their town was something quite out of the ordinary even in that troubled land. At one point a man approached me from the crowd to enquire if there was going to be a curfew, and I made some sort of fatuous answer to the effect that if everybody behaved in a sensible manner a curfew would not be imposed.

It was over two hours before a breakdown truck arrived with a party of armed men and we were soon back on the road again. I think now that the officer who was responsible for leaving one of the guns in such a situation, under the protection of one unarmed soldier, deserved a reprimand. In the Royal Artillery the care and protection of the guns is of paramount importance because without its guns an artillery regiment serves no useful purpose. In times of extreme danger the cry has always been the same: 'Disregard the men – save the guns'. This officer had ignored all the traditions of the Royal Artillery in abandoning a gun in such a careless way.

* * *

We remained at Gedera until the end of March and most of our time was spent on drill orders. This meant moving about the countryside with our guns and vehicles and bringing the guns into action against numerous imaginary enemy concentrations. Everyone was involved: gunners, drivers, signallers and specialists, each learning how to react in a variety of situations, and during a day's activities we would drop into action many times in all kinds of ground conditions. Much of the time we were working on soft sand and we gained a lot of useful practice in dealing with this kind of terrain. The drivers became quite skilful in keeping their vehicles moving and the gun teams learned the value and the necessity of working as a team as they heaved on drag ropes and strained to pull the guns into position.

I served in a gun sub-section under a sergeant named Clifford Smedley, who was an excellent man in every respect. He was extremely well read and intelligent and a born leader, who commanded respect and deserved the affection and loyalty we all felt towards him. Under his leadership we became a happy and highly skilled gun crew and there was no dissension of any kind. We were all firm friends. A particular friend of mine was Reginald Leigh, known to all as 'Tansy'. He was an ex-regular soldier, and a man of enormous strength, but in common with many such men he was quite gentle by nature. Tansy had a sparkling sense of humour and we often played the fool – I would pretend to order him about, picking fault with his drill and smartness. Sometimes I would threaten to give him a 'bloody good hiding' if he didn't liven up his ideas. After such baiting he would turn and grab me and lift me high above his head, threatening to dash me to the ground, but it was all in fun and we always finished up laughing together.

Whilst we were at Gedera I celebrated my twentieth birthday. It was the first time in my life that I had spent a birthday away from home and I remember feeling rather homesick, but I still had my good friends. One gift I received was from Bob Paulson; it was a round tin containing fifty Players cigarettes and in the lid he had placed a small piece of paper bearing the words 'Happy birthday old Herm'. Dear old Bob – apart from George, he was my best friend.

Towards the end of March we made another move, this time to a place called Hadera. It was a pleasant camp, almost surrounded by plantations of eucalyptus trees; it was not very far from the sea and quite close to the little town. We pitched camp in a high wind. The limber gunners had been allocated a marquee, but the strong wind and the soft sand made its erection an almost impossible task. After a great deal of tugging and pulling and swearing we had everything secure and we settled ourselves down for what was to be a very pleasant interlude before we were introduced to the real horrors of war.

By this time we had all been fitted out with tropical kit. The uniform was made of khaki drill, a light cotton material much more suitable to the climate of the Middle East than the khaki serge we had previously worn. We wore pith helmets, shirts and puttees most of the time, but for more formal occasions the dress was tunics and slacks. In this camp we were also issued with bed boards and trestles that raised us about four inches from the ground when sleeping; this was a big improvement. Also we each had a mosquito net under which we could lie listening to the croaking of thousands of frogs in the nearby plantations; they sang us to sleep each night.

It was a period of intensive training, and we went out on manoeuvres with other elements of the 1st Cavalry Division of which we were a part. It should be pointed out that this division was fully horsed at this time and it was often very thrilling to be training alongside some famous regiments such as the Life Guards, the Horse Guards and the Scots Greys with their beautiful grey horses. There were regiments of lancers, hussars and dragoons, and what a magnificent sight it was to see them trotting with lances high and pennants fluttering or to hear the thunder of hooves as they galloped into action with sabres drawn or lances levelled. It must have been a terrifying experience to face a cavalry charge: a line of galloping horses with sabres and lances glinting in the sunshine must have chilled many a heart. I am very glad that we were a part of this division and that I was able to witness such scenes before they passed into history. The 1st Cavalry Division was soon to be mechanised and such sights will never be seen again.

As well as being busy with constant drill orders, night occupations and regimental schemes, we also had a succession of inspections by high-ranking officers. The General Office Commanding, Palestine, the Commander of the 1st Cavalry Division and the General Officer Commanding in Chief, General Wavell, inspected us. As he walked along the ranks General Wavell stopped from time to time to exchange a few words with various soldiers and he chose me as one of them. Our conversation ran as follows:

General Wavell: 'Do you feel confident to go out and face the enemy'?

Me: 'Yes, Sir'.

General Wavell: 'Good man.'

[There can be no doubt that this conversation had a salutary effect upon the future conduct and outcome of the war. It must have struck terror into the hearts of both Hitler and Mussolini to know that Ray Ellis was now prepared to do battle against them!]

In spite of all the training activities, we had a fair amount of leisure time and it was possible to walk into Hadera, a delightful little town lying midway between Haifa and Jaffa. There were several good cafés and also a cinema, and it made a pleasant break to be able to get out of camp for a few hours in the evening. The sea was quite close and there was excellent bathing. George and I spent a couple of Sundays on the beach, just he and I with a huge stretch of deserted beach all to ourselves. There were rocks also, poised above pools of clear, warm, shimmering water. We spent hours diving from the rocks and trying to reach the bottom but the water was too deep and we could never get down far enough to touch the white sand beneath. When we tired of diving and swimming, we just lay in the hot sunshine and talked of brotherly things: it was absolutely idyllic.

Whilst in Palestine I visited many of the holy places that had featured in the bible stories of my youth. I went to Bethlehem, where I saw what was reputed to be the stable where Jesus was born, and to Jerusalem and the Church of the Holy Sepulchre that stands over the site of Calvary. I found it an emotional experience to be standing in the places that had featured in the Christian teachings of my boyhood: especially the place of the crucifixion and the riven rocks, split asunder during the ensuing earthquake, and what was said to be the tomb where Jesus was laid and from which He arose from the dead. I stood awhile outside that tomb and imagined Mary Magdalene standing in the same spot and weeping, and then turning to find Jesus standing behind her. It was very moving.

What an exciting experience to walk through the old city of Jerusalem. The streets were as narrow as an arm's span and were filled with people, animals and birds. Many of the shop fronts were open and almost everywhere there seemed to be food cooking on spits over little charcoal fires. It was noisy and colourful and to my eyes it seemed very strange and foreign. There were Jews with long beards and black suits, and Arabs in turbans and long robes; some wore the red fez and some carried long, curved knives attached to their belts. I felt as if I was back in the pages of a childhood storybook. I was able to walk along the Via Dolorosa where Jesus had carried His cross, and to stand in wonder as I watched the Jews at prayer in the shadow of the Wailing Wall. I walked on the Mount of Olives and swam in the Dead Sea; I talked with Bedouin Arabs outside their black tents and watched overburdened little donkeys carrying their heavy masters, whilst obedient wives walked behind in dutiful procession carrying an assortment of goods balanced on their heads. It was a wonderful education and I enjoyed every minute to the full.

It was too good to last. Good friends surrounded me, I was fit and healthy, living in a pleasant camp where food was plentiful and the sunshine was warm and kindly. My stay in Hadera was, without any doubt, the happiest of all my wartime experiences. But the time passed all too quickly and towards the end of

April we had two full regimental schemes before moving to a dreadful place called Bir Asluj for the purpose of training with live ammunition.

When an artillery regiment needs to fire live rounds of ammunition it is necessary to find some remote, uninhabited spot where this can be carried out in safety. Bir Asluj was not only remote and uninhabited, it was also decidedly unpleasant. Situated in the Sinai Desert eighty miles beyond Gaza, it was the most God-forsaken spot imaginable. The only thing that made it habitable was a well that provided the necessary water. The sand in this baked and arid wilderness was a fine alkaline dust, very, very fine, like powder, so that the merest breath of wind produced a dust storm of these suffocating particles. The temperature maintained a constant 35° C in the shade throughout the daylight hours and fell almost to freezing point during the night. There was no escape from this unfriendly environment because we were under canvas, which offered no protection from the heat, or from the cold or the dust.

There was a water tower set about fifty feet above the ground, into which water from the well was automatically pumped, and from this elevated tank water was fed to the various parts of the camp. Some time prior to our arrival, primitive showers had been rigged. The water for each shower was held in a petrol tin about eight feet from the ground and when a string was pulled it discharged its contents into a second tin, the bottom of which had been perforated with many tiny holes. The water sprayed out of these holes to provide a shower of limited duration. The first man to use one of these contraptions rushed out from under the spray screaming because the water in the tin had been under the sun's rays all day and it was scalding hot.

After a day out in the merciless sun, firing on the ranges, we returned in the evening covered with dust to find a meal of the same old corned beef stew, also covered with dust. There was a bar in the camp, under canvas, and it was here that we met Australian soldiers for the first time. They were from an Australian field regiment and, like us, were here to fire on the ranges. We got on quite well together, although their manner of behaviour and their type of discipline were very different from our own. One thing we did have in common was a dislike of this particular place and the experience of drinking warm beer in a hot, dusty tent.

In this awful place my dear friend Bob Paulson took ill. He suffered violent pains in his lower abdomen and he lay in a little bivouac tent untended for most of the time. Harry Day, the medical orderly, was convinced that Bob was suffering from appendicitis and he tried to persuade the medical officer that this was so. But the doctor would have none of it, saying that it was merely a stomach disorder. Harry pleaded for Bob to be sent to hospital, but it was all to no avail. Our doctor was a very conceited man with a notable indifference to the well-being of the troops in his care. In this case at least, he was also incompetent, as he failed to diagnose a dangerous condition that was all too obvious to his orderly.

Poor Bob, he lay in ever-increasing agony and we had to watch in helpless despair as he tossed about on his blanket in a dirty, sweaty little tent until at last the doctor realised his mistake and ordered him to be removed to hospital. Alas, it was too late. The hospital was two hundred and fifty miles away across bumpy desert tracks and Bob had a burst appendix. He died in Jerusalem hospital on 16 May 1940. He was only nineteen years of age.

When the news reached us that Bob had died, the bottom seemed to drop out of my life. I could not believe that anybody so young and so full of life could be so suddenly snatched away. It made me feel very vulnerable and far from home, and the sadness of losing my dear old friend was too much for me. I was sitting on my blanket sobbing quietly when the sergeant major came into the tent and found me. He was a kindly man, old enough to be my father, and he had served in the First World War. He put his arm across my shoulder and said, 'You're going to shed a great many more tears before this lot is over, my lad.'

I was chosen to be one of the funeral party, which set off for Jerusalem the following day. There was no proper road across the desert from Bir Asluj, just a bumpy track. We were by now accustomed to riding over bumpy ground in bouncing trucks, but during this journey I was thrown up into the air and hit my head on the steel canvas support. My head was cut and my nose started to bleed and it became a nightmare journey as I was covered in dust and blood and had no way to clean myself. This was bad enough – but what must it have been like for Bob Paulson making the same journey with a perforated appendix. The Sister at Jerusalem Hospital told us that she had never known anyone fight so hard for their life as Bob had done. Had he been admitted at an earlier stage in his illness, his life could easily have been saved.

We laid Robert Paulson to rest in Ramleh Cemetery. The trumpeters sounded the Last Post and Reveille, and a firing party from the Hampshire Regiment fired a farewell salute over his grave. Then we sadly turned away to leave him there, our first casualty of the war. I was never to return to that unhappy place, but it has remained in my memory all my life as a symbol of the heartache and the futility of war. Bob's name is carved on the war memorial in the village of Woodborough, where he lived. Far better that he had lived and that as I sit typing these words his grandchildren were filling that churchyard with their laughter. Bob was denied the joy of marrying his girlfriend Mary and sharing with her the upbringing of a family. His life was thrown away before it had properly begun.

\* \* \*

I returned to Bir Asluj, where we continued with our training for some time before returning once more to Hadera. There was news that fierce fighting was taking place on the Western Front, and that the British and French Armies were being heavily defeated. Then came the news that Italy had entered the war in support of Germany, and that Italian troops were advancing in tremendous strength towards the Libyan border with Egypt. The South Notts. Hussars were ordered to come up to fighting trim and be prepared to move within seven days. We were to be the first troops of the 1st Cavalry Division to be sent into action.

These were to be our last days of comparative comfort. There was a great deal of activity and excitement as extra guns, vehicles and equipment were sent from other regiments to bring us up to fighting strength. Eventually, on 23 June 1940, we said goodbye for ever to our friendly camp at Hadera and were soon entrained and on our way via Kantara on the Suez Canal to Egypt and into the Western Desert.

## Chapter 3

# Mersa Matruh – a First Taste of War

Now, at last, we were moving into a war zone where we would be under fire from the enemy, and the thought of this was quite exciting. I don't remember any feelings of fear or apprehension; on the contrary, there was almost a holiday atmosphere in the air, with lots of singing as the train made its way towards the Suez Canal. Here, at Kantara, we were detrained and there was some confusion as the guns and vehicles were all unloaded. I think that originally we had been en route for Cairo, but urgent orders had been received for us to proceed with all haste into the Western Desert. We were to take up positions in Mersa Matruh, which had been established as the main centre of defence against any attack by Italian forces from the west.

We had arrived at Kantara during the early hours of the morning and all the unloading and the ferrying of equipment across the Suez Canal had to be carried out in complete darkness. There was an air raid alarm in progress at the time and this heightened the excitement to some extent, but we got everything across without mishap, and then it all had to be reloaded onto Egyptian State Railways trains. It was mid-afternoon before we were ready to move again. There were two trains, one carrying RHQ, 425 Battery and the light vehicles, and the other loaded with 426 Battery, the guns and the gun-towing vehicles.

The Egyptian State Railways were not renowned for speed and efficiency, and the journey across the Nile Delta and eventually into the Western Desert was very slow and uncomfortable. In spite of this, it was interesting to see the irrigation canals carrying water from the Nile and the water buffaloes turning in endless circles to pump water into the fields. Whenever we stopped in a station the train was invaded by scores of youths carrying baskets full of hard-boiled eggs and crusty bread rolls. They shouted, '*Eggs i bread, eggs i bread,*' as they tried to sell their wares. It was very cheap and I sampled my first '*eggs i bread*' and found it to be very good, but once we had moved out of the Delta and into the desert the egg vendors were seen no more. We were full of confidence and chalked the message, *Mussolini Here We Come,* on the side of the carriage in which we were travelling. The stops, which were long and frequent, gave us the opportunity to visit the locomotive at the head of the train, where we could beg scalding-hot water with which to brew our tea.

When we arrived in Mersa Matruh we were immediately rushed off into a desolate wind-swept wilderness near the coast and about five miles out of the town. Matruh was under constant aerial bombardment and it was wisely decided to put us in a place of comparative safety until we were ready to take over our positions in the fortress. It was a dreadful place; there was no cover of any kind and we arrived in the middle of a severe sandstorm. This was my first experience of a sandstorm. The sand was everywhere: in our eyes, in our throats, in our hair; there was no escape from it. The searing-hot wind continued to blow for hours on end; it was a choking, stifling heat, and visibility was reduced to just a few metres. There was no water available and we all developed raging thirsts; and it was impossible to even think of preparing food in such conditions. I called to mind a picture I had seen as a schoolboy years before showing just such a sandstorm, with the Arabs lying on the sand covered by their cloaks. I decided to follow their example by crawling under my blanket, where I lay sweating and thinking about big jugs of cool spring water and the tinkling of ice cubes.

The following morning I was ordered to go as part of a fatigue party into Mersa Matruh to help with the unloading of stores. By this time the wind had eased somewhat and the worst of the storm was over, but it was still very hot and dusty as we made our way towards the cluster of buildings and I realised that Mersa Matruh was a very small town. The air raid damage was immediately apparent: shattered houses, splintered trees and huge blackened craters bore testimony to the fact that this place had been under heavy attack.

We parked by the side of the road and the officer in charge of the party went off in search of orders. I decided to have a closer look at the damage and so I dismounted and wandered off a little way down the street. I heard the noise of aircraft very high in the sky and I saw people running for cover and then suddenly there was a succession of tremendous explosions and it seemed as if the whole world had gone mad all around me. The noise was ear-splitting, the ground shook and the air was filled with flame and smoke. There had been no warning at all, just a screaming, whistling sound and then this terrifying series of detonations. It was my first experience of any type of bombardment and I was totally unprepared and just stood transfixed as everything seemed to blow up all around me. Then, just as suddenly, it was all over and the noise stopped, only to be replaced by a different kind of shriek; this time it was made by a human voice and a figure lurched into view from behind a building. It was a soldier and he was screaming. He had his hands pressed against his stomach and his entrails were spilling out between his fingers. I watched, horrified, as he sank to his knees, his screams changing to a whine, and then he toppled over, kicking and gurgling in a pool of blood and slime. Within seconds I was on the ground beside him as a second stick of bombs came whistling down to explode nearby. I had never been so frightened in my life as I lay there trembling and bewildered; it had all been so sudden and I couldn't believe that it was all happening. When it was all over I climbed to my feet. The air was filled with dust and smoke, the soldier was lying in a grotesque heap and I could hear a lot of shouting. My first impulse was to run away as far as possible from this awful place. In those few minutes the war had become a reality.

I was thankful to find that none of our party had been injured in the attack and we were able to continue with our duties. It was significant that we were no longer singing and our work was punctuated by repeated fearful glances into the cloudless blue sky. I could not get the sight of the dying soldier out of my mind. Although I was to witness a great many horrifying scenes in the years that followed, that poor man has always remained in my memory.

[*As the account of my experiences over the next few years must be concerned with warfare and battles, I would like to make it clear that it is not my intention to fill the pages of this book with details of horrific scenes such as the one I have just described. Such things are bound to happen in war, but it is not my purpose here to shock. I mention this particular episode because it was my 'baptism of fire' and my first encounter with the realities of death in battle.*]

\* \* \*

The following day we moved into the fortress of Mersa Matruh and took over a gun position from the 1st Field Regiment Royal Artillery. As they pulled their guns out of the gun pits, we were surprised to see that they were equipped with 18-pounder guns, Mark 1. This particular gun had been obsolete at the *outbreak* of the First World War. It says something about the state of our country's lack of preparedness for war when the senior field regiment of the British Army was equipped with guns which had been out of date before the previous war had even started.

Our gun position was on a ridge overlooking the bay to the north and the airfield to the south, which meant that we were able to bring fire to the defence of either, but we were powerless to defend ourselves from the aerial bombardment which continued with unabating fury. The Italians had practically no opposition at all. They did not have very far to come from their bases in Libya, and as we had no fighter planes capable of attacking them, it was a simple matter for them to make their raids without any danger to themselves. Their three-engined Savoia bombers had a distinctive, ominous engine note as they approached and they always came in at maximum height so that they could only be seen as tiny silver dots against the blue of the sky.

There were six anti-aircraft guns at Mersa Matruh, manned by the Egyptian Army. They put hundreds of shells into the air but were never successful in bringing down an enemy plane. Our fighter protection was limited to three Gloster Gladiators. They were very old-fashioned single-engined biplanes that were no faster than the bombers they were chasing, and so they had no hope of ever catching them. In any case they were stationed at Fuka airfield, many miles to the east, and they always arrived five minutes after a raid had taken place, to be met with a barrage from the Egyptian gunners. Fortunately the Egyptians had the same lack of success as in their encounters with the Italians, and as far as I know the little biplanes suffered no damage. One of the reasons for this ridiculous state of affairs was the fact that the RAF changed their recognition signals every two hours, so it is not surprising that mistakes were made.

There was no warning system in the early days and no such thing as radar or radio-location. If the wind was in the wrong direction and we failed to hear the noise of the approaching aircraft engines, the first knowledge we had of an air raid was the exploding of the first bombs. The raids went on pretty well all round the clock and so we had no peace of mind, and we spent much of our time scurrying to our slit trenches and cowering there whilst a raid was in progress. The worst thing about it was the fact that we could do nothing in retaliation, and this feeling of helplessness played havoc with our nerves. The enemy planes usually came over in waves in numbers that were small when compared with the thousand-bomber raids on principal cities later in the war, but it must be remembered that Mersa Matruh by comparison was only a tiny village and the raids were continual.

George and I shared this new experience of being bombed, crouching together in the bottom of a trench we had dug just behind the gun position. One morning he told me that he had a strong premonition that this particular trench was going to receive a direct hit. I needed no further encouragement to start digging a new trench, which was only half completed when the bombs started to fall again. We threw ourselves into the bottom of this shallow hole and hugged the ground as the bombs exploded all around us. Fortunately the guns were untouched and there were no casualties, but when we went to look at our old trench there was nothing there but a big, smoke-blackened crater. I told George that if ever he had the merest suggestion of a premonition in the future, to be sure and let me know immediately!

We lived in a rough and ready manner, as we were to do for the next few years. There was no accommodation of any kind and our home was wherever the gun was placed. There we ate, washed, shaved and slept; everything was centred on the gun. There was no shortage of food, but it was a monotonous repetition of bully stew, tinned pilchards and tinned bacon. These three things between them formed the main ingredients of our diet, together with bread or army biscuits of course. The tinned bacon was wrapped in what looked like a thin plastic wrapper, and in a more temperate climate I believe it would possibly have been quite appetising. In the heat of the desert the opened tin revealed a revolting mixture of melted fat and pieces of pink meat. Our salvation was tea: hot, strong, sweet tea. How we loved our tea! We called it 'char', a Hindustani word borrowed, like so many 'army words' of the time, by the British Army in India. We were also issued with a special type of margarine that had a high melting point; it looked like axle grease and tasted very much the same. We did little grumbling about the food, however; we were young and fit, and we had healthy appetites, so that the quantity was far more important to us than was the taste.

The things that I recall most vividly about our stay in Mersa Matruh are the bombing and the digging. During the months we were stationed there I did enough digging to last me for a lifetime, and if we weren't digging, we were filling sandbags or dragging guns about. The constant exercise was in itself no bad thing and I developed physically to such an extent that when we eventually went back down the line and collected our kit bags, my old tunic would not fit around my chest.

After some time we moved from our position on the ridge and dug new positions nearer the town. Close by was a fairly large, pink building which we knew as Senussi House, and this we used as a canteen. It was only about twenty-five yards behind the guns and at the end of the day it was easy to stroll across to spend the evening talking and drinking bottles of Stella beer. There were no chairs or tables, just upturned crates to serve in their place on the dirt floor, but we found it a pleasant change from sitting in a gun pit. One night we were having a singsong in this apology for a canteen when the bombs began to fall, without warning as usual. We rushed from the room, across a courtyard and back across the sand towards the gun pits and our trenches, diving into them as the bombs exploded close by. As Fred Lamb ran across the courtyard he brushed against a pile of beer crates that were stacked there and a piece of wire became entangled with his pullover. He struggled wildly to free himself but could not escape, and so, without more ado, he picked up the crate, plus the two others piled above it, all of them full of beer bottles, and ran, carrying all three, to the comparative safety of the trenches. It is really surprising, the strength that fear can give.

\* \* \*

One good thing about our regiment was that there was always a good selection of literature available even in the most unlikely spots, such as Mersa Matruh. I did a lot of reading during my off-duty hours and I can clearly remember lying in the ventilation shaft of our dugout on hot, airless afternoons and losing myself in the pages of many, many books. Another recollection I have of this dugout is of a regular soldier who had been drafted to us. He was not a man renowned for his courage and whenever a raid was in progress he would put on his steel helmet, and over this he held a little cardboard attaché case in which he kept his writing materials. Whilst in this ludicrous pose he kept repeating the words, 'Can ye hear 'em, Mon?' over and over again as the bombs came crashing down. This same man eventually made his escape from the bombing and the privations of life in the desert by wrapping a wet towel tightly around his knee and then beating it soundly with the back of a spoon. He continued with this treatment until his leg became so swollen that he could not walk. In this way he achieved his objective of being sent down the line and out of danger.

It was during this period that I had one of the narrowest escapes of my life. It happened in a Royal Engineers' dump, where I had been sent to collect some stores. This dump was situated on a mound; it was irregular in shape, but was roughly a circle of about two hundred yards in diameter. I drove there in a fifteen-hundredweight truck that I parked just inside the compound and I was on my way in search of someone to contact when I heard the first bombs come whistling down. They crashed into the dump with intense ferocity and were so close that I had no time to do more than crouch down where I stood. It was a terrible raid, every bomb landing within the area, and I was convinced that my end had come. I remember repeating to myself, 'I shan't feel anything, I shan't feel anything,' as the ground rocked and heaved beneath me.

The Italian Air Force had chosen this moment to destroy this stores dump and they were making a good job of things. After what seemed an eternity the bombs ceased to fall, the aircraft flew away and I was able to look around me. What I saw was complete devastation: the dump had been virtually destroyed. I found myself standing within a circle of bomb craters, all of them within a few yards of where I had been crouching, frozen by fear. In each case the blast had gone outwards from the centre and by some quirk of fate I had not been harmed by either blast or splinters. I should have been blown to pieces but in fact I had not even been blown over. My guardian angel certainly worked very hard for me on that day.

I do not know what casualties were sustained in that raid, but my own escape was nothing short of miraculous. The truck I had been driving had simply disappeared and I had to walk back to our gun position. The air was heavy with smoke and dust and I kept turning to look at the smoking ruin of the dump, very conscious of the fact that I was extremely fortunate to be still alive.

Obviously, everybody had their near-misses and there were few of us without a story to tell of some narrow escape, but others were not so fortunate. I still feel sorry for our second-in-command, Major Batt, who received wounds that necessitated the amputation of one of his legs. This operation was carried out successfully in the field hospital and he should have recovered, but they failed to notice that he had also been wounded in the other leg. This wound, left untreated, turned gangrenous and it killed him.

George and I remained together in the same troop and on adjoining guns. We shared many experiences in those frightening days and it was good to have him around. One night we were walking back towards the gun position after being on some errand when we were caught in an air raid. Running for safety, we spotted a deep hole in the light of the bomb flashes and dived for cover as the explosions continued all around us. We saw that we had dived into a hole full of stout wooden containers each bearing the notice 'DANGER – AMATOL – HIGH EXPLOSIVE'. We were sheltering in an ammunition dump! It seemed to be a very long raid indeed and we were very glad to leave our refuge at the earliest possible moment.

Cliff Smedley was still my sergeant and a fine man he was in every respect. We once went together to the coast for a swim. Mersa Matruh in peacetime must have been a delightful place: the bay was fringed with white sand and the water was warm and clear and deep, an ideal spot for a holiday. Cliff was a very strong swimmer; he had been a friend of Tom Blower, the Channel swimmer, and the two of them had trained together. He suggested that we swim across the bay and as it didn't look very far I agreed. It was, in fact, a distance of about three miles, which was far beyond my capabilities and so it was not surprising that when we were halfway across I began to tire. Realising that I didn't have the strength to reach the shore whichever way I went, I began to panic and thrash about wildly. Had Cliff not been there I would most certainly have drowned, but he rose to the occasion as he always did. He actually ordered me, in military fashion, to obey him and to lie on my back. Thank God discipline prevailed over panic and I turned onto my back as he had ordered. Then he swam beside me and reasoned with me, telling me to rest quietly for a while. When I had rested and calmed down a little, he told me to swim very gently and after a short time he made me turn onto my back and rest again. In this way, swimming and resting, we slowly made our way towards the opposite shore, which we reached in safety. I knew that I owed my life to this splendid man, who always remained calm no matter what the situation.

The continual bombing began to have its effect upon morale and we were all becoming highly charged and jumpy. There were rare occasions when a man's nerve would fail for a short time. This happened one afternoon in a heavy raid when we were sheltering in the gun pit. A member of our gun crew became hysterical and tried to jump over the edge of the sandbags. He was screaming with fright as I jumped after him and pulled him back onto the ground at the side of the gun. During the whole raid he clung to me in terror as I tried to be reassuring, with my arm protectively over his shoulders. If this gives the impression that I was fearless and brave, then let me hasten to dispel any such illusion. There was no soldier in Mersa Matruh more scared than Ray Ellis; I was absolutely terrified and not one jot braver than the man I was trying to help. It was just that we had become like a family of brothers, so that his need at that time gave me added strength to help him. We all needed each other and that was part of the bond that held us together,

There was a rather amusing incident when I ran for the safety of a trench during an air attack. I took a flying leap into the trench and landed astride Fred Lamb's shoulders, because he was already in the trench and running for the shelter of a dugout. He never broke stride as I dropped onto his shoulders, he just grabbed my ankles and kept on running, and this meant that my head and shoulders were above ground level as he carried me along the trench. Desperate to get under cover, I was beating him about the head and shouting to be released, but all to no avail. He ran straight into the dugout and I smacked into the sandbag wall before falling backwards into the trench.

The ensuing conversation does not bear repeating. Everyone except Fred and me thought it was very funny and after a short time we also joined in the laughing. He was a dear old friend.

Such episodes serve to illustrate the demoralising effect of being under continual bombardment and having no means of either escape or retaliation. Had we been able to hit back in some way we would have felt far less vulnerable and would have had the satisfaction of knowing that the enemy was receiving blow for blow. In the situation as it was, we were well aware that the Italian airmen were in practically no danger at all. We were just sitting ducks!

Apart from the activities of the enemy, there were two main adversaries to overcome when living in the desert under active service conditions: the heat during the day and the intense cold at night. There could be a very wide temperature change between the two, sometimes as much as 40° C, and it was necessary to make sure during the heat of the day that greatcoats and blankets were not left on a vehicle which might be parked for the night several miles away.

Sentry duty was always very unpopular and to be avoided whenever possible. It was a cold, lonely and unpleasant duty made all the worse by the silly arrangement of the daily password. This was given in two languages, English and Arabic, because it was possible, in the pitch dark, to meet an Egyptian soldier also on sentry duty. It could be a nerve-wracking experience to be prowling about in the darkness and suddenly realising that you had forgotten the Arabic word that would establish you as a friend if you bumped into a nervous and trigger-happy Egyptian soldier.

We knew that the Italians had amassed three armies in Cyrenaica and that they were building up a huge force just over the border. We were also very much aware of our own weakness in men and materials, both on the ground and in the air. An overwhelming attack was expected daily, which meant that we had to remain in a constant state of readiness. Any soldier who has been on active service will agree that the most miserable task of the day is 'Stand To'. This is the name given to a period of duty just before dawn – the most likely time for an attack to commence. When snugly wrapped in warm blankets and sound asleep, it is a hateful experience to be roughly awakened by repeated shouts of 'Stand toooo! Stand toooo!' It would still be dark and bitterly cold as we forced ourselves awake and hurried to sit, shivering, on the gun as we awaited the first rays of light to appear. It usually lasted for about an hour and then we 'Stood Down' and another day had begun.

At last the Italians moved forward over the border into Egypt and we braced ourselves for the assault, but for some obscure reason they did not continue with their advance but settled themselves down in strongly defended camps in the vicinity of Sidi Barani. Had they come forward with aggression and determination, they would most likely have overcome the pitiful force that stood against them and the course of the war would have been very different – but that is something for military historians to grapple with.

The Italian move coincided with a change in our defence strategy at Mersa Matruh, and this meant another new gun position. The guns were moved from the gun pits near the coast and spread very thinly along a perimeter about two miles out from the town. Here they were placed in sections of two guns, each section forming the nucleus of a 'strong point'. My brother George and I were once more together on one of these sections; he was with Jim Hardy's gun crew and I was in Cliff Smedley's crew. There was also a small detachment of men from the Cheshire Regiment, who were equipped with one water-cooled Vickers machine gun. It is a sobering reflection of our unpreparedness at that time that two field guns, one machine gun and a total of twenty men were to try to hold a section of the front some two miles long and be ready to repel an attack by both armour and infantry. We needed no encouragement to start digging with a vengeance because in reality there was no 'strong point', just a patch of open desert.

It seems strange to me, looking back, that the design and construction of these defences were left almost entirely to the initiative of the sergeants in charge of the gun detachments. When one considers that this was the main line of defence to protect Egypt, the Suez Canal and the oil fields of the Middle East against three Italian armies already over the border and poised to strike, it becomes even more incredible.

In a very short time the gun pits were dug and the guns made ready for action, and when this had been accomplished other factors were taken into consideration. We began to turn our thoughts and energies towards added protection for both gun and crew, and the construction of underground living quarters. All this time the bombing continued both by day and by night, and the sandstorms came and went as we waited in vain for the Italians to open their offensive. Nine months had passed since we had left England and as yet no one had been granted leave, and under the prevailing circumstances the likelihood of leave seemed very remote. By this time we were well experienced in the art of rough living in the desert, but there was one aspect of desert life that we all found very disconcerting and that was the way in which our hair was always matted with sand.

George had the brilliant idea that we should all shave our heads. I was the first to volunteer, sitting on an upturned petrol tin whilst George got busy with the scissors and cut off all my hair. When the others saw the final result they decided that it was not such a good idea after all! It had to be that day that the first leave rota was posted. Starting the following week, small groups were to be sent off to Cairo every week for seven days' leave – and my name appeared at the top of the first list. I took one sorrowful look in my small shaving mirror and then asked to be transferred to the end of the queue. I was the only man in the regiment with a shaven head.

One of the consequences of Italy's entry into the war was the cessation of mail services between Britain and the Middle East by air mail or via the Mediterranean Sea. This meant that all our mail had to go by boat right round the Cape of Good Hope, and for several months we received no mail at all and were completely cut off from our families at home. Eventually letters did begin to filter through but it was very unsatisfactory. It only takes a few seconds to write these words but the effect of this lack of mail on our morale was very far-reaching. Even when the system was established it still had the effect of making us feel very remote, because if a topic were raised in a letter home, several months would elapse before the reply was received. Apart from the delays of sorting, a letter would have to await the formation of a convoy before making the long sea journey at the speed of the slowest ship, and any reply would have the same delays in reverse. Later on in the war other means were found to allow short messages to pass more quickly, but for the bulk of the mail the slow sea-mail service was our only means of contact. Letters from home never lost their place as the most important single aspect of our lives, except the hope of surviving to return to those we loved.

The spirit of comradeship grew amongst us to fill the emotional gap left by the separation from our families. In small, close-knit groups we shared our thoughts and talked incessantly of mothers, wives, sweethearts, fathers, sisters and brothers, and it was inevitable that private family matters were gradually divulged in a desperate attempt to maintain a feeling of being immediately involved with home life. Within the group all letters were shared, even the most intimate, and we each became involved in the affairs of the others in our small community. It was a most extraordinary relationship that allowed us to lie in our dugout at night discussing matters that in normal circumstances would have been strictly private and personal. I do not recall a single instance of these confidences ever being abused in any way. What I do remember is the pleasure, when a batch of mail arrived, of having so many letters to read and of being able to share in the warm relationships, hopes and aspirations of several families.

As the weeks passed, we toiled away building our defensive position. We excavated a huge hole that was to be our underground shelter and when it was deep enough we made plans to cover it in such a way that it would be shell-proof. We had spotted some girders in a dump on the other side of the fortress and these we intended to steal. The Royal Engineers were engaged in building a concrete pillbox for the machine gunners who were sharing the post with us, and each evening they left all their equipment and returned to their quarters just outside the town.

When the opportune moment arrived we set off in our gun-towing vehicle, and under cover of darkness we dragged the girders one at a time across the desert, manoeuvred them into position over the hole and covered them with corrugated iron sheets. Using the equipment left by the Royal Engineers, we worked right through the night mixing concrete and laying it over the top, and by morning we had a solid concrete roof supported by strong girders. Later that day an irate major from the Royal Engineers drove across the desert following the tracks made by the stolen girders. He demanded that we return them immediately, but alas for his hopes, the concrete was already set and there was little he could do apart from swear and grumble. I dare say that those same girders are still lying buried in the sand somewhere on the outskirts of Mersa Matruh.

Just up the coast a few miles to the west of Mersa Matruh is a small village called Mersa um el Rakham, which at that stage of the war was deserted. It was here that we found the next protective layer for the roof of our shelter in the form of large slabs of rock that had obviously been fashioned for some purpose, but long, long ago. Tansy Leigh insisted that they were old tombstones and he said that to place them on the roof would be a bad omen, but he was overruled and we loaded them onto the gun-tower and took them back to be piled on the roof. In this deserted village we also found lots of tomatoes growing in patches beside the empty mud houses, and these made an excellent supplement to our boring diet. We did not share this knowledge but made frequent journeys to replenish our stocks and enjoyed many a tasty evening meal of toast and pilchards with fresh tomatoes.

When the strong point was completed, it was quite an elaborate piece of work. The gun was under cover and well camouflaged, and a tunnel ran from the gun pit down into our shell-proof living quarters, in which we had constructed bunks of hessian stretched over timber frames. We had even managed to install a large cistern below ground level, and as this could be filled by the water bowser we had the unheard-of luxury of water on tap – the dream of every desert rat!

Over my bunk I built a little shelf on which I kept my favourite photographs, and above that was a hook for my equipment. My steel helmet dangled from another hook within easy reach and with a candle burning on the shelf I could relax quite comfortably. It was here that I read a very interesting book called *How Green was my Valley*, which was a bestseller in England at that time. The only snag with this dugout was the fact that it quickly became infested with fleas, which caused endless discomfort to everyone except me. For some obscure reason fleas did not find me in any way attractive, and I could lie in my bunk in peace whilst my pals were continuously slapping various parts of their bodies.

Jim Hardy and his gun team had been just as busy building their own gun position adjacent to ours. With the detachment of the Cheshire Regiment and their machine guns in the now-finished concrete pillbox, and the two eighteen-pounder guns sitting snugly in their gun pits, we prepared ourselves to help repel the expected attack by the Italian armies poised on the Libyan border.

There was a lot of friendly rivalry between the machine gunners and us. We maintained (in fun) that they were incompetent and therefore placing our lives at risk. One day we challenged them to strip and reassemble their machine guns, which they did with incredible speed and efficiency. Unfortunately for them, probably because we were watching them closely, they omitted to fit some little part and when they filled the cooling system the water just leaked away. There was a great deal of ribald laughter and they were never allowed to forget their mistake. In fact we were all very good friends and it was all taken in good part.

As we had now been toiling day after day in the scorching sun for several months wearing nothing but shorts and boots, it was not surprising that our skins were deeply tanned. This caused some embarrassment when a visiting general questioned the wisdom of having 'native' troops in such an advanced position. Our colonel quickly put him right and he was profuse in his apologies. It is significant that we were still at the stage of using such phrases as 'native troops', and using the word 'native' in such a context and in such a disparaging manner, but of course I am writing about 1940, which is now over half a century ago.

We did not remain static and often the guns were hauled from their pits so that we could go off into the desert on patrol. It was at about this time that I was selected to be trained as an artillery spotter and I was to become an OP ack. The letters OP stood for observation post, and ack meant assistant. An OP party in those days usually consisted of an officer, his assistant and a signaller. These three were usually in company with the infantry and sometimes even in front of them, anywhere where they could have a good view of the enemy positions. I had to learn how to register Zero Lines, observe the fall of shot, make corrections to line, range and angle of sight, bracket targets and bring down shell fire on the enemy. I found it most interesting and worked hard to become proficient. It involved a certain degree of skill in mathematics and I found myself involved with angles and bearings and back bearings, geometry and trigonometry. It all added a touch of spice to the endless digging and diving for cover from the endless raids which made our lives a torment.

One day I was crossing an expanse of open desert with no cover at all when I spotted a fighter plane flying low and coming towards me. It was a biplane and not very fast, but as it approached I knew that I had no hope of escape. The pilot obviously had me in his sights – but then he waggled his wings and flew over me and as he did so I saw the RAF roundels on his wings. It was one of the three Gladiators from Fuka aerodrome. Lucky me! Had he been an Italian I would have met my maker that day.

It was to be September before my name came up again for leave, and by this time my hair had grown to a reasonable length. We travelled down to Cairo from the railhead at Mersa Matruh in a train that resembled a pepperpot it was so riddled with holes made by bomb splinters and machine-gun bullets. What a delight it was when we reached the Nile Delta to travel through green and cultivated countryside and to see towns and villages again.

On arrival at Cairo station my first duty was to hand in my rifle and ammunition to the Military Police. A receipt was given so that it would be possible for me to collect them on my return. This was normal practice. Then we went off to find a hotel. I do not recollect the name of the hotel we used, only that it was somewhere near Abbasia. I shared this leave with Ian Sinclair and Bob Foulds, and we spent practically all our time together. This was our first visit to Cairo, so there was much to be seen and discovered. Cairo in the 1940s was very much smaller than it is today and so we soon came to know the Sharia Fuad el Awal and the Sharia Malika el Farida, which were the two main streets. There was Opera Square with its Opera House and a well-known cabaret called the Bardia; Emad el Dine, terminus of an express tram route to Heliopolis; the Gezira Sporting Club; and Groppi's Rotunda. We even ventured into Sharia Wogh el Burkah, the infamous street of brothels, but we did little more than peep inside one or two of its establishments, as at that time we were still fresh-faced and innocent.

Needless to say a visit had to be made to the Pyramids and the Temple of the Sphinx. In those days it was possible to make the pleasant journey from the centre of Cairo to Giza and the site of the Great Pyramids through miles of open countryside, all under cultivation and with little villages scattered here and there, whereas today it is one vast conurbation teeming with people and traffic and noise all the way to the foot of the Pyramids. I shall never forget my amazement when I caught my first glimpse of them: they were so much bigger than I had expected. They towered into the sky, belittling all my expectations. I climbed to the top of the Great Pyramid of Cheops (no longer permitted) and gazed down with awe at the clear line separating the arid, lifeless desert from the lush, green delta as it stretched away into the distance as far as the eye could see.

Inside the Pyramid it was dark and forbidding; there were no electric lights in those days, just the occasional flash of a magnesium flare which left one blinded and fearful to take another step, whilst the crafty guides demanded an extortionate amount for each flare they lit. We toured the Temple of the Sphinx and I still wonder how they managed to carve those huge blocks of hard stone with such breathtaking precision. We all three had our photographs taken sitting on camels with these wonders of the ancient world as a backdrop. Bob sent all three copies in a parcel to his mother, requesting that she forward them to our parents. My photograph never arrived home, which disappointed me greatly, as it would have been a wonderful souvenir.

It is hard to imagine the sheer delight we found in living again as civilised human beings. To be able to shower, and to wear clothes that were freshly laundered and smartly creased, gave us a wonderful feeling of well-being, whilst to sit down to a properly laid table with a crisp, white tablecloth was joy beyond belief. The food: real butter, newly baked rolls, steak, chips, strawberries and cream – it was like something out of *Alice in Wonderland*. We ate well and slept quietly in clean, soft beds, far from the crash of battle and the fear of imminent death. It was my first leave in over nine months and I enjoyed it to the full.

There was one incident that remains in my mind concerning a very pretty Egyptian girl who served in one of the big stores in the middle of the city. I had caught her eye whilst walking round the store one morning at the start of our leave and later that day I returned and asked her for a date. The girl was rather surprised and confused, and she shook her head saying that it was not possible. I was not to be put off so easily and I threatened to remain standing beside her counter until she changed her mind. After some time my persistence caught the notice of the floorwalker, who informed the store manager that one of his assistants was being harassed. The manager duly arrived on the scene and after a polite and gentle argument said he had no option but to call the Military Police.

At this juncture the girl spoke rapidly to him in Arabic, and as a result of this conversation we all retired to a private room in the staff quarters. Here she explained to me in excellent English that it was not possible for a girl like her to be seen out with a British soldier because it would mean that she would lose her good name. However, she said that if I could get hold of some civilian clothes she would be glad to meet me. I realised her position and was sorry to have caused her so much embarrassment. I apologised to everyone for my stupid behaviour and in my turn I explained that it was impossible for me to find civilian clothes and that in any case it was strictly forbidden for British soldiers to wear anything but uniform. That being the case we parted the best of friends and the manager shook my hand before I left. For the remainder of my leave I could be sure of a little wave and a smile whenever I visited that store. I have often wondered what the girl's name was and what happened to her.

This incident reflects the abnormal life that we were living. This was the first time that I had been in conversation with a girl since leaving England many months before and in common with all my friends I was starved of feminine company. It was not physical sex that I was seeking – that was easy enough to obtain in Cairo; I merely wanted to spend some time in the company of a pretty girl: not an unnatural thing for a healthy nineteen-year-old. I think that the girl had realised this and maybe the manager did too. They were both very kind, because it would have been a simple thing for them to have me arrested and had they done so I would have been in serious trouble.

This very enjoyable leave ended all too quickly and it seemed no time at all before we were back at the station and I was handing in my receipt and collecting my rifle. Soon I was climbing aboard the bullet-riddled train which always pulled out of Cairo at midnight to start the long, miserable journey back into the desert, leaving all the delights and comforts of normal living far behind. I fell asleep on one of the hard wooden benches that served as seats and when I awoke it was daylight and we were back in the wilderness and heading in the direction of Mersa Matruh.

## Chapter 4

# In Action near Sidi Barani

Back at the gun position I was soon into the old routine, with the luxury living of Cairo nothing more than a warm memory. The bombing continued unabated and occasionally a group of Italian fighter planes would swoop down from nowhere with their machine guns blazing, and woe betide anyone found out in the open when this happened because there was no cover to be found anywhere on the open ground. This continual bombardment day after day was very wearing on the nerves. It is one thing to go swiftly into action and take part in a fierce battle, but to be continually under attack for many months is a much more searching experience, even for the bravest of men. There were times when almost everyone found himself weakening under the strain. In the First World War a large number of men were executed for cowardice and we were now beginning to appreciate the fact that many of them had probably been brave men who, in a moment of weakness, succumbed to the pressures of continual danger.

I well remember occasions when, with bombs exploding all around me, I would gladly have surrendered the Suez Canal and all the oil in the Middle East for the opportunity to escape. Sick parades became lengthy as men sought for some legitimate reason to be sent away to a place of safety. Poor old Tansy Leigh, who was a great friend of mine, went through one of these stages. He became as nervous as a kitten and kept reporting sick with imaginary complaints in the hope of being evacuated, but he was always declared fit and sent back to the gun position. He was one of many. One day he was ordered to carry some equipment to another gun position, and this meant that he had to cover about half a mile of open desert. He was absolutely terrified and refused to go. This was an awful situation and we all stopped dead in our tracks because here was one of our close friends placing himself in a position where he could be charged with cowardice in the face of the enemy. Three times he was ordered to go and three times he refused. It was Sergeant Smedley who had given the original order, but soon Captain Porter was involved. They were both reasonable men, and both were anxious to find some way of resolving the situation, but there seemed to be no way of escaping some dreadful outcome. Desperate to save my friend, I volunteered to make the journey myself and after a short council of war between the captain and the sergeant it was decided that I should be allowed to do so and that Tansy would be charged with the relatively minor offence of insubordination. I set off across the desert with all the speed of a startled hare and was able to deliver the equipment and return in safety. Tansy received seven days' field punishment.

I tell the above story because it is a perfect example of how men can react to extremes of pressure in ways totally foreign to their normal modes of conduct. It is certainly not my intention to portray Tansy as a coward and myself as a hero, because we were neither of these things and on another day the situation could easily have been reversed.

Several years after the war I was on holiday in Devonshire and went to seek out my old friend Tansy in his home town. He invited my wife Irene and me to supper and there, in front of his wife and his son, he recounted the above episode in absolute truth, finishing with the words, 'You're a better man than I am, my old mate.' But this was not really the case, for I believe it must have taken far more courage to relate that story than I had managed to summon up to cross that bit of open desert. Tansy (his real name was Reg) was no coward; it was just that the constant bombardment had shattered his nerves. I have heard many stories of medals being awarded to men who were far from deserving of such honours, and I often wonder how many cowards have received medals and how many heroes have been shot or disgraced as cowards in the total folly of warfare.

It is a strange fact that very few men actually confront the enemy in time of war. Keeping one man in the front line requires the backing of hundreds. Even in a unit like our own, which was constantly on active service, there were certain people who were always that little bit safer and a great deal more comfortable than the men at the sharp end. This was true in Mersa Matruh, where our regimental headquarters was established in a deep, bomb-proof, concrete shelter where the staff could work all day and sleep in safety each night. We did not object to this, but we certainly envied them their good fortune. What did cause resentment was the fact that each night we gunners had to take turns on sentry duty at the entrance, still exposed to danger whilst they slept peacefully beneath.

During the month of October I was promoted to the rank of lance bombardier, which entitled me to wear one stripe on my arm. The battery commander, Major Birkin, summoned me to his dugout to tell me of this decision and was in the process of giving me the usual talk that accompanied such promotions. He had just reached the point where he was telling me that it had been noticed that I was 'cool under fire', when a huge bomb exploded a few yards away. The ground heaved, the dugout shook violently and the noise was ear-shattering – and we found ourselves peering at each other through the dust because we had both dived under the table! There was no further talk of coolness under fire.

Now I was nearing the end of my service in 'B' Sub with Sergeant Smedley and my close friends in the gun team. When we went out on patrol, I was constantly being detached to act as an OP ack instead of working as one of the gun team. I found it a refreshing change of occupation because it was very different in almost every way from working on a gun. I quickly came to terms with what was required and soon I found myself proficient in the necessary skills of observing and directing gunfire.

One day I found myself attached to a hastily formed unit of men selected from both batteries, largely from 426 Battery I think, because most of the men were strangers to me. There was a great deal of confusion and the usual rumours were running rife. We had some guns, which seemed to me to be in dubious condition. They appeared to be eighteen-pounders adapted to fire a twenty-five pound shell, but I am not sure of this because I was not a member of any gun team. I cannot remember the actual date, but it was either late November or early December and the weather was very cold as we made our way south into the desert and then west in the general direction of the Libyan border. Many people think of the desert as a place of constant blazing heat, but in fact during the winter it can become quite cold and desolate, and even in the middle of summer the temperature can fall almost to freezing point during the night. To live and sleep in the open calls for a great deal of endurance at any time of the year, but at that particular time we were beset mainly by the cold. It was late in the year and our uniforms of shorts and shirts were made from khaki drill, which was a light material designed for the heat of summer.

In those days it was not military policy to tell the soldiers who were to fight in a battle anything about the strategy. In this instance we were not even told that there was going to be a battle. I thought we were on a normal patrol and I had no idea that the British Army was poised to make a desperate strike against a much more powerful adversary. It was perhaps a good thing that I didn't know because if I had realised that we were going to take on three Italian armies with the pitiful forces at our disposal I would most probably have run away and hidden behind a pyramid. As it was, I shivered in the cold, ate my bully beef and hard tack (army biscuit) and cursed whoever had dreamed up this particular scheme.

As we made our way further west it soon became apparent that a large number of troops were on the move. We saw tanks and a large number of large trucks camouflaged to look like tanks. Amongst the guns in our own column were trucks carrying replicas of field guns which appeared to have been constructed mainly from ply-wood, and the men with them had been supplied with flash bombs called 'Thunderflashes'. It was all very puzzling, but as usual we just shrugged it off as another exercise designed to make us suffer.

Later in the war it became the normal procedure before a battle to inform all troops of the strength and disposition of the enemy and of the general strategy behind the plan of attack. This must have been far better for everybody concerned. To have such knowledge must have enabled them to face their own small part in the battle with a shrewd idea of its importance within the master plan. It also made it possible for them to make intelligent decisions in order to improve the situation whenever this became necessary. For us there was no such information available. As I made my way forwards in company with an officer and a signaller to man a forward observation post overlooking the enemy positions, I honestly believed that it was a training exercise. There was a cold wind, which picked up the sand and lashed it into our faces as we crawled forwards to the top of a mound. I peered cautiously over the top as I had been trained to do – and to my complete astonishment found myself gazing into an Italian military camp.

At the time I knew that the Italians had advanced in large numbers into Egypt and that they had established themselves just over the border. I did not know that they had built several huge defensive camps or how the camps were designed or where they were situated. In fact I had no knowledge of what I was looking at other than the obvious fact that they were Italian troops. Through field glasses I watched them going about their business, obviously completely unaware of our presence. Their uniforms were of a greeny-blue colour; some of them were wearing steel helmets, some had pith helmets and others were wearing side hats.

There appeared to be thousands of them stretching away on either side. Those closest to us were going about their duties in a normal manner, walking about, chatting in small groups or engaged in a variety of tasks and there was no sign amongst them of urgency or alarm. Another fact, far removed from the extent of my knowledge at that time, was that whilst we had been moving towards the Libyan border, the Royal Navy had also been busy steaming up the coast. I now know that HMS *Warspite*, *Terror*, *Aphis* and *Daffodil* were all on station out to sea and like us were waiting for the battle to commence, but it was not until the battle was in progress that I became aware of their presence.

It started with a deafening roar of guns. As the first shells exploded amongst them, the enemy was galvanised into action. We were busy in those first moments establishing our zero line and sending down the first fire orders, and it was not long before we were listening to the scream of our shells as they passed overhead on their way to explode within the enemy camp. Just over to our right a small detachment of Northumberland Fusiliers had established themselves with a large machine gun and they began pouring bullets into the enemy positions. The Italians were taken completely by surprise and it was some minutes before they got to grips with the situation. Then they began to respond with ferocity and the air became filled with the sound of rifle fire, the chatter of machine guns, the crash of mortars and the screams and heavy thumps of exploding shells.

At some time in the midst of all this confusion there was a loud explosion close by and looking over we could see amidst a cloud of dust that the machine gunners were slumped over and around their gun. The officer motioned for me to go over to them and I crawled across, but there was nothing I could do because all four men were dead. It was at this time that the Royal Navy joined in the battle, opening up with their huge guns – the sound of those shells coming over must have been really terrifying for the Italians. The fire was very accurate and we could see the heavy shells bursting with deadly effect within the enemy strongpoint. We watched, fascinated, as shell after shell from both the Navy and from our own guns smashed into their positions. The bombardment continued until dark.

There was little sleep that night, for although the shooting died down to some extent, there was a great deal of desultory fire going on all the time. During the hours of darkness we twice changed position and had some trouble with the telephone cable but by daybreak we were situated in another OP quite close to the enemy lines. A busy day followed. At one period we were able to bracket an artillery position where we caused great devastation, scoring at least two direct hits and inflicting what must have been a large number of casualties.

Soon after this we ourselves came under shellfire. There was no real cover so we could only lie flat on the ground and pray. We survived without casualties and later were able to give covering fire to some attacking infantry (I think they were Coldstream Guards). Some time after this we put down smoke shells to protect some tanks caught in the open. All kinds of orders were being issued and then cancelled again almost immediately. We seemed to be dashing hither and thither amongst sand, shells and bullets and to me, in my lack of knowledge of the general situation, it appeared to be just utter confusion. There was an occasion when we were following some of our tanks and we ran into a hail of machine-gun fire. We had to abandon our vehicle and dive for cover, and the tanks disappeared into the sand and smoke leaving us hugging the ground. We heard the Navy open up again and the ground trembled beneath us as we lay there. Within minutes the machine-gun fire lifted and we were able to regain our vehicle that had been hit several times but still functioned admirably. So it went on and I remember passing a remark to the signaller that I hoped somebody knew what was going on because I certainly did not.

One thing I remember clearly was the inadequacy of our maps. They were 1/25,000 scale and had been compiled, I think, from air photographs. A fully comprehensive map of the desert does not contain a wealth of information, for obvious reasons, but the maps we were trying to work with gave us no help at all. At one point I was crouching behind some rocks with the signaller when I overheard a radio conversation between two tank commanders who were trying to establish their positions. One said to the other, 'I am about two miles south of the second Buq in Buq Buq.' (Buq Buq is the name of a small Arab village just south-east of Sidi Barrani.)

By nightfall we were very tired, but again there was little opportunity for rest. Under cover of darkness we moved to take up new positions and dawn found us in an OP that was quickly spotted by the enemy; we came under heavy shellfire but fortunately were able to extricate ourselves without loss. When we moved to a new position we were quick to register our zero lines, and although the Italian gunners were still active we were this time able to return their fire.

From our position we had a good overall view of the front and were able to gain an impression of the situation as it must have appeared to the Italians. They must have been convinced that they were under attack from a very formidable force. In front of them they could see the flashes of innumerable guns firing almost continuously and behind them were numerous tanks churning up the dust with their tracks. With heavy naval shells landing with devastating effect amongst them, as well as everything the army could throw at them, it must have been very disconcerting. They were not to know that the large majority of the guns were made of plywood, that the gun flashes were merely flash bombs, and nor did they know that most of the tanks they could see were merely camouflaged trucks plying back and forth.

We changed targets to engage the Italian forward positions as tanks of the 6th Royal Tank Regiment advanced with all their guns blazing and the Guards charged down the hill behind them with bayonets fixed. The Italians opened fire with everything they had and for a few minutes all hell was let loose. Then, apart from our own guns, the firing gradually died away and we were mystified as to what had happened. Gradually we began to realise the truth of the situation: the Italians were surrendering.

We ordered our guns to cease firing and stood up to witness an astonishing sight. The Italian troops were giving themselves up not just in platoons or companies but in droves. The whole front had collapsed and hundreds of men were streaming forwards with their hands held in the air. I couldn't believe my eyes, there were so many of them. Later, other groups began to appear until the whole desert seemed to be full of Italian soldiers of all ranks eager to surrender. It was incredible; in a matter of minutes the whole situation had changed beyond recognition and the battle was over. Watching all those men walking into captivity, I could not help getting the impression that it was the end of the war.

There was now confusion of another kind because no plans had been made to cope with such a mass surrender. It seemed to be taken for granted that the prisoners should be marched away to the rear of our positions, away from all their arms and equipment, but there were insufficient men to carry out the task.

By this time we had moved forwards and I found myself in a press of bodies being ordered by an officer to take charge of a large group of prisoners and march them away to the rear.

There must have been over a hundred men and I only had a rifle, but there was no danger and it was not a case of trying to prevent their escape – they didn't want to escape – and so I just walked in front and they all followed behind. I had not the slightest idea where I was going but there were so many similar groups that it was just a question of heading in the same direction as everybody else. After a time we all shuffled to a halt and the prisoners sat in groups on the desert floor as more and more men arrived. How strange it seemed to be in the midst of all these men who were wearing strange uniforms and jabbering together in a foreign language that I did not understand. Here and there could be seen the occasional British soldier but there was no evidence of any proper organisation until eventually a convoy of lorries arrived in a swirl of dust and troops began to dismount. Commands were shouted, order and discipline were obviously being restored and it was a great relief to realise that someone had taken control of the situation.

Things did not happen quickly and by the time I was able to hand over my charges it was almost nightfall. It seemed pointless to go wandering about the desert in the darkness and so I just walked some distance to find a quiet spot before rolling myself in my blanket; being very tired, I was soon fast asleep. The following morning I retraced my steps to the area where I had become separated from my unit, but could find no trace of them; I discovered later that they had returned to Mersa Matruh. This meant that I had no food or water and no form of transport. Hearing of my predicament, some infantrymen shared their rations with me and I was thankful to hold a mug of hot, sweet tea in my hand. It was one of those rare moments in army life when I was under no one's command and so I took myself off to have a look at the Italian positions.

Few people have had the experience of walking through a battlefield within hours of the final shot being fired, and I was filled with curiosity as I made my way towards the stone ramparts that formed the boundary of the camp we had attacked the previous day. In their panic the Italian soldiers had deserted their posts, their equipment, their personal belongings and their dead. Huge shell craters testified to the weight of the naval bombardment and hundreds of bodies in a thousand grotesque poses gave evidence to the accuracy of our fire.

The wounded had been removed and there was a deathly silence over the whole area. I was to read later that an Italian general had explained the mass capitulation on the fact that they had run out of ammunition, but this was nonsense because the whole camp was fully equipped. There were guns by the score, machine guns, mortars, tanks, armoured cars, huge lorries, piles of shells, food dumps, water trucks: everything necessary to wage war. It was obvious from just looking round the camp that with all this equipment and the men they had at their disposal the Italian Army should have been able to sweep our pitiful little force aside and march into Egypt without difficulty. They had everything necessary for victory except one vital factor: for some reason they lacked the resolution and the will to fight.

My solitary tour of this ghastly, windswept place of death was short-lived. A number of lorries arrived and an officer of the Royal Engineers recruited me without ceremony. He put me in charge of a group of men and told me to form a burial party. Other groups were set to work collecting various items of equipment or ammunition, and more lorries arrived carrying prisoners who were to act as labourers.

Being put in charge of a burial party on a battlefield is not an enviable task and it is not one that I would recommend to anyone with a weak stomach. My original intention was to get the men to dig a long series of individual graves but that idea came to nothing because we quickly discovered that beneath a light covering of sand the ground was composed of huge slabs of solid rock. Eventually we found that the only way to deal with the situation was to drag the bodies into some nearby hole or trench that had been previously excavated by the Italians themselves and then shovel rocks and sand down onto them. There was no pretence at any religious ceremony – such a thing never even occurred to me – and nor did I make any effort to establish a record of the men we were burying. There were so many bodies and I was totally inexperienced in such matters. The majority of dead were Italian, but there were also quite a number of Libyans, who were distinguishable by their uniforms and the highly coloured headdresses they wore of scarves in wide stripes of red and blue or black and green or some similar combination of colours. We put rough markers over some of these mass graves, but they merely said things like, 'Ten Ities' or 'Eight Libyans'. In those days we always referred to Italians as 'Ities'.

We were several days engaged in this dreadful work and we grew more callous by the hour. Many of the corpses were decidedly unpleasant and we were glad when a member of our party found some large meat hooks among a pile of discarded equipment. With these we were able to drag the bodies along without having to touch them with our hands. I am not particularly proud of the way we dealt with these poor remains and I now wonder at my own heartless behaviour. I was probably overwhelmed by the horror of it all and anxious to put it behind me. Our own dead were less numerous and they were each given individual graves, usually marked with a rifle stuck into the ground and topped with a steel helmet. The man's identity discs (known as 'dog tags') were also fastened to the rifle.

Eventually I was able to make contact with a group of men from 425 Battery, who had come to help with the task of clearing up after the battle. It was good to be with my old friends again and I was delighted that George was amongst them. The work of burying the dead and salvaging guns, ammunition and equipment continued. It was a very unpleasant period; the weather was bleak and cold and rations were sometimes in short supply, especially water. I was thankful to be issued with some warmer clothes, and as there was plenty of timber in the camps we were able to build small campfires to keep ourselves warm. There was now little danger of attack from the air as the defeated Italian Army was fleeing westwards along the coast into Cyrenaica.

My next promotion came through whilst we were there. Just before Christmas I was made a Bombardier with two stripes. George was also promoted to the same rank, and it was at this time that we shared an odd little escapade. A Hurricane fighter plane had been compelled to make a forced landing way out in the desert, but fortunately the pilot had been able to radio his position before coming down and a rescue party had rescued him. George and I were given the job of going out to guard this solitary plane. We were taken out in a truck with a couple of days' rations and dumped beside the aircraft that stood forlornly in the most desolate wilderness one could possibly imagine. It was like being in the middle of a dusty ocean; nothing broke the skyline in any direction except the departing truck as it dwindled away to a speck in the far distance and then disappeared over the horizon.

Having watched the departure of our friends, we turned our attention to the little area in this barren waste that was to be our home for the next few days. The first thing to become apparent was that there had obviously been a skirmish there in the not too distant past. It must have taken place before the recent battles because the area had been cleared of everything worthy of salvage and only small items of equipment and the odd rifle and bayonet were left to mark the spot where the fighting had taken place.

We were very keen to examine the Hurricane. George climbed into the cockpit whilst I walked around the machine. We had heard a great deal about this famous Hawker fighter, but this was the first time either of us had ever been really close to one. I was examining one of the eight machine guns set in the wings when George called out, 'What's this button on the joystick marked safe and fire?' He roared with laughter as I leapt to one side.

Like almost every other British soldier who had been engaged in clearing up the battlefields around Sidi Barrani, we had both equipped ourselves with one of the excellent Italian groundsheets, which were to be found in abundance. They were vastly superior to the British groundsheet, which was an abomination. The Italian version was of a closely woven fabric which was wind- and waterproof and skilfully designed to be used not merely as a groundsheet but also as a sleeping bag and as a cloak. In addition to this there were buttons and buttonholes that enabled them to be easily fastened together to make anything from a two-man tent to a small marquee. We quickly set to work to construct a little tent for ourselves and when we had done so we fastened the ridge to the wing of the aeroplane and skewered the four corners to the ground with old bayonets we found lying in the sand.

It was a beautiful night, with a huge moon shining in a clear sky, as we bedded down, crawling into our little shelter to lie talking about the folks at home and wishing that we were with them. I have always been a restless person and as we lay there chatting in the moonlight I was idly digging a little hole in the sand with my fingers. Suddenly my finger touched something solid and it only needed a few moments' exploration to discover that it was a human hand. I sat bolt upright and had just finished telling George that there was a body beneath us when the tent was mysteriously lifted and carried away. Nowhere in the world at that moment were there two more terrified men. The absolute silence, the loneliness, the moonlight, a dead body and a ghostly tent that moved of its own accord all combined to scare us out of our wits. We leapt from our blankets and ran several yards before turning and I am sure we expected to see the grim reaper himself standing there in the moonlight. Instead everything was calm and still and we quickly returned to a more rational state of mind. A sudden gust of wind had caused the aircraft to move slightly, and this explained the mystery of the moving tent. And we now knew why there were no bodies to mark the spot where the fighting had taken place: they had all been buried in shallow graves. Needless to say we found a different place to finish our night's rest, without the shelter of a tent.

The gusts of wind during the night had been heralds of a developing Khamsin and as the day progressed so the wind became stronger and we soon found ourselves in the middle of a blinding sandstorm. As we had no shelter it was absolute misery. We took turns sitting in the cockpit of the plane, but with the canopy closed it was like sitting in a furnace. It was a fierce storm that raged without abating into the second day, and we realised that there was no hope of anyone finding us whilst it continued. We had very little food and water, and decided to ration what little we had in case we became stranded for any length of time. The second day turned into the third without any let-up and it was a frightening experience to watch our precious water dwindling as we lay on the ground covered by our groundsheets and tried to shield ourselves from the stinging sand. By the fourth day we were very alarmed and very thirsty; the last of the water had gone and still the wind was sweeping relentlessly across the desert, reducing the visibility to little more than a few yards. It was mid-day before we noticed any slackening of its power and then it gradually died away and things returned to normal. Hot and desperately thirsty, we scanned the horizon impatiently until at last the long-awaited little dust cloud appeared on the skyline. It became a speck, which quickly transformed itself into a truck bearing our relief and water, precious water. I have often wondered since just what we were doing there in the first place. Who on earth did they think was going to steal an aeroplane in the middle of a desert? There wasn't a living soul for miles and miles and miles, and in any case the plane was unable to fly. Why did it have to be guarded? Only the army knows the answer.

* * *

We spent Christmas in a desolate place known as Tumar West, which had been one of the outlying Italian camps. Somebody had obviously made an effort to brighten our lives a little because the ration truck brought us each a parcel from 'Friends in England & Cairo'. The parcels contained cigarettes and a few goodies, and there was also a small consignment of beer and some meat, which was said to be turkey. We had strong doubts about this, but at least it wasn't corned beef! We made the best of things, thankful to be alive and out of danger, but it was a dreadful place, featureless and desolate, with a cold and searching wind moaning through the remains of the Italian defences and over the shallow graves of the men who had recently died there. As we sat, dirty and rather disconsolate around a little fire of shattered timber, I couldn't help recalling the previous Christmas that I had spent with Binkie. Her sparkling eyes and the warm glow of the fire in her comfortable home seemed to be further away than the crescent moon that shone so coldly over the benighted battlefield which spread around us.

A particular incident occurred in that awful place, and has remained vividly in my memory ever since. It concerned the body of an Italian officer that I discovered in a dugout. I clambered down the steps to find him sitting bolt upright in the half-light. He was facing me from behind a wooden structure that had served him as a desk, his eyes were wide open and for a few seconds I believed him to be still alive. Then I realised that he was frozen in death and was covered with a fine layer of dust. There were no obvious signs of injury and I decided that he must have been killed by the concussion of a heavy shell. It was most eerie and I just climbed back up the steps and left him sitting there, silent and alone. I don't doubt that he is still where I left him.

Soon afterwards we were relieved of these unpleasant duties and returned to Mersa Matruh, where to my delight I discovered that I was to go on leave to Cairo. The train pulled out from the battered station in the afternoon of New Year's Eve and I happily settled myself down for the long journey down to the Nile Delta. I can recall that journey with particular clarity, not because anything very exciting happened – in fact it was a very peaceful and uneventful trip – but for the thoughts that went through my mind as the train carried me away from the horrors and hardships of the previous months.

I believe that many men, before going into battle, harbour a secret fear that they may fall short on courage when the testing time arrives, and I had been no exception. It is one thing to be strutting about in uniform posing as a gallant and fearless warrior when there is no element of danger to contend with. It is quite a different matter when you are actually under fire and crouching in some lonely corner, cold and dirty and afraid. Now I drew satisfaction from the knowledge that I had cleared that particular obstacle. Whilst I had done nothing very courageous, and certainly could not lay claim to any deeds of glory, that was of little importance. What mattered to me was that I had proved to myself that I could withstand the hardships and overcome my fear, and having done so I would never again feel the need to prove myself. Six months previously I had gone into the desert as a youth, but now my youth was over and I knew that the train was carrying at least one man who would never be the same again.

## Chapter 5

# Gennia

In common with most leave parties we were a dirty and rather dishevelled group, but very happy to be leaving the desert behind us for a few days. It was New Year's Day 1941 and for us it was a marvellous start to another year. Arriving at Cairo station very early in the morning, we went through the usual procedure of handing in weapons and ammunition to the Military Police before making our way by taxi to a hotel that we had been able to book at a special bureau on the station forecourt. The hotel staff were well geared up to the situation and dirty clothes were whisked away, laundered, dried and ironed in the time it took me to shave and to loiter for a while in a hot, relaxing, soapy bath. Then, in newly starched uniforms, we experienced the delight of sitting down to a hearty breakfast of bacon and eggs, toast and marmalade, and deep cups of delicious coffee, just revelling in all the unaccustomed luxury of chairs and tables and crisp white tablecloths. Breakfast over, we took a leisurely stroll through the city, happily conscious of the fact that for a whole week we were free to follow our own desires.

That same evening, my desires took me in the direction of Opera Square and the Bardia, a high-class restaurant and cabaret. My friends had tried to persuade me to join them for a tour of the bars and the nightclubs, which was just another way of saying a glorious binge, but I had other ideas. I wanted to spend a little time in a more refined atmosphere, where the hum of quiet conversation mingled with the tinkle of glasses and the entertainment matched the high quality of the food. In a normal situation the Bardia would have been far beyond my reach financially, but I had not spent a penny for over three months and so I decided to do myself proud on this first evening back in civilisation.

It was a splendid place, full of chandeliers and mirrors and lights; everything was extravagant. The bars were stocked with every drink imaginable and the floors were scattered with rich carpets and deep, leather divans. After a couple of drinks at the bar I was escorted into the restaurant by a huge, jet-black

Sudanese waiter, who wore a long, spotless robe with a scarlet cummerbund and the inevitable fez perched above his enormous face. I noticed that obviously wealthy civilians of many nationalities mainly occupied the tables but there was also a goodly sprinkling of British officers. As far as I could ascertain, I was the only non-commissioned rank in the restaurant and my presence there caused a few eyebrows to be raised, but my experiences during the previous weeks had so hardened me that I was impervious to their unfriendly curiosity and their cold, unwelcoming stares left me completely unmoved. I sat comfortably at a table for two, ordered my meal, enjoyed my drinks and watched the floor-show as I waited for my dinner to be served.

In common with everything else in that establishment, the floor-show was of a very high standard, and the meal, when it arrived, was absolutely delicious. When I was halfway through my main course the lights were dimmed and the spotlights picked out the figure of a girl who was about to perform a solo act. She was exquisite, so elegant and dainty that I felt that I could have picked her up with one hand and thrown her up to the stars. I have never professed to know much about dancing, but she held me spellbound and my food was forgotten as she swept and twirled around the floor with an effortless grace that was a pleasure to behold. By the time her act was over I was completely captivated and throwing all caution to the winds I beckoned a waiter and told him to pass my compliments to the dancer and to invite her to join me at my table.

To my immense surprise, about ten minutes later I saw her threading her way through the tables in my direction. I stood politely and we both smiled as I held the chair for her and then I resumed my seat and gazed across at her. She was beautiful, with large, dark eyes that looked straight into mine with just the trace of a twinkle, and then I realised that I was completely out of my depth. All my recently acquired confidence evaporated into the smoke-filled air and I just sat tongue-tied, realising that I didn't know how to cope with the situation I had provoked. I was trying desperately to find some apposite remark to end the dreadful silence, and she watched me quizzically for a few moments before turning her head slightly to one side to say kindly. 'Suppose you start by telling me your name.'

I breathed a sigh of relief as she rescued me from my embarrassment and the situation was saved. She spoke impeccable English with a delightful accent, and soon we were chatting away like old friends. I quickly discovered that she had a bubbly sense of humour and the twinkle in her eye proved to be a true indication of her sense of fun. She joked about the situation of me being the only non-commissioned soldier in the room and mimicked a haughty person registering disapproval. It sounded so funny to hear an Egyptian girl trying to imitate an affected English accent. She screwed up her face and said, 'The demmed impertinence of the mayrn.'

In the flow of conversation I learned that her name was Gennia (pronounced Je-nee-ya) and that she was nineteen years of age. She was very natural and open in her manner. She explained how she had trained as a dancer, and I gathered that she was very proud of her achievement in securing her own act at the Bardia and that it was very remunerative. Quite innocently I asked her if she did anything else apart from dancing. This stopped her short. She looked hard at me for a moment before making that characteristic little gesture of turning her head slightly and then she said, 'Are you asking to go to bed with me?'

Her directness took me by surprise and my confusion returned, but I managed to convey that such a thing would be very much to my liking. She looked at me for a few seconds and then smiled and said, 'It would cost much more than you can afford, I should imagine.'

This set me wondering and so I queried, 'How much is that?'

She looked at me for a few seconds and then said, with a broad smile, 'Five hundred piastres.'

'Five hundred piastres,' I echoed. 'Phew, that is far beyond my pocket.' It was indeed: five hundred piastres was the equivalent of more than two months' pay for me at that time.

'Never mind,' she said. 'It doesn't matter. I am enjoying your company and just sitting here chatting together.'

Having got that little matter out of the way, we continued in friendly conversation until I happened to look up and see Frank Birkinshaw, one of my pals, standing just inside one of the entrances beckoning to me. I excused myself and went over to him.

'Wherever did you manage to pick up that dreamboat?' he asked. I told him that the operative word was certainly 'dream' because she was way out of our class with a price tag of five hundred piastres. He whistled in amazement, and after a few seconds he left and I made my way back to the table, only to find that Gennia had disappeared. I thought that would be the last I would ever see of her, but in fact she had merely gone to prepare for the second part of her act. This I watched with even greater interest than before and I was delighted when she later returned to join me again at the table.

Much later in the evening Frank Birkinshaw returned and again beckoned me over to the entrance where he held out his hand. 'The lads have had a whip-round,' he said and placed five hundred piastres into the palm of my hand. 'Go on, mate,' he grinned. 'Go and enjoy yourself!' Has anyone ever had better friends than I?

I left the Bardia with Gennia sometime after midnight and she told me to remove my hat because it marked me immediately as a soldier and we were going into a part of the city that was strictly out of bounds to British troops. Soon the familiar part of Cairo was left behind and we walked hand in hand through a maze of tiny streets, most of which were empty of both people and traffic. It became an exciting experience to be hurrying along these silent streets in the moonlight with a pretty girl holding me by the hand and guiding me confidently towards her flat. It was quite some distance and we turned many corners before she stopped before a huge wrought-iron gate and spoke through the bars to a watchman who was hidden just inside. Slowly the gate opened and she whispered, 'Give him ten piastres.'

I slid the money into the man's hand as we passed into a large courtyard. In the misty moonlight I could see gardens and a fountain playing as we made our way through, but it was mostly shadows and I was content to follow where she led. A door was opened and she spoke softly to an old woman before passing inside with me close behind her. Another door was opened and she switched on the light as we entered a room – and I got the shock of my life.

I had half-expected to find myself in some poor dwelling but instead it was the lap of luxury. The flat was beautifully appointed and spotlessly clean and tidy. She poured me a drink and we sat awhile smoking and talking before she led me into the bedroom. It contained a huge bed and there was a magnificent walnut bedroom suite that must have cost a small fortune, and the floor was covered with a soft, white fluffy carpet.

'The bathroom is over there,' she said pointing to a door in the corner and I found myself in a tiled bathroom that actually shone. When I returned to the bedroom she was half lying on the bed wearing nothing but a tiny, gold wristwatch. This was the first time in my life that I had seen a naked girl and I remember feeling clumsy and awkward because she was so dainty and petite. When I sat down and removed my army boots and placed them beside her tiny shoes she started to giggle and soon we were both laughing. I felt very happy and relaxed because I knew that aside from any other aspect of our relationship, we had become friends.

The following morning I returned to my hotel to be greeted by all the expected catcalls and banter. I took a bath and tumbled into bed and they all went out laughing and left me in peace. I met Gennia at lunchtime in the Kursall bar, where we had a drink before lunch, and then we went to Heliopolis and spent the afternoon sunbathing and swimming in the huge open-air pool. When we were preparing to leave she started making plans for the evening: I was to go to the Bardia at about eight o'clock … I stopped her before she could go on and began to explain that I was in no position to repeat the previous night's extravagances. I was just pointing out that it would take me several months to save sufficient money to do so when she, in turn, stopped me. Placing a finger on my lips, she said, 'We will not talk about money any more, you and me.' She handed me the five hundred piastres and told me to give the money back to my friends.

We spent the whole of my leave together and it was one of the happiest times of my life. We visited the Gezira Sporting Club and the Pyramids, went to the open-air cinema in Ezbikhia Gardens, lunched at the Kursall, took afternoon tea at Groppi's Rotunda, sunbathed and swam at Heliopolis and dined each night together at the Bardia between her acts. I never paid for another meal at the Bardia, but I never discovered whether she paid for our meals or whether the waiters forgot to produce the bills! She certainly seemed to have a lot of influence there. Then each night we walked back, hand in hand, to her flat and the comforts and delights of that huge bed. One night as we lay talking quietly in the dark she said, 'You will never forget me as long as you live and I shall never forget you.' This narrative confirms the validity of at least the first part of this prophecy, but I shall never know about the second.

Apart from being an accomplished dancer and an extraordinarily beautiful girl, Gennia was also an extremely kind and generous creature. She was gentle and loving by nature and she had the most delightful and ready sense of humour, which meant that in her company I always found myself smiling and happy. Sometimes I still think of that tiny, winsome Egyptian girl and I feel sorry for those people whose experience of life has denied them the privilege of ever knowing someone as kind and as honest as Gennia. I have always remembered her as a bright, warm, sunny afternoon during a long period of bleak, wet weather.

It was a sad moment when my leave came to an end. I left her where I had found her, in the Bardia. We had a final drink, squeezed hands and blinked back a few tears as we kissed goodbye. I had to run all the way to the station and was only just in time to collect my rifle and jump aboard the dreaded midnight train that was to carry me back into the desert.

## Chapter 6

# Suez

The battle was won, the enemy destroyed and we were leaving it all behind us: the heat and the thirst, the crash of bombs and shells, the fear, the weariness and the desolation of those vast, open spaces. We had entrained at the railhead in Mersa Matruh in the early afternoon and now darkness was approaching. We were tired and dirty, hungry and uncomfortable as the train rumbled on through the unchanging scenery. No one complained. It was nothing unusual for us to be in this condition and we had come to accept such situations as normal. Nor did we show any surprise when the train jolted to a halt, for this was a common enough occurrence, but we stirred ourselves sufficiently to look out of the windows … It was a sight to behold! There, along the side of the track, was a long line of Aldershot ovens, glowing red and issuing smoke and sparks in abundance.

We lost no time in clambering down from the train with our mess tins and enamel mugs and soon we were being served with hot, delicious food. Huge slices of newly baked bread, fat sausages bursting with goodness, piles of floury, mashed potatoes and gallons of hot, sweet tea. It was like something from a dream as we crouched there in the darkness and ate our fill. I can recall certain meals during my lifetime that rank high above any others, and strangely enough all of them were very simple. This was one such meal: it was nothing more than a few sausages and mashed potatoes, but it outshone the finest banquet ever provided. Who arranged it I shall never know, but it was one of those rare occasions when the army managed to spring a surprise that was actually pleasant.

The following morning we arrived back in the Nile Delta and slowly made our way through Alexandria and countless small towns, going ever eastwards in the direction of the Suez Canal. There was the usual speculation about our final destination and the inevitable rumours circulated to fill the void and stir our imaginations. This time we had it on good authority (the colonel's batman, no less) that we were going into barracks at Ismailia. Most rumours were said to have their origin in the words of the colonel's batman, but had this unfortunate fellow been as guilty of leaking secrets as he was purported to be, he would have been 'shot at dawn' every new day. However, in spite of our understandable doubts, the rumour gained credence, as rumours will, and the thought of going into barracks lifted our spirits greatly, for barrack life meant a return to something approaching civilised living conditions. We had by this time experienced nearly eighteen months of army life and never during that time had we enjoyed proper sanitary arrangements or washing facilities. We had never had a bed in which to sleep and never been housed in reasonably comfortable conditions. It was hardly surprising then that we welcomed a rumour that promised to restore such luxuries.

Imagine then, our great delight when we eventually detrained at Moascar, a small town on the Suez Canal, and marched into barracks there. We were singing happily as we thought of beds with sheets, wardrobes and lockers, dining rooms with tables from which to eat, showers, water closets, sports fields for our leisure hours, to say nothing of the proximity of a town. Try to imagine our dismay as we continued to march past all the building blocks and finished up on a dusty sports field. We halted and stood in ranks, half-hoping that there had been some ghastly mistake, but no. From somewhere down the line we heard the voice of the sergeant major bellowing, 'Right – that's it, lads. Get yer beds down!'

There were to be no barrack-room facilities, no taps gushing forth clean water, none of the things of which we had been dreaming. It had been just another rumour after all. Later that evening, when we were able to venture into the canteen, we gazed in wonder at the men who were spending their army life with all these luxuries that they seemed to take for granted. We bore them no ill will, but we certainly did envy them as we trudged back to sleep rough on the playing field. At least, we told ourselves, we are in the middle of a town and that is something to be thankful for. But the following morning even this disappeared into the mists of unreality as a convoy of trucks arrived to carry us away.

We found ourselves travelling south alongside the Suez Canal. The Canal was a vital communications link which the enemy was anxious to disrupt and his method of doing so was to send aircraft, at night, to drop sea mines into the water. A special type of magnetic mine was being used. These mines lay on the bottom and as each ship passed over them a needle would click over, one notch at a time, until it reached a pre-set point whereupon the mine would explode with devastating force. This made it difficult to sweep the channel clean. A minesweeper could pass up and down several times without exploding a single mine and then a cargo ship would pass and be blown out of the water.

Our job, we learned, was to be twofold: we were to try to shoot down the enemy planes as they came in very low, and secondly, we were to watch the mines as they descended by parachute, and pinpoint their positions in the water. To perform these operations we were split into parties of four men. These parties, each under the command of an NCO, were established at quarter-mile intervals along the banks of the Canal. I found myself in charge of Number 16 Post. We had four rifles, a Bren gun, some ammunition and precious little else, but we set to work with a will and by nightfall we had constructed a new home for ourselves. We dug four slit trenches in which to sleep and a gun-pit for the Bren gun. So much for our dreams of barrack-rooms and beds.

The enemy was not slow to make an appearance, and on that first night they came in flying low and at fantastic speed. As they flew down the Canal they raked the banks with machine-gun fire and we responded in like manner. It was a dangerous occupation and very noisy and colourful because most of the ammunition was in the form of tracer bullets. As well as dodging bullets and firing at the planes, we had to keep a close watch for the white parachutes, which spread themselves as they carried their deadly loads down into the waters of the Canal. On that first night we discovered to our horror that not all the mines landed in the water – some landed on the banks triggering the most fearsome explosions.

It was not at all a pleasant job but it did have its compensations. The enemy only came at night and this meant that we had the whole of the day to enjoy ourselves in safety. We discovered that lying in the sun on the banks of the Suez Canal could be a very pleasant occupation indeed. We spent several weeks in this fashion and we were never bored because there were so many interesting diversions to occupy our minds. We were told that over 250,000 tons of shipping was being held up in the Canal and the Bitter Lakes at that time because of the danger from mines. One memorable event was the passage of the aircraft carrier *Illustrious* as it made its way slowly towards the Mediterranean Sea. We held our breath as it passed our position in case it exploded a mine, but it made its way safely along the whole length of the Canal – a distance of some ninety miles.

One calm and peaceful afternoon we were watching a freighter as it sailed silently past our position when, without warning, there was the most dreadful explosion and the ship seemed to heave itself out of the water. What followed was complete pandemonium; there was frenzied shouting, the ringing of bells and the shriek of escaping steam as the crew tried desperately to bring the stricken vessel to the side of the Canal. They got a boat over the side and managed to fasten a huge wire cable to one of the bollards set at intervals along the bank. A steam winch began the task of hauling the ship to safety, but by this time it was listing heavily and the strain was terrific. We watched with horror as the wire cable snapped and snaked with incredible speed along the deck, cutting down two crew members as it went. In the midst of all this confusion another sailor had fallen overboard and we could see him struggling in the rush of water that was swirling around the listing vessel. By this time we had left our post and rushed to offer whatever help we could; without stopping to think, we all four jumped into the water to try to save the drowning sailor. It was a desperate struggle, but somehow we managed to drag him clear of the ship and into calmer water. With the help of some sailors who had scrambled ashore, we got him to safety. They managed to keep the ship reasonably upright, either afloat or resting on the bottom – I never did find out which, but it was still there when our tour of duty finished.

As we were stationed at the southern end of the Canal, it meant that we were fairly close to the town of Suez. Permission was given for one man from each post to visit the town every afternoon. In order to do this it was necessary first to walk to the end of the Canal, a distance of about two miles from my post, and then to take a ferry across the bay. Unfortunately this ferry sailed very infrequently and to miss it was to forfeit the afternoon's outing. This happened to me one day when I arrived at the jetty only to see the little boat's wake disappearing in the direction of Suez. This was most infuriating and I cast around in search of other means of transporting myself across the bay. I spotted a little steamer making its way along the coast, very close to the shore, and as a last resort I hailed it in the very unseamanlike way of thumbing a lift. To my complete surprise it turned into the jetty and stopped long enough for me to jump aboard.

The small crew greeted me with friendly smiles. They were all Sudanese, with black, shining faces, but none of them could speak a word of English. Feeling very pleased with myself, I settled down on the deck on a pile of sacks to enjoy the sunshine and the prospect of a free trip across the bay, but my complacency was short-lived. It soon became apparent that we were not heading for Suez; in fact the town of Suez was fast disappearing abaft the beam on the starboard side. In a sudden panic I rushed to the little wheelhouse to explain that I wanted to go to Suez. All I got for my trouble was friendly nods and smiles, and as the afternoon passed I realised from the position of the sun that we were heading south in the direction of the Gulf of Suez.

I was to remain on that little ship for three nights and four days as it made deliveries and collections of goods from tiny village ports along the Gulf. I slept on the deck covered by sacks and ate in company with my smiling hosts. The food was quite enjoyable: a sort of flat, unleavened bread and a vegetarian diet of beans, tomatoes and fresh, green leaves which were very tasty.

What a strange experience it was; I had no idea of the names of the villages we visited, only that whenever I went ashore I was always treated with friendliness and courtesy. I was extremely careful not to stray too far in case the ship left without me. It was a great relief when we started to sail north again and I was very thankful one day to see that we were approaching the familiar jetty from which we had left. They pulled in and I jumped ashore and the little steamer sailed away as I stood waving farewell to my smiling friends with whom I had never been able to exchange a single word.

Making my way back along the canal bank, my first task was to report to battery headquarters where, complete with four days' growth of beard, I explained to the orderly officer the reason for my absence from duty. There was some deliberation, but it was quickly decided that the matter should be dropped. I don't think anybody could find anything suitable to say under the circumstances. I never did manage to spend a pleasant afternoon in Suez.

The planes continued to arrive at various times of the night according to the phases of the moon. It was always very noisy and fast-moving action with lots of tracer bullets and the explosions of mines that detonated on impact with the bank. One night we had a very near-miss when a mine hit the bank dangerously close to our position. We were all blown clean out of our post and over the silt bank. We were badly shaken but no one was injured and we were soon back in position and digging new trenches for ourselves. None of our weapons had been damaged, but we did lose some personal belongings.

During our time there I must have fired thousands of rounds at aircraft that were very low and well within range, but I never had any known success. It is surprisingly difficult to hit a low-flying aircraft, particularly in the dark. There were times when I was convinced that I had scored many direct hits but it was all to no effect.

The swimming was excellent and as we were sitting all day at the water's edge swimming became a common pastime. There was just one snag, however. As we were stationed at the southern end of the Canal, there was always the danger, we were told, of sharks making their way out of the Red Sea and into the waters of the Canal. Although this danger was slight, we always had to mount a watch whenever a member of the party was swimming. It happened one day that I was enjoying a swim when the lad on watch shouted, 'SHARKS!' Turning to look in the direction of his pointing finger, I saw to my horror a black fin skimming through the water. My swimming ability has never been more than average, but I am convinced that during the next few seconds I broke the world's water speed record in my dash for safety. In spite of this I was far too slow and long before I reached the bank I felt a hard, smooth body brush against me. It is a good thing that I did not die of heart failure because I was in no danger at all. They were not sharks but porpoises, and these friendly creatures enjoyed nothing more than to play with anyone they found swimming. I did not remain to play on that day, though, being quite content just to sit on the bank and watch them. Actually we never did see any sharks whilst we were there.

Our next move was to a camp called El Tahag, which was situated in a desert area somewhere between Cairo and the Suez Canal. Shortly after our arrival there, we were issued with brand-new twenty-five- pounder guns that had just arrived from England. There was great excitement as the new guns were lined up on the gun park, and we were keen to examine them. Then there was a grand parade and the colonel addressed the regiment. He told us that we were shortly to form part of an invasion force that was to land on the island of Rhodes. We had been selected to be amongst the spearhead troops, and very high casualties were to be expected. He further informed us that there would be an acute shortage of vehicles during the first days after the landings and we would most probably have to manhandle our guns into position. In view of this we were to start immediately with a hard training programme. He knew that we would all be very proud that we had been selected for this important role. Needless to say, we had very different ideas about that. Our preference would have been for something slightly less glorious, such as taking charge of a rest camp near some shady, Mediterranean lagoon.

The next two or three weeks were spent in hard, physical labour. We ran up and down steep sand hills carrying full packs. We went on long, tiring route marches through the sand carrying full kit in full Field Service Marching Order. We dragged guns for long distances with drag ropes until our hands were sore and our backs ached. It was very wearying but we were very hard and fit and well able to cope with all these things, especially as we usually returned to camp in the evening for a good meal and an hour or two to spend in the canteen.

One evening I was summoned to the tent that served as a battery office for an interview with the battery commander. He explained to me that the senior officers had been considering the situation of my brother and I both being in the same troop. They were concerned because it presented the possibility of us both being killed by the same burst of machine-gun fire or the same fall of bomb or shell. In order to prevent such an occurrence, it had been decided that I should be transferred to 'A' Troop immediately. I was to move all my kit into 'A' Troop lines and report to the gun crew of a certain sergeant (who will remain nameless) on number four gun.

I left the tent in a state of complete and utter bewilderment. The thought of leaving 'B' Troop was an unexpected and shattering blow. No one reading this book will ever realise the effect this move was to have upon my life. 'B' Troop had become my home. In an existence such as ours at that time the word home no longer represented simply a dwelling place – it had a wider connotation. The group of men whom I had come to think of collectively as 'B' Troop had become my home. Now I had to leave them. George, Fred Lamb, Clifford Smedley, Bob Foulds, Jim Hardy, Tansy Leigh, Arthur Fox, Wag. Harris, Danny Lamb: they were all passing before my eyes. We had shared everything since the moment of our call-up nearly two years previously. It was like being deported to a foreign land. In fact it was worse because it meant that I would have to go into action again with a group of comparative strangers. There can be no doubting that it was a wise and considerate decision by the officers concerned, because for two brothers to be killed simultaneously would have been a terrible thing for our parents to have to face, but it left me in a dreadfully lonely situation. I was quickly to find that the men in 'A' Troop already had their own well-established friends and they were a tightly knit community. They gave me a friendly enough welcome, but there was no real warmth – that would have to be kindled. I visited my old friends whenever it was possible to do so, but things were never the same again. The old days had gone for ever.

It was during this period that I celebrated my twenty-first birthday. I spent the morning of that day working out the angles and figures necessary for an artillery barrage and after lunch we set off on a twenty-mile route march. It being my birthday, I felt entitled to use a bit of cunning to lighten my load. I cut a piece of cardboard to the exact shape of my pack and fitted it inside so that the empty pack gave the appearance of being full. After marching several miles we stopped for a rest and I foolishly lay back on my pack like everybody else. The cardboard crumpled and the pack flattened and gave the game away. There was a great deal of laughing and banter as the lads filled my pack with heavy rocks which, as a point of honour, I had to carry for the remainder of the march.

That evening George went into the canteen to try to win some money on the Crown and Anchor Board, so that he could give me a birthday treat of some kind. The fact is that nobody ever wins on the Crown and Anchor Board except the man who is running it, and so George lost what little he had. He then came to me and borrowed my money, which he lost in like fashion. So it happened that my twenty-first birthday fizzled out with the two of us sitting in the darkness of my tent talking about home.

Our next move was to Kabrit, which was to be our final camp before we embarked on the invasion of Rhodes. The boats which were to ferry us across the Mediterranean were already at anchor in the Bitter Lakes that form part of the Suez Canal. Some members of the regiment and a large quantity of stores and equipment were already on board when everything was suddenly cancelled. We heard that a large force of German troops – the Afrika Corps – had been landed in Libya in support of the Italian armies already there. This powerful force had already broken through our line at Ajedabia and was said to be advancing rapidly, sweeping all before it. This was very worrying news because since the start of the war the Germans had never been repulsed and their armies seemed to be impregnable.

Orders had been received for the South Notts. Hussars to abandon all plans for the invasion of Rhodes and to prepare for desert warfare. We were to come up to fighting strength immediately and other regiments in the Delta were instructed to send us the best of anything we needed, without quibble. The equipment gathered for the invasion was cast aside and there was a mad flurry of activity as vehicles, stores, equipment and reinforcements began to arrive from all directions. New gun-towing vehicles such as we had never seen before were delivered; they were called 'Quads' and we quickly loaded them with stores and equipment. The limbers were loaded with ammunition and we all worked like demons to prepare for battle. It was only a matter of hours before we were ready to move and on the morning of 5 April 1941 we set off on the first leg of the seven hundred mile journey that was to terminate in the desert fortress of Tobruk, at the start of what was to become the longest siege in British military history.

## Chapter 7

# Tobruk – The First Battle

The first stage of the journey to Tobruk took us through part of the Nile Delta and as far as Mena, where we bivouacked for the night not far from the Pyramids. It was tantalising to see the lights of Cairo so near and to imagine the nightlife, the restaurants and all the bustle and glitter of city life. Most of the officers went off to spend the evening there but we were not allowed to leave the guns. The following day, which was a Sunday, we were addressed by the colonel, who told us that there was every likelihood of us being dive-bombed during the journey ahead. He said that on no account were we to scatter, as it was vitally important for us to reach our destination as quickly as possible. Later that day we reached Bahie, and Monday took us on again as far as Qasaba. Tuesday found us well into the desert and we drove through a strangely deserted Mersa Matruh and headed in the direction of Sidi Barani.

The deeper we got into the desert, the more alarmed we became. We began to meet columns of lorries laden with troops and equipment, and also many ambulances, all of them travelling at speed and heading eastwards. We passed desert airfields where huge, wooden crates, as yet unpacked and containing new aircraft engines, were being set on fire. There was more than a hint of panic in the air and the further west we travelled the more disorderly it became. It soon became obvious that the British Army of the Nile was in headlong flight; everybody seemed to be sharing but one thought and that was to put as much distance as possible between themselves and the enemy.

On Wednesday we passed Buq Buq and were heading towards Solumn, Halfaya Pass and the Libyan border when despatch riders rode down the length of the convoy carrying large messages which read: '**CLOSE UP – DRIVE AS FAST AS POSSIBLE.**' It did not escape our notice that we were being urged to drive as quickly as possible in the opposite direction to that being taken by everybody else.

The frontier between Egypt and Libya at this point is situated close to the top of a high escarpment, which is negotiated by means of a narrow, snaking road known as Halfaya Pass. To British troops it was always known as 'Hell Fire Pass'. Here we found the road almost completely blocked by every imaginable type of vehicle. They were coming down the pass sometimes two abreast and it was only with the greatest difficulty that we were able to make our way slowly to the top. We saw evidence that many trucks had gone over the edge of the road and crashed down onto the rocks hundreds of feet below.

At the top of the escarpment we drove into a large fuel dump that was about to be blown up. We didn't stop to fill our petrol tanks, but just threw as many cans of petrol into the back of the gun-tower as we could in the short time allowed. It was only a matter of minutes before we were on the road again and heading in the direction of Fort Capuzzo and Bardia. Our orders were to get as far as Tobruk before it was taken by the enemy. We knew that Benghazi had already fallen and that there had been sightings of German tanks in the area of desert we had to cross. This meant that we were faced with a very hazardous journey indeed, for to be caught by German panzers whilst still moving in convoy would mean certain disaster. It was dark before we passed Fort Capuzzo, but we pressed on at speed along the shell-pocked road that crossed the desolate stretch of desert that lies between the frontier and Tobruk. The strain of driving at speed in convoy in the dark along a bumpy road was exacerbated by the knowledge that at any moment we were liable to come under attack by enemy tanks.

We all took turns at the wheel. It is certain that the drivers could not have survived our journey of the previous few days had we not all taken our share of the driving. As we drew nearer Tobruk, the sky ahead became alight with continuous flashes and the noise of bombing and shell fire grew ever louder. Away to the south were many flickering lights that we knew to be German troops on the move. The sight of retreating British troops had long ceased and we realised that the main body of the army was now behind us and that we were hurrying to the aid of the rearguard.

From the frontier to Tobruk is a distance of about eighty miles and this was all covered in darkness. In spite of our weariness we were alert and watchful as we bumped and bounced along the uneven road. It was one of those journeys that seem to have no end, but at some time during that long night we drove slowly through a gap in a minefield and then through a corridor of tangled barbed wire and we knew that we had reached our destination. After we had passed into the fortress, the mines were relaid and the barbed wire pulled back into position; although we didn't know it at the time, the Siege of Tobruk had begun.

We carried on in the darkness until we came to a junction, where the road from Derna to the frontier met the road from Tobruk to El Adam. This junction was to become known as Eagle Crossroads and it was here that we met up with two other artillery regiments. It was complete chaos! Three artillery regiments all mixed up in the darkness in a highly vulnerable position with the enemy knocking at the gate. There was much shouting and swearing and revving of engines as we tried to sort things out. If the Luftwaffe had chosen that moment to mount a bombing raid complete with flares, the main power that was to defeat them in the coming battle would have been destroyed in a matter of minutes.

Eventually we managed to extricate ourselves and to bring the guns into action in the dark in an anti-tank role. A strong wind got up during the latter part of the night and by dawn a sandstorm had developed which reduced visibility to a few hundred yards. We manned the guns and waited for the enemy tanks to appear through the blowing dust. It was a moment fraught with danger, but the colonel coolly equipped himself with a rifle and walked up and down in front of the guns. We all greatly appreciated the significance of this gesture. He was a very brave man.

An order was circulated that Tobruk was to be held at all costs and we knew that we were in for a fight. The wind dropped somewhat as the day progressed and the visibility increased, so that later in the morning we were able to move forward in the direction of a heavy bombardment that was going on over to the west. As the dust-storm cleared it became very hot, and we got our first sight of German aircraft when Stuka dive-bombers made their appearance; the noise was deafening as the ground began to erupt with great fountains of dust and smoke which marked the fall of their bombs. We swung the guns into line and prepared for action, and in a matter of minutes our first shells were winging their way in the direction of the advancing enemy.

We engaged the enemy several times that day and then, after nightfall, we made preparations to move again, this time into what proved to be the central sector. We took up our positions here on the morning of Good Friday and although we did come under some sporadic shellfire during the early afternoon, the front remained fairly quiet. We used this time to try to build some protection around the gun. It was difficult to dig because the ground was very rocky, but it is surprising the amount of encouragement a few shells dropping in the vicinity can give.

The officer commanding 'A' Troop, Captain Slinn, was an excellent man in every way. He had come to us from the Honourable Artillery Company (HAC), a prestigious regiment based in London. I have reason to believe that in private life he was a very wealthy man and it was said that his family owned a shipping company and that he was also involved in merchant banking. Maybe so, but more important to us on the battlefield in Tobruk was his quiet, confident manner in times of danger. Captain Slinn was always a perfect gentleman; he treated everyone with the greatest courtesy and he had the admiration and respect of every man who served under him. He called us together on the gun position that afternoon and began to explain the situation to us. He told us that we were about to face a massive onslaught as the German Army made its attack to secure the port of Tobruk. Whatever the cost, he remarked, they must not be allowed to succeed. He pointed out that if the Germans were not stopped they could go on to conquer Egypt, take the Suez Canal and then the door would be open for them to move into the oilfields of the Middle East. With a large percentage of the world's oil at their disposal, they would become virtually invincible. He said that the fate of England and the free world was in our hands that day and we must not fail. Captain Slinn concluded his stirring little talk by quoting the final passage from the speech of Henry V before the Battle of Agincourt: 'You know your places; go to them and God be with you.' Few people realise how much we owe to men like Graham Slinn, those quiet, courageous English gentlemen who always seem to appear when they are needed to lead by example. He was to be twice awarded the Military Cross before being killed in action later in the war.

We returned to our guns with a different attitude of mind, as we were now fully aware of the gravity of the situation. It was almost as if he had known the precise moment to boost our morale, for within minutes all hell was let loose. The expected attack had begun and the German troops moved forwards to engage the defences on the central sector where we were stationed. Soon the sky was black with smoke and the air was alive with screaming shells as German tanks, supported by waves of infantry, tried to break through the thinly held line manned by troops of the 9th Australian Division. These men, who had barely had the time to reach the defensive positions before the start of the battle, needed all the artillery support we could give them. The guns glowed red as we put down a defensive barrage that was fearsome in its intensity.

This was a desperate battle, and it went on without break from Good Friday afternoon until the evening of Easter Monday. I spent the remainder of the first day as a gun layer, the man who aims and actually fires the gun. For the first few hours we were firing continuously, and even during the hours of darkness there was no respite. We never really relished the prospect of a night action, being very much alive to the fact that the German artillery could roughly locate our position from the flashes as the guns fired. By counting the seconds from flash to bang they could also calculate the range. (We of course used the same tactics against them.) We were not surprised therefore to hear the scream of approaching shells, which began to explode threateningly close to our gun positions. Enemy planes were almost constantly overhead both by day and by night, when they dropped parachute flares that lit up the whole area. The thud of exploding bombs was constantly heard and there were repeated dive-bombing attacks along the whole front. Thankfully most of the high-altitude bombing was directed somewhere behind us, probably on the harbour.

The following morning I began a tour of duty at the observation post. It should perhaps be pointed out that the guns were usually positioned several thousand yards behind the front line and therefore the target was not visible to the gun crews. We had to have spotters up forward who could observe the enemy and send back the necessary commands for the guns to be properly aimed and set with the correct angle for the range. Our observation post at that time was in a front-line trench that we shared with the Australian infantry, and it was here that I had my first taste of trench warfare.

The line in the central sector ran along the crest of a ridge and so we were able, for part of the way, to travel in a fifteen-hundredweight truck, but the last part had to be covered on foot. With shells and mortars falling all around us, we entered the trench system and made our way on foot towards the firing line. It was something I had done a thousand times before in my childhood play, but this was no game. Amidst the sound of bursting shells I could hear the crackle of machine-gun fire as we stumbled along the trench carrying our equipment, blankets and rations. We found the party we were to relieve in the front-line trench and they were not slow in handing over to us and making their departure. The Australian infantrymen were all grim-faced as they manned the parapets; they all had their bayonets fixed and were hung around with hand grenades. I took my place on the firing step and very cautiously searched the ground in front of us with my field glasses. It was important for us to become familiar with the territory in this sector, and we soon became busy making sketches and marking in any points of reference that we considered likely to be of help in future ranging on targets.

The thunder of guns, the whine of approaching shells and the ground erupting on all sides heralded another German attack. The noise was ear-splitting and terrifying, and my instinctive reaction was to dive for cover, but this had to be overcome. The job of artillery spotters is to direct the fire of the guns in the rear so that the shells land to the best advantage. Through the dust and smoke I could see men moving, running in little bursts from one piece of cover to another, and I could hardly believe my senses that I was actually standing there, under shellfire, watching German infantry advancing towards me over no-man's-land.

As most men who have seen action will confirm, there is no time to be afraid in the midst of a battle. Fear is usually experienced before and after the conflict but rarely whilst it is taking place because at that time the mind is fully occupied with the job in hand. We were busy observing the fall of our shells and sending back corrections to the guns as the enemy crept ever closer. The trenches we were defending had been originally constructed by the Italian Army; they were well built and cleverly designed in the form of strong points well protected by several rows of barbed wire entanglements, and in front was a deep anti-tank ditch. In order to reach us the Germans had to cross the ditch and blast their way through the wire. In attempting to accomplish this they were suffering heavy casualties as our gunfire was both accurate and deadly, and the Australian infantry were blazing away with both rifles and machine guns. After the first attacks were repulsed, the medical orderlies were busy dealing with the wounded in our section of the trenches, but they had little time to complete their duties before another attack was launched – and this time it came with armoured support. I could see the black crosses on the German tanks as they came thundering across the rocky terrain in a headlong assault with all their guns blazing. It was a daunting sight, and as we put down fire among them we could see their infantry following close behind. We continued to decrease the range of our guns as the tanks advanced towards us, but they came on menacingly to bridge the anti-tank ditch and to grind their way through the barbed wire – and then they were upon us.

It was a dreadful situation. We were now bringing down fire onto our own positions – something I was never to witness again. It was absolute carnage as the German infantry made their frontal attack into this maelstrom of smoke and fire. There was a cacophony of rifle fire and machine-gun fire, bursting shells, hand grenades exploding, and there was much shouting and screaming as men fell stricken. All around us we could see men fighting desperately, hand to hand, with bayonets and it was altogether a heart-stopping experience. Whilst this was taking place in the front line, the tanks had passed through and were marauding at will in the open ground to the rear. Realising this, we lost no time in redirecting our fire and we were soon in the situation where our own shells were bursting behind us.

Looking back on that episode it seems incredible that anyone could have lived through such murderous, close-quarter combat. I know that I owe my survival on that day to the courage and the fighting spirit of the Australian infantry, who finally repulsed the German troops in a bloody and hard-fought battle. Had they failed, my companions and I would have stood no chance at all – as artillery crew, we were not trained in the skills of bayonet fighting.

Having failed to break the Australian line, the survivors of the German infantry started to withdraw and so we quickly changed targets again and began to rain down shells upon them as they fell back. They were also being swept with rifle and machine-gun fire, and many sought shelter in the anti-tank ditch just beyond our shattered wire. They engaged us in a similar way and the sound of their rapid firing Spandau machine guns will always live in my memory. Those in the ditch had little chance of escape and a very large number of German soldiers were to die in that place. The German tanks made a foray for some time behind our lines, but when they realised that the main attack had failed they started to withdraw. This meant that we had to face them yet again as they charged at us once more, this time from the opposite direction with all their guns firing wildly.

It is impossible to describe what it feels like to have a huge tank grinding its way towards you and to be within feet of those menacing steel tracks that could so easily grind you into the ground. That is to say nothing of the machine guns spitting bullets in all directions. It was a great relief when they had lurched over our trenches and were making their way back into their own lines with our shells bursting amongst them.

During the lull that followed we began the sickening task of tending the wounded and moving them to a place of comparative safety. The dead had to remain where they lay because it was but a short time before the enemy launched yet another assault, which was again beaten back with heavy losses. It seemed that the Germans were determined to capture Tobruk no matter what the cost; they were accustomed to winning battles and until this time no one had ever stopped them. Now they were to suffer their first reverse at the hands of the Australian infantry and the British artillery, but it was a very close-run thing.

I learned during this battle for Tobruk that forward observation posts had a very special significance as regards to rank. Danger was a great leveller! When huddled together for hours in great discomfort and exposed to all kinds of danger, men tend to develop special relationships that pay little regard to differences in rank. During the long siege that was to follow I was to accompany many different signallers and officers to a variety of OPs and almost invariably we became three friends, each equally dependent on the other two.

The battle continued with unabating ferocity. When my stint at the OP was over, I returned to the gun position to find that behind each gun there was a huge pile of empty cartridge cases. The guns were rocking back and forth as shell after shell was poured onto the attacking German troops, and in order to keep the guns fed, RASC (Royal Army Service Corps) troops were driving directly onto the gun position and unloading the boxes of ammunition behind the guns. Still the Germans continued to force the attack and we were all absolutely worn out, not having slept for several days and nights. Food was brought to the gun crews and was snatched whenever possible. Our faces were masks of sweat and sand with little red slits which served as eyes as we staggered around the guns like robots, laying, loading and firing without proper conscious thought of what we were doing. It was just a mechanical repetition of actions we had been trained to perform. Towards the end of the battle I remember someone coming to our gun with a bottle of whisky and we all paused long enough to take long, stinging gulps of the raw liquid. We were reaching the end of our stamina and how much longer we could have continued is difficult to assess, but on the Monday evening the guns fell silent and the first battle of Tobruk was over.

In a state of complete exhaustion, we just dropped where we were around the gun, wrapped ourselves in our blankets and slept. The German Army had met a great reverse. It was a great boost for the Allied cause and, for a while at least, the Suez Canal and the oil-fields of the Middle East were safe, but we were not aware of any of this. Oblivious to the fact that we were under siege, short of ammunition, men and food, and that much bitter fighting lay ahead of us, we were happy to lose ourselves in the embrace of sleep, that great healer and restorer. The guns were left to cool themselves in the cold night air.

## Chapter 8

# Life During the Siege of Tobruk

As the siege of Tobruk was to last from Easter until Christmas it would be a very boring exercise to try to give a day-to-day account of those months spent in the fortress. A great deal has been written about the siege, some of it nothing more than embroidered nonsense, so I will try to give an honest impression as to what it was like to live as a combatant soldier during those dangerous days. I will also endeavour to select certain incidents that may help to colour the scene and sometimes add a little light relief.

It has to be remembered that this was trench warfare, with all the trappings of barbed-wire entanglements, dugouts, machine-gun nests, strong points and of course, no-man's-land – that deadly stretch of land between the two opposing forces. It had all the hallmarks of the First World War in France and Flanders with the notable exception of the mud and the cold. In place of this we had rocky, scrubby desert and intense heat, at least during the day. There was also the greater danger from air raids. The Germans had powerful forces and we had no aircraft whatsoever after the first few days. Another difference was the distance from home and the fact that we were besieged, which meant that for us there could be no home leave. In fact there could be no leave at all, not even for a period of rest behind the line, because there was nowhere for us to go. This meant being on duty for twenty-four hours a day, seven days each week, and for a period of nine months we were never to be out of the line even for a brief period.

Another aspect of life in Tobruk during the siege concerns the lack of any form of diversion. There was no entertainment of any kind. There were few books to be found, no music, no radio, no newspapers, no sport, nothing but continual warfare, night and day, seven days a week. Mail from home, so very vital to morale, was very hit and miss. If a letter was sent home at the beginning of May, one could not expect to receive an answer until the following September. Also, as we had now been abroad for over two years, only a faithful few continued to write on a regular basis; their letters were to become the most important facet of our lives.

The food was boringly repetitive and consisted mainly of corned beef served either cold or as a stew known as Bully Stew. It was cooked on the gun position in an open kitchen about one hundred yards behind the guns and at mealtimes we lined up with our mess tins into which the stew was ladled. Bread was rarely seen and when it did appear it was invariably green with mildew; why this was so I was never able to discover, because it must have been baked within the confines of the fortress. In place of bread we were issued with army biscuits known to the troops as 'hard tack'. One way of eating these unsavoury, bullet-hard biscuits was to soak them in water for several hours and then heat the resulting mush over a small fire; this made a tasteless porridge that we called 'biscuit burgoo'. Butter we never saw; it was replaced by a thick, yellow concoction that had been produced to withstand high temperatures. Tinned pilchards often made an appearance, as did a dreadful thing bearing the label 'Hunters Tinned Bacon'. It may have been acceptable in cooler climes but not in the heat of the desert. Each tin contained bacon slices wrapped in thin greaseproof paper, but when the tins were opened there was nothing but a greasy, runny mixture of bacon fat and paper. There was no fresh fruit and no vegetables of any kind, and apart from the very early days, no chocolate or other form of confection. We never saw cake or sweets and things like pastry and meat pies were only memories of happier times. Existing on a diet that was so deficient in Vitamin C over so long a period could have produced diseases such as scurvy, and to prevent this we were issued with ascorbic acid tablets which had to be taken daily.

Water came from wells situated very close to the sea, from which they found their origin; because of this the water was brackish and never properly quenched the thirst. We carried our personal ration of drinking water in water bottles that were continuously exposed to the sun's rays, so our water was always warm and just a tiny bit salty. We were always hungry, for food was in short supply, and we were constantly thirsty on account of the heat and the brackish water. In this matter of food and drink we were quite powerless to improve our lot. There were no shops from which to supplement our rations and no little café or bar where we might sit down for a good meal with a pint of beer or a glass of wine. Such places did not exist. The town of Tobruk was empty of civilians and consisted of nothing more than a huddle of empty, shattered buildings.

During the whole of our stay in Tobruk the front was never silent for more than a few minutes. There was never a day without the sound of bursting shells and mortars, and the rattle of rifle and machine-gun fire was almost continuous. The German Stukas (dive-bombers) were stationed on El Adam airfield which was only a few miles away – so close in fact that it was possible for men at the OP to watch them taking off and landing. As we had no air cover to protect us, it is not surprising that the fortress was dive-bombed continually, sometimes three or four times in a day. High-level bombing became so commonplace, both by day and by night, as to pass almost unnoticed unless the bombs were falling very close.

To live in such an environment for nine months without a break was very stressful, and there were some who were unable to cope. They found their own ways of escaping into safer spheres, but the majority just had to grit their teeth and find some way of overcoming their fears and the continual hardships. Fortunately man is very adaptable, and within a short period of time we found ourselves able to deal with our problems and to accept them as part of a daily routine. We became very wise in the ways of war. We learned to tell from the sound of the enemy's guns whether or not the shells were likely to fall close, in which case we would dive for cover, but we taught ourselves to ignore the sound of any bombardment that did not immediately concern us. We discovered the art of sleeping through all kinds of noise and we typically made fun of the surrounding dangers. It became common practice when settling down for the night to say, 'Don't wake me for anything less than three Panzer divisions through the wire.' In this way a pattern of life gradually emerged which allowed us to contend with the hardships, the perils and the boredom that were to be our constant companions for the next nine months.

After the initial offensive had been repelled, the Germans did not lick their wounds for very long. They began a series of attacks, which were to continue for many months, and for much of the period I settled down to a routine which meant that I shared my time between the gun position and the observation post. There were many hazardous incidents in both these locations and there was an occasion when the Victoria Cross was posthumously awarded to a brave Australian soldier who lost his life only a few hundred yards away to our left of our observation post. The danger was not all confined to the front-line trenches, however; the gun positions also endured their fair share of the enemy's wrath. The dive-bombers made repeated attacks on the guns and the scream as they went into their bombing dive became a familiar sound. They usually dropped five bombs, four in a circle and one in the middle. It was very frightening to be crouched in a trench as the planes came screaming down from directly above and to watch the bombs fall as the pilot pulled out from his dive.

For me it was a shattering experience whenever 'B' Troop was attacked because they were less than quarter of a mile away from our position and my brother and my best friends were all there. One day in particular stands out in my mind: I remember watching with dismay as plane after plane dived into the attack, screaming down to deliver their deadly load onto 'B' Troop's position. The whole area became obscured beneath a huge cloud of smoke and dust, and when it was over we waited to be informed of the casualties. I learned that two of my friends had gone: Philip Collihole and Clifford Smedley had both lost their lives in the attack.

I was devastated to learn of the death of my dear old friend Sergeant Smedley. During the raid he, like everybody else, had dived for cover into a slit trench, and had he remained there he might have been spared. Unfortunately Clifford Smedley was not the type of man to lie shivering in a trench, and as the raid progressed he noticed that the Bren gun was not being manned to give protective fire. Without a thought for his own safety, he jumped out of the trench and ran towards the Bren gun pit, but alas he was not to make it. A salvo of bombs crashed down before he could reach the gun pit and his life ended.

It was May Day 1941 when he died and now, over seventy years later, I still weep for his passing. A finer man I would never meet and our nation was the poorer for his loss. How many men of the calibre of Clifford Smedley and Philip Collihole have we sacrificed on the field of battle in the last century? On the Somme, in the mud at Passchendaele, in the Western Desert, in Burma and again in France and the Low Countries. Men of courage and integrity, men of high intelligence, men who would have grown in wisdom to the betterment of our country; so many of them were left to lie under neat white stones in far-off lands. Most were so young that they died without progeny, and so we shall never see their like again. These two men lie close together in the lonely, rarely visited cemetery in Tobruk. My very dear friend Clifford Smedley left no child to mourn him or to grow in his image, but for as long as I live he will be remembered as a true and gallant friend who died bravely for his country. I sometimes sadly wonder if the country has proved worthy of his sacrifice.

\* \* \*

The majority of the men in 'A' Troop were both friendly and efficient, and I was happy in their company. One bonus was the sergeant major, Jim Hardy. Jim had been my first sergeant immediately before and at the outbreak of war, and by this time we had been good friends for over three years. I still saw George and my friends in the other troop fairly frequently. When things were quiet I would make my way across to their gun position for a chat. I was over there one day when we came under fire from a battery of heavy Italian guns. I took cover in a slit trench together with David Boe and as we crouched there a huge shell made a direct hit straight into our trench. It plunged into the ground between us – but failed to explode. It took several seconds for us to come to terms with the situation and then we moved with the speed of light. It was a narrow escape that left us shaking from fright but it was not altogether uncommon for shells to fail to explode, particularly Italian shells. I read recently that quite a high percentage of the shells fired on the Somme in the First World War failed to explode.

As the weeks passed I got to know our sector of the front very well because I spent so much time at the OP. I was also on very friendly terms with the Australian soldiers holding that part of the line. In front of our wire the ground sloped slightly upwards towards the German trenches, and then it fell away again, leaving a lot of dead ground that was out of our vision. The Italian engineers who had designed the defences had hit upon the bright idea of erecting an observation platform about twenty feet high just behind the line. Built of steel, it was protected by an armour-plated shield and had a platform reached by a vertical ladder. The platform was large enough for two men and we used it daily to keep a watch on the enemy's movements and to direct fire when necessary. Once inside it was not too bad, but climbing the ladder could be a hazardous business because it was in full view of the enemy trenches only a few hundred yards away. We found it best to climb up before daybreak and then stay there until the heat haze began to play tricks with visibility.

During the day it was often possible to walk about with impunity even in the front line because in the desert strange things happen. I had always been rather sceptical about mirages, considering them to be things of the imagination, but I quickly discovered that mirages do frequently appear on the horizon. Clumps of palm trees, pools of shining water, even buildings all stand out most realistically in regions that are known to be completely arid and deserted. What is more, they appear in exactly the same places day after day; on occasions we used them as gun aiming points and found them to be most accurate and reliable. During the heat of the day we could often see German soldiers quite clearly – but they appeared to be walking upside down about fifteen feet above the ground. I have not the slightest doubt that they could see us in a similar situation. There was no point in aiming at such targets and so we had a certain freedom of movement. It did not pay to be too careless, however, because the situation could change within seconds and without any warning everything would be crystal clear again.

Some men suffered greatly from exposure to the sun's rays because every day was cloudless and there was no shade to be found anywhere. We spent the whole of every day under the pitiless glare of the sun because we had no cover whatsoever and in most cases our skins had turned to a deep shade of copper, but there was an unfortunate minority for whom this did not happen. They were usually very fair-complexioned and their skins turned to a fiery red and then peeled and this process was repeated time after time. Ginger Barker, a friend of mine, was one such case and he was in continual torment from this constant sunburn. I firmly believe now, as I did at the time, that such men should have been returned to base on medical grounds. Another condition that caused a great deal of discomfort was that known as 'desert sores'. These were open wounds that appeared on the skin and they were very common in Tobruk during the siege. Their cause was a mystery and so was their cure. They were probably the result of dirt or dietary deficiency, or both. We were certainly dirty: I never had a bath or a proper wash during the whole of the time we were there and that was a period of over nine months, but I was fortunate never to suffer with desert sores.

One day, to my intense delight, I received a parcel from home. It had been nearly six months in transit and it contained a strange variety of articles. There was a cake, which had gone hard and stale, and some chocolate that had turned white and lost its flavour. My father had included a tin of salve that he had made from an old recipe left by my grandfather, and, to my complete amazement, I discovered two packets of balloons! I am still pondering the reason for their inclusion, but mothers have strange ideas about warfare, and they did provide us with some light relief. The cake and chocolate were quickly despatched in spite of their poor condition but the salve remained in my dugout until one day I decided to try it out on one of my friends who had desert sores. Within a few days his wounds began to heal and the news quickly spread so that I had a queue of men demanding treatment. It worked splendidly in every case until, alas, my stock dwindled to nothing. I now regret never having asked my father for the recipe of this unique ointment that my grandfather had acquired from somewhere.

I do not recall feeling any personal animosity towards the Germans facing us across the wire. It seemed to me that they were more or less in the same unhappy situation as us. This feeling was to some extent mutual, I believe, for one could often hear the machine gunners from either side signalling to each other with the familiar rhythm of 'da diddley da da' from one side, answered by 'da da' from the other. It was in this spirit that, in league with the Australians on our post, we one day decided to use my two packets of balloons. We blew up a balloon, tied the neck and kept popping it up in the air over the parapet. The front immediately fell silent. All firing in the vicinity stopped. The enemy must have wondered what on earth it was and their field glasses must have been working overtime before they realised that it was a joke. They were quick to respond and to join in the fun, and as we popped up the balloons, one at a time, they fired at them with their rifles. They entered into the spirit of the thing by not using machine guns. It went on until all the balloons were burst and then we sent up a red flare and they fired a flare in return. At least it made a change from trying to kill each other and the balloons had served a purpose after all: they had shown that we were all stupid human beings.

For a short distance in front of our sector the German line had been established along the edge of a ridge and this meant that in places we had difficulty in observing movement behind their line. Someone in a safe region somewhere in the rear, who would never have to climb it, dreamed up the idea of building a high tower just to the rear of our lines. From the top of this tower the artillery observers would have a splendid view and be able to direct fire accurately on the enemy emplacements that were otherwise out of view. The Royal Engineers worked throughout the night, using metal scaffold poles to erect this high tower. It was surmounted by a metal platform and it had to be climbed by means of a vertical ladder. It was decided that Lieutenant London should climb this tower in order to direct the guns in support of an attack that was going to be made, and that I should accompany him as his assistant. No signaller was needed because a line had already been laid to the top of the platform, and we were to carry a radiotelephone as well. As it would have been suicide to climb this ladder in daylight we had to make the ascent before daybreak. I have always had a horror of heights and to be scaling a vertical ladder in the dark to such a height had me in a state of absolute terror. We were both wearing greatcoats because it was bitterly cold and when I climbed onto the metal platform with the desert far below, I was shaking visibly and not only from the cold. There was no armour plating because at this height we were out of the range of small arms fire and too high to be affected by shellfire.

When dawn broke and the battle commenced, we had an excellent view of the enemy troop dispositions and we were able to shell them with great accuracy. The Germans quickly became aware of the fact that we were responsible for their losses and they made every effort to dislodge us, using artillery fire as a means of knocking down the tower. At one period during the morning we estimated that there were three enemy batteries concentrating their fire solely on our position. The air was filled with the scream of approaching shells and the ground below was a seething mass of smoke and flame as shell after shell exploded all around the base of the tower. I remember we felt the wind of some shells as they passed between our heads to fall and explode somewhere below.

As the morning progressed the sun's heat became unbearable and the shellfire increased in intensity as we continued to direct the fire of our guns onto various enemy concentrations. By this time the tower was rocking violently and we were both terrified because we were convinced that it was only a matter of time before it fell. We were sure that one of the legs had already gone when we were told via the radio that we were the 'mean point of impact' and that the tower was expected to fall at any moment. Lieutenant London was ordered to remain where he was, but I was to descend and make my way to the forward observation post. When I was in that position and ready to take over the shoot, he too was to leave the tower.

We both thought that we were facing certain death. We said goodbye to each other, solemnly shaking hands, before I heaved my body over the side and began the hair-raising descent of this swaying death-trap. I was descending into a maelstrom of fire and destruction: it was like climbing down into an active volcano. No one ever moved faster than I did on that day and as I neared the bottom I could feel the heat and the blast of the bursting shells. By some miracle I reached the ground in safety and commenced my mad dash through the shellfire in the direction of the forward observation post. It was a distance of about a hundred and fifty yards, but the ground was pulverised and pitted with shell holes and I kept stumbling and falling. Fear lent me wings and I emerged unscathed from the worst of the inferno, racing across the open ground to reach the forward observation post ready to take over the shoot. The field telephone was always kept in a state of readiness so I was able to report my safe arrival to the battery command post.

My first task was to engage a couple of tanks, and then I caught sight of a column of vehicles moving from left to right just behind their line. Being so very familiar with that section of the front, it was an easy task for me to estimate the line and range of this target and to send fire orders for five rounds gunfire. That meant forty shells, because at that time I was observing for the whole battery of eight guns. Within seconds the first salvo of shells came whistling over to land accurately on the target, and it was only then that through the swirling smoke and dust I caught a glimpse of a Red Cross on the side of one of the vehicles and knew them to be ambulances. I gave the order 'STOP', which all artillerymen know to be a special order that literally means just what it says. It is an order reserved for such emergencies and the guns stopped firing immediately, but not before several of the ambulances had been destroyed. There was no time for remorse; it was unintentional, but such things are bound to happen in the heat of battle and at that moment the whole front was alive with targets that had to be engaged.

During the late afternoon things began to quieten down but it had been a hectic day and one that I shall never forget. When we were back in the comparative safety of the trench once again, an Australian officer came up to me and said, 'Do you know that you ran straight through the bloody minefield?' I stared at him in horror. In my terror I had forgotten all about the minefield. I looked at the tower, still leaning drunkenly on its three legs, and at the mine-sown ground over which I had stumbled in my eagerness to escape the shellfire. My knees went weak when I realised what I had done. I was astonishingly fortunate on that day, for I had survived without so much as a scratch. The officer was less fortunate and lost his left arm.

I learned a great many lessons during the siege of Tobruk which were to affect my thinking in future years. One of these occurred during the ferocious fighting of the early weeks and it was concerned with nothing more than a simple bar of chocolate. There were still a few goodies left in the food stores and these included a stock of Cadbury's plain Bourneville chocolate bars that were issued with the daily rations as long as the stocks lasted. They were small bars in the familiar red wrapping that they still carry today. Each evening at about six o'clock, when the rations were brought up to the guns, they contained one bar of chocolate for each man. It was our only luxury, and when it was issued we all did the same thing: we ate it all straight away. There was no saving a bit until later, no hoarding to build up a private stock for the future. We realised that for us there was likely to be no future and so we ate our chocolate at six o'clock in the knowledge that by six-thirty we could easily be dead.

I have carried this philosophy with me for the rest of my life; it has served me well and it is to be recommended. Take the good things that life offers and use them at once, do not delay, for a pleasure deferred is a pleasure lost forever. Be neither greedy nor selfish, but gratefully accept the good things that come your way; they are yours to enjoy. Always make sensible provision for tomorrow, but never to the detriment of today, because today holds the passing moment of your life. Eat your chocolate at six o'clock – six-thirty may be too late!

Apart from mentioning my closest friends, I have consciously refrained from giving lurid details of men who were killed or wounded in action, but there was always a steady thinning of the ranks from this cause and the gaps had to be filled. It happened at one point during the summer that I was called to fill one of these gaps and it caused me a great deal of consternation. I mentioned earlier, in connection with our training, that there was a group of men known as specialists, whose work was concentrated on the mathematics of ballistics. They were trained in the surveying of the land, working out angles of line and sight, plotting zero lines, and converting meteorological data so that it could be applied to the angles and ranges set on the guns. They were required to have a sound mathematical background and a sure knowledge of trigonometry, and one of the positions they filled was that of GPOA, or gun position officer's assistant.

One morning I was called to the command post on the gun position and told that I was going to become the GPOA as the man presently filling the post was needed elsewhere and there was no properly trained man available to take his place. He was to spend the remainder of the morning giving me instruction and after that I was to take over his position. I was horrified, and protested that this was a job that required months of training and that I was in no way equipped to carry the responsibility commensurate with the job. All my protests were brushed aside; I was told to obey orders, get on with learning the job and stop making difficulties.

What a morning! Fortunately for us the front remained reasonably quiet and I was able to concentrate my mind as I had never done before. I had to learn first how to use a 'director', which was a surveying instrument. Then we discussed bearings and back bearings, the artillery board and its arc, meteorological telegrams and how to decipher them, programmed shoots and registered targets. I remember discussing Pythagoras's Theorem and drawing triangles in the dust on the mudguard of a lorry as we discussed sines and cosines, tangents and logarithms, and the use of the slide rule: a long, bewildering exposition of facts that had my brain reeling. Of course it was absolutely ridiculous; to absorb all that knowledge and its application in one morning would have required the intellect of a mathematical genius. Foolish though it was, however, the fact remained that I had become the GPOA and as such I carried a great deal of responsibility for the accuracy of four guns that were constantly in action. It was an awful thought that a mistake on my part could quite easily have resulted in our shells falling amongst our own forward troops.

Never in my life have I had such headaches as I did on the days that followed. Together with Jim Hardy, the sergeant major, I used to sit in the dugout for hours swotting and trying to work things out. Jim was of little help, for he knew no more than I did, and he too was a gunner rather than a specialist. Somehow or other I managed to come to grips with the essentials and I wrote down the basic methods to follow when working out various problems, particularly those which required immediate answers, such as when firing on registered targets. Obviously, much of this work had to be done whilst the guns were in action and I often found myself trying to solve mathematical problems whilst shells or bombs were exploding all around us. It was a terrible strain, but I managed to survive and there was no major catastrophe due to any error of mine. I was very thankful, however, when after about six weeks some reinforcements arrived and I was able to relinquish the post and resume my normal duties as a gunner and an OPA.

Without the Royal Navy we could not have survived for very long. They did a marvellous job and kept us supplied with the essentials of food and ammunition. They also ferried the badly wounded down to the delta and brought in reinforcements. This work was carried out mainly by the destroyers and no one envied them their task of making the very dangerous journey from Alexandria, which invariably concluded with them being bombed in Tobruk harbour. The anti-aircraft fire to be seen each night over the harbour was a fantastic display of light, colour and sound. It was said, with some justification, that there were so many wrecked ships in Tobruk harbour that it was almost possible to walk dryshod from one side to the other. One of the wrecks was that of the Italian cruiser *San Giorgio*, which had been sunk earlier in the war. The naval ships always timed their voyages so that they arrived during the hours of darkness and they made sure of being well out to sea again before daybreak.

I fell ill with sandfly fever during the hot summer. I felt very weak and could not find the strength to carry on, so I went and lay in a slit trench just behind the guns. I stayed there for a couple of days and on the second day a sandstorm began. I had eaten nothing and my water bottle was almost empty, and the hot sand was gradually covering me as I lay there. It occurred to me that I could lie there and die, the sand would cover me and no one would shed a tear on my behalf. In other words, I was indulging in self-pity. It was another of those lessons I had yet to learn: 'Do not expect other people to run about after you, they are far too busy looking after themselves. If you want food and water, get up and find it.' And that is exactly what I did. I staggered across to where the cooks were boiling the eternal 'bully stew', drank a mug of tea and stopped feeling sorry for myself. I still have to remind myself of that episode from time to time when I feel that the world is being especially unkind to me.

We had long since given up the habit of wearing steel helmets. For most of us it became a matter of pride to wear some other form of headgear, usually something informal. Some liked to wear the knitted cap comforter, others the normal khaki side hat; I had my favourite peaked cap with the wire removed, and there were some who preferred to wear the RHA dress side hat of red, blue and gold. Whatever hat we wore, it usually carried the regimental cap badge, of which we were all very proud. It was one of the very few cap badges in the British Army that carried neither name nor motto, and where other badges were made of brass, ours was silver in colour.

One of my friends, who had been wounded in one of the earlier battles and sent back to Egypt in a destroyer for hospital treatment, was convalescing in Cairo prior to being sent back to the unit. One morning, whilst walking along one of the busy streets, he was stopped by a girl who touched his arm and said: 'Excuse me, but I recognise your cap badge. You are from the South Notts. Hussars.' She asked him if the regiment was stationed nearby, but he told her that they were up at the front and explained that he was waiting to rejoin them. 'I know someone from your regiment', she confided. 'His name is Ray Ellis. Do you know him?' He quickly explained that we were friends, whereupon she opened her handbag and took from it a small photograph, which she handed to him. 'Will you please give this to him with my love,' she said and then she disappeared into the crowd. He handed me the photograph and of course it was Gennia. 'Did she give you an address?' I asked him, but he replied that she had just slipped away and he never saw her again. That was the last contact I was ever to have with Gennia, but I have always remembered her with a great deal of affection.

Because of political pressure from Australia, arrangements had to be made to withdraw the 9th Australian Division from Tobruk and replace it with the 70th British Infantry Division. This operation had to be carried out by the Royal Navy and it lasted from the end of August until well into October. There was to be no such relief for the British troops who were already a part of the garrison; we had to remain and fight, but those of us who survived were proud to be amongst the very few who served throughout the whole siege of Tobruk. It proved to be the longest-ever siege in British military history.

At first it seemed strange to be fighting alongside British troops again. It was the first time that the 70th Division had ever been in action and they were very uneasy under fire, which was perfectly natural – we had once been the same. By this time, however, we were battle-hardened and we could not understand why they were always diving for cover at the slightest sound. For a while it seemed to us that they had little idea what it was all about, but they soon settled down to life at the front and proved themselves to be both efficient and courageous.

As the months dragged on, we became rather weary of it all; the dreadful monotony of spending so much time in such an environment was beginning to tell. It was in the search for some means of brightening our existence that I discovered I had a talent for telling stories. Most nights the gun team would gather round me in the gun-pit and I would tell them a story. It became almost a ritual for someone to say, 'Come on, Bomb. Tell us a story.' 'Bomb', of course, was short for Bombardier, which was my rank at that time. Always having been an avid reader, I had no shortage of ideas to draw upon and I became adept at making up my own stories, which were usually based upon the characters and plots of the many novels I had read. I enjoyed telling stories and the telling of them filled many a dreary hour for my friends, who had so little to break the monotony of their lives.

Another of my ideas at that time was to build up a little library. I borrowed a fifteen-hundredweight truck and drove round to every section of the regiment and to other units as well, asking if anyone had a book in their kit for which they had no further use. It was surprising how many books I was able to collect over a very short period. After making a list of them all I arranged them in my dugout and then organised a library session of one hour during the hottest part of the day when things were usually at their quietest, when books could be exchanged. It was a very popular venture and very much appreciated by the lads in the troop.

The months dragged on and I was promoted to the rank of lance sergeant. I was well settled in 'A' Troop, where I had made many friends, but I still made frequent visits to 'B' Troop's position to spend some time with George and my old pals. By this time I had lost the irritation I had previously felt at the uncaring attitude of our officers. Several months of continual action had brought us all much closer together and they had become less remote and more concerned about our well-being. I had become very friendly with several of our officers through spending so much time with them at the OP. I got on very well with the battery commander; Peter Birkin and I discovered that when the barriers were down they were all decent fellows at heart. I was particularly fond of Captain Slinn, who was a splendid soldier and a perfect gentleman; another officer with whom I struck up quite a rapport was a lieutenant named Geoffrey Timms. Both these excellent men were to be killed by the same shell burst later in the war.

During one of the battles in which we were engaged the gun next to ours received a direct hit. We saw the flash of the explosion and at the first opportunity we rushed over to help the gun crew, who were in a sorry state. Amongst these stricken men was another old pal and he was in dire distress. Dear old Ginger Barker, who had been one of the limber gunners in Palestine, was lying across the trail of the gun with his legs all shattered. I could see the splintered white bones protruding through the bloody, tangled flesh, and I knew that he would never walk again. The wounded were taken back to the field hospital and we later heard that both of Ginger's legs had been amputated at the thigh. He survived the operation and when he was strong enough to be moved he was placed aboard a Royal Navy destroyer for evacuation to a place of safety in Egypt. During the passage to Alexandria, however, the ship was attacked by enemy aircraft and sunk. I still shudder at the thought of my old friend's last moments, lying below decks with no legs, helpless and unable to move, and knowing that he was on a sinking ship. Poor old Ginger, he was a good man who deserved a better fate. With his passing I had lost yet another good friend and it seemed that the old pals of earlier days were all gradually slipping away.

In spite of the dangers involved in the sea journey, it was everybody's dream that they would be sent back to Cairo for some reason. One day I was told that I had been selected to attend a course on the art of camouflage and for a fleeting moment I thought that fortune had smiled on me. One glance at the map coordinates, however, dispelled any such airy hopes. I recognised them as being in the region of Tobruk and closer scrutiny identified the location as a place we called Stuka Wadi. It was the site of one of the water points down near the coast and as such it was frequently the target of German dive-bombers.

I packed my kit and climbed into the back of a fifteen-hundredweight truck to be driven from the gun position, down the two escarpments and along the dry wadi almost to its end. Here I found the spot the Royal Engineers had chosen for their course. I was the last to arrive. There were about a dozen men attending and from their cap badges I could see that they came from various regiments in the garrison. There was a deep cave under the cliffs in which to sleep but unfortunately for me every space had been taken. This meant sleeping outside in an area that was regularly bombed; it was pitted with bomb craters and obviously a very dangerous spot and no place to make one's bed. The cave's entrance offered a modicum of safety from any air raid that might happen, but there was one big snag. In the rocky walls were many holes in which sand vipers sheltered from the sun during the heat of the day. These poisonous snakes emerged from their holes during the hours of darkness to forage for food. Not surprisingly I hesitated to lay my bed down in such a place, but it was either that or sleep outside and risk the bombing. It was a case of casting my lot with either snakes or men, and I chose the snakes. I slept there every night during the course and although each morning I found many traces in the sand of their nocturnal wanderings, they caused me no harm. In common with most wild creatures, snakes only attack humans if they are startled or afraid.

The course was interesting enough and I learned, amongst other things, that it was most important to disguise shadows that stand out boldly on aerial photographs. These shadow lines could be broken by the skilful use of paint. The idea was to attract the eye along different lines and so break up the familiar shape of, say, a lorry or a gun or a tank, and to present a different shadowy outline that was not immediately recognisable. It was all very well in theory, but I was not wholly convinced and after studying many aerial photographs it seemed to me that there was no way of camouflaging a gun position in a desert.

I enjoyed my few days down on the coast and the dive-bombers did not put in too many appearances. I was able to swim in the sea, which was a great delight, and there were plants growing there, huge cactus and other such green vegetation. After months of nothing but glaring sand I found it most restful to the eyes. As we were several miles from the front it was relatively peaceful and the pleasure of being able to lie listening to the lap of the waves was sheer delight. Best of all though was the escape from the eternal noise of gunfire, the tedium of the gun position and the danger of the front line.

Returning to the gun position, I was soon back into the old routine. We were forever digging alternative gun pits so that when we were shelled out of one position we had another ready to be occupied. It was hard work as the ground was very rocky, but it had to go on all the time, two men from each gun detachment being allocated to the task.

On one of these many gun positions I built for myself a splendid dugout. Nearby I had discovered the remains of an Italian lorry that had been knocked out many months before and I had salvaged sufficient wood from it to line the sides of my shallow hole in the ground. One night I was sitting in this dugout leaning my head against the walls when something slipped between the boards and bit me on the back of my head. Knowing that there were many sand vipers in the vicinity of this post, I ran out into the darkness calling out that a snake had bitten me. The lads came running up to stand around me in dismay as I waited for the poison to take effect. Frank Birkinshaw went into the dugout and began tearing away at the wooden boards and we heard him shout, 'I've found the bastard. It's a black scorpion.' I never thought that I would be delighted to know that a scorpion had stung me. It was very painful and swollen for a few days, but at least it wasn't terminal. In spite of the prevalence of snakes in the desert, I never heard of anyone being bitten by one.

## Chapter 9

# The Break-out from Tobruk

As the months continued to pass, we began to wonder if Tobruk would ever be relieved. There had been one attempt during the summer: in Operation Battle-axe British troops based in Egypt had made a valiant effort to reach us, but they had been beaten back. We felt very isolated but morale was still high and there was no talk or thought of surrender. In fact the garrison, far from being merely on the defensive, continually attacked the German positions and we gave them little peace.

Now, as winter was approaching, there was talk of another offensive and rumour had it that we were going to take an active part in our own relief. Soldiers live on rumours, many of them completely spurious, but this one persisted and it began to have a ring of truth about it when we started digging gun pits over on the Bardia Road Sector. This was highly significant because during the whole of the siege we had defended the central section of the perimeter, and to be preparing positions behind the part of the line that faced towards Egypt suggested that we were going to fight a battle in that area. Then, to our complete surprise, we were actually told of the battle plan that had been formulated.

The Eighth Army was to attack from the Egyptian frontier with the purpose of destroying the enemy forces in Eastern Cyrenaica, Tobruk was to be relieved and in the next stage Tripolitania was to be occupied. Our role in the battle was to advance out of the perimeter and occupy two ridges known as El Duda and Sidi Rezegh. Here we were to meet up with 30 Corps, and in so doing cut off Rommel's communications with the west. The battle was due to start on 17 November. What we did not know was that Rommel was simultaneously preparing to launch an offensive against us. He was planning an all-out attack on Tobruk and his forces were already grouped and ready to strike on 23 November. This was to have serious consequences because it meant that when our attack went in, the Germans were already in position and equipped for battle. Whilst all these preparations were under way, the weather took a turn for the worse; it became bitterly cold and we experienced our first rainstorms for many, many months.

The battle began with the usual crash of an artillery barrage and it turned out to be a long and bitter struggle with heavy losses on both sides. One thing was proved beyond doubt: the German tanks were far superior to our own in mechanical efficiency, and the guns they carried were larger and more powerful, as well as having a longer range. British tanks were greatly inferior under battle conditions. Another weapon that was to have a large impact on this and many later battles was the German 88mm gun, which had no rival.

At first things seemed to be going well, but within a week the Germans had launched a decisive counter-attack, which drove 30 Corps back from Sidi Rezegh with the loss of two-thirds of its tanks. It also cut off the 7th Armoured Brigade and the support group, annihilated the 5th South African Infantry Brigade and left us, the Tobruk Garrison, with a huge salient to defend.

For most of the time through this battle I was the sergeant in charge of No. 1 Gun in 'A' Troop. We moved into our new positions in the most terrible conditions of biting cold and heavy rain. We had not had time to do more than dig slit trenches behind the guns before the battle commenced. There was no shelter from the bitter wind and continual rain, the ground was churned up into a deep clogging mud and everything we possessed was soaking wet.

We opened up with a heavy bombardment, and during the first day of the battle each gun fired over 900 shells. The enemy quickly found our range and returned fire, and their shells began to fall around us. The sky seemed to be filled with enemy aircraft that attacked our positions with both high-altitude bombing and dive-bombers and we began to suffer heavy casualties. By nightfall on that first day we were chilled to the bone, soaking wet through and very, very tired.

It is not often realised that manning a gun during a fierce battle is very hard work. In order to engage different targets the gun has to be constantly dragged into position by hand. When the gun fires, the force of the explosion drives the gun carriage backwards and downwards so that the spade is buried deeply into the ground. When this has happened, and the wheels have also sunk into the mud, it is an exhausting labour to pull it clear so that it can be pointed in another direction. The shells have to be fetched from the ammunition pits dug to the rear of the gun position, and each metal box of four shells weighs over a hundredweight. Loading the gun can also be very tiring and it takes a very strong man to go on loading hundreds of shells one after another. Even artillerymen, if they have never seen active service, do not realise the physical effort required to man a gun in battle. To continually serve a gun in conditions I have just described is gruelling work even for fit and strong men.

I, however, was anything but fit. In fact I was feeling very ill at the start of this battle and in normal circumstances I would probably have been in hospital. For a few days previously I had been feeling off colour and in the end I had to go and see the MO, who examined me and concluded that I was suffering from enteritis. He went on to say that I should be ordered to bed, but in view of the fact that a battle was about to commence in which every man would be needed, it was my duty to remain at my post. As I turned to leave he advised me not to eat corned beef or army biscuits, and to go easy on the tea. As our rations comprised little else, he was really telling me to fast.

When we were told about the coming battle we were led to expect that it would probably last for about three days, but as so often happened it turned into a bitter slog with each side refusing to give an inch of ground. For me it was a miserable battle, not merely because of the danger but because in the early stages I felt so weak and ill. The continual driving rain and the bitter wind made life a misery for us all. During periods when the gun was not actually firing we tried to get some sleep, but this meant lying in a shallow slit trench that was half full of cold water. It was far too dangerous to stay above ground for anything other than manning the gun. It was a great relief when after the battle had been raging for about a week I began to feel better and was able to start eating again. A weak man in a gun team is a liability and I was supposed to be in charge and setting an example. I must have been very fit and sound of constitution to have recovered so quickly under such conditions.

When I recall the bombing and the shelling that took place at that time, there are two aspects that stand out clearly in my mind. The first concerns a remarkable combination of angles and chance that resulted in a hair-raising form of bombardment. At one period during the battle a German battery was firing on our position and many of the shells were striking a ridge in front of us at such an angle that the shoulder of the shell was hitting the ground instead of the nose cap. This resulted in the shells ricocheting in such a way that they flew towards us at tremendous speed, screaming and bouncing end over end. Sometimes they would explode before reaching us and sometimes they would bounce over or between the guns to burst in the air or upon striking some object that lay in their path. The noise they made was horrendous and we hated them. The second was another form of missile that was unusual and highly unpopular: the Italian Breda gun. The Breda was really an anti-aircraft gun that fired shells from a belt in rapid succession. Although the shells were small in comparison to our own, they could be quite devastating in their effect. The Italian gunners hit upon the novel idea of firing their guns into the air at such an angle that the shells all fell onto our position. They came down almost vertically and so there was no protection from them even in a slit trench.

In the initial attack we supported the Black Watch and the Beds. & Herts. The men from these two infantry battalions had advanced behind our creeping barrage, but they had run into stiff opposition from the enemy, who were in full strength, well dug in and manning a series of defensive posts. After much bitter fighting they were able to gain their objective but not without heavy losses. A great friend of mine, Stanley Keeton, always known as 'Buster', had followed close behind these troops in an open vehicle in order to lay a telephone line for the observation party. For this he was later awarded the Military Medal and it was a decoration well and truly earned.

After several days of fighting the garrison troops had reached El Duda, but 30 Corps had been forced to retreat and this meant that we were out on a limb. The commanding general considered it imperative that the captured ground should be held whatever the cost, so that if the troops from the 8th Army did manage to fight their way forwards, there would be a corridor for them to enter Tobruk. As may be imagined, holding on to this ground, encircled the enemy on three sides, was a dangerous and costly business and the guns were seldom silent either by day or by night. There was always the danger that one of the German counter-attacks would be successful and that they would retake the ground they had lost and be able to recover the equipment which had been abandoned during our advance.

There had been a battery of medium artillery behind the ridge where our attack had gone in, and in the heat of the fighting the German gunners had deserted their guns and fled. These guns were now in the middle of no-man's-land, halfway between the opposing forces. It was expected that the enemy would make a desperate attempt to recover them, and plans were made to prevent this happening. It was decided that an NCO should make his way across no-man's-land to where the guns were situated. Once in position, he was to prepare one of the guns so that it could be towed. Then a driver was to make a mad dash across the open ground in a sandbagged gun-tower, hitch up the gun and tow it speedily back to our own lines. The NCO would remain behind to prepare another gun and so on until all the guns had been retrieved.

Volunteers were called for, and I was foolish enough to step forward. Jim Martin volunteered to be the driver. Jim had been our driver when I was in Cliff Smedley's gun team back in the old days at Mersa Matruh. The Royal Engineers were ordered to prepare a path through the barbed wire and the minefield so that the gun-tower would not be impeded in any way. There was no time to lose and so Jim set about packing sandbags into his gun-tower and I started to make my way towards a point in our lines from which I could make a dash for the deserted German guns. There was almost continuous mortar fire coming over at the time and also a great deal of shellfire that became so heavy at one point that I had to dive for cover. I found myself sharing a rough shelter of sandbags and piled-up rocks with a party of men from the 2nd Battalion, the Black Watch. They had suffered heavy casualties already and were now holding this part of the line with our support.

It was still bitterly cold, although they had rigged a roof over their shelter from Italian groundsheets that did give some protection from the biting wind. I was sitting on an ammunition box next to one of their officers and telling them about my mission with the German guns when a shell came whistling down straight into the shelter. It plunged into the ground between the officer and myself and failed to explode. We all finished up in a heap, and when I picked myself up I discovered that, in passing, the shell had torn the sleeve of my greatcoat. The officer had not been so lucky: it had taken off his right arm.

There was a great deal of confusion, and the injured man was bleeding profusely as they pulled him away from the unexploded shell to tend his wounds. I also lost no time in climbing out of the hole and with shouts of 'Stretcher-bearers' ringing in my ears, I made my way along the line to find a suitable jumping-off point. I was very conscious of the fact that this was the second time in just a few months that a shell had landed right beside me and failed to explode, but I had little time to dwell on such matters – that would come later. My main concern at the time was finding any available cover as I dodged across the windswept ground that was no-man's-land, towards those horribly exposed guns, wishing all the time that I had not been so foolhardy as to volunteer for such a dangerous escapade.

The ground was littered with the bodies of men who had fallen in the attack, and I felt very vulnerable, imagining that every soldier in the German Army had me in his sights and was about to pull the trigger. In spite of my fears I reached the gun position unscathed, and it felt strange to be amongst German guns. There were eight of them in a staggered line, each one surrounded by the usual equipment which is to be found on a gun site: ammunition, gun stores, men's equipment, empty cartridge cases and, in this particular case, the bodies of fallen men.

There was a good deal of crossfire whizzing about but no one seemed to be firing especially at me; the shells and mortars were all falling either on the British troops on one side or on the Germans on the other, and I was in between the two. It was not the happiest of places to be but I did not appear to be the centre of interest and so I went towards the gun on the right of the line. After a quick inspection of the piece and the gun carriage, I was able to make a start in lowering the gun barrel, fastening the clamps, releasing the brakes and generally preparing the gun for movement. This done I hurriedly made my way towards a pile of rocks that lay in front of the guns; it was the only bit of cover in the area. I threw myself down behind them to wait for the gun-tower and found myself in company with the body of a British soldier.

I have never forgotten this man because I spent so many hours lying beside him that day. He was a private soldier from the Beds. & Herts. Regiment and he had been badly wounded in the lower abdomen. Someone had tied a shell dressing over his wound and dragged him into the cover of the small pile of rocks during the battle. There he had been left to die, alone in that bleak, God-forsaken desolation. Judging by the condition of the ground beneath him, he had obviously bled to death. I did not look at his dog tags to discover his name – I had other things on my mind, such as trying to stay alive myself – and in fact I did not disturb his body at all, but I remember him clearly.

It was not long before I saw Jim Martin start on his hazardous journey towards me. He came at great speed, swerving from side to side as he crossed the open ground, but I was not the only person to see him: the Germans also had him in their view and they were quick to respond. Although he did not have far to travel, their artillery had opened fire on him before he managed to arrive and with shells beginning to explode all around him he came charging onto the gun position as I ran forward to indicate which gun we were going to move. It called for great accuracy because there were only two of us; there was no gun team to help swing the trail about. Fortunately, Jim was an excellent driver and we had both performed this operation hundreds of times both in training and in action. All our experience paid dividends that day as he swung the vehicle round and backed up to the gun in seconds, stopping with the towing hook exactly in the right position over the trail eye. He jumped from the truck and the two of us hoisted the trail and hitched it onto the towing hook in a matter of moments and then he was back in the driving seat and on his way with the gun bouncing behind him.

All the time shells had been falling around us and so I lost no time in scurrying back to my shelter behind the rocks where I waited until things quietened down a bit before dashing across to prepare the second gun. It was about ten minutes' work to prepare each gun, but it took me longer than this because I was trying to work from a prone position whenever possible. As soon as the gun was ready and any debris cleared away to give free access to the gun-tower, I scampered back into cover again to await the next mad dash. This sequence of events continued for the remainder of the day because there was about an hour between each recovery.

At first the enemy concentrated on trying to knock out the truck as it went back and forth, but after we had got four of the guns away without mishap they changed their tactics and brought their fire down onto the guns themselves. It seemed they were hoping to destroy them rather than allow them to fall into our hands. This made my position doubly dangerous and the afternoon became a veritable nightmare as I spent my time hugging the ground beside my silent companion and making terrified dashes to prepare each gun in turn.

During the hours I spent lying there in my rocky shelter I had a spectacular view of the battle that was in progress all around me and I only wish that I had the literary skills to describe the scene adequately. The noise alone was beyond imagination: the whine of bullets, the scream and crash of shellfire, the roar of aircraft engines overhead and from time to time the shriek of the Stukas as they dived to hurl their bombs against the British lines. My senses were assailed by columns of smoke, the smell of cordite, tracer bullets describing arcs of colour against the grey sky and the rattle of tank tracks somewhere out of sight.

It was a frightening but fascinating experience and I shall never forget watching the dive-bombers peeling off, one after another, to scream down into what seemed to be an impenetrable mass of tracer and exploding Bofors shells. It was a paradoxical situation: although I was in a certain amount of danger, lying in the middle of no-man's-land, I was comparatively safe. Apart from the shells being fired in the attempt to destroy the remaining guns, most of the missiles were passing above my head and I could watch the Stuka raids with a certain amount of detachment.

In spite of the incessant shelling, the enemy failed to destroy any of the guns and by the end of the day we had removed them all beyond their reach. It was just getting dark as Jim made his last brave sortie, and as I saw him weaving towards me I said goodbye to the soul of the unknown man whose body had shared my cold and lonely day. No doubt his name appears on a war memorial somewhere in either Bedfordshire or Hertfordshire, but I shall never know. Within seconds of securing the final gun I was climbing aboard the gun-tower, anxious to be away and back behind our own lines. Jim Martin had made eight journeys, each one fraught with the greatest danger, and it was largely due to his skill and courage that the enemy was deprived of eight valuable guns. Without any doubt he deserved a medal for his work that day, but I don't think he received so much as a word of commendation. In the Regimental History his name appears but once – in the list of the fallen. He fell at Knightsbridge on 6 June 1942.

Having taken the last gun to a place well behind the line, we made our way back towards the battery gun positions. Darkness had now fallen but we had no difficulty in finding our way because the sky seemed to be alive with flares, some fired from the ground and others dropped from aircraft. We had to pass over a crossroads that was well known to the enemy and they were shelling it with salvo fire from time to time. We halted just short of the crossing and waited until the shells landed and then made a quick dash to get across before the next salvo. Right in the middle of the junction we hit a shell hole, the wheels started to spin and we ground to a halt just as the gun flashes told us that another salvo was on the way. We leapt from the vehicle and threw ourselves down on the ground and the shells exploded all around us. Neither of us was hit and Jim climbed back into the truck whilst I pushed with all my might. By a piece of superb driving skill he got it going again and I hung onto the back as he drove clear.

Jim dropped me off at 'B' Troop gun position and then made his way back to the wagon lines. I went to find my brother George, who took me into a dugout he had rigged for himself and pulled out a stone bottle of proof rum. (We had a rum ration almost every night during the siege and a double ration if there was to be a battle.) He poured me half a mugful, saying, 'Here, drink this. You'll need it after the day you have had.' I stopped for a while with George and Fred Lamb, and then made my way back to 'A' Troop position; when I arrived there Jim Hardy was waiting for me, and he also had a bottle of rum from which he poured me another half mugful. Considering the fact that I had eaten nothing since early morning and also the fact that I had just recovered from a bout of enteritis, a mugful of proof rum was bound to have some effect and it did. I rolled myself in my wet blanket, curled up in my soggy slit trench and fell into an exhausted rum-induced sleep. The guns were in action several times during the night, but I heard nothing of it; the lads just let me sleep and for a few hours I was able to escape from all the turmoil.

With every day that passed, the battle to hold the corridor became more desperate. The Germans put in one attack after another; they had complete control of the air and their tanks outmatched our own in every way, but their every effort was to fail. We had never fired so many shells in so short a period of time, and orders for fifty rounds of gunfire became almost commonplace. Our guns had been in action now for nine months and it was estimated that each gun had fired nearly ten thousand shells. The guns were worn out and we began to suffer premature explosions, which is when a shell bursts in the chamber of the gun. This is a terrible thing for the gun crew, who are inevitably either killed or badly injured. I lost another old friend in this way: Arthur Fox, dear old Foxy who had been such a staunch member of Cliff Smedley's gun team back in the days of Mersa Matruh. The gun overheated and exploded, and Arthur was killed.

[*The above notes are not intended as a historical record of the Corridor Battle, as it became known. By describing some of my own experiences, I have tried to give some idea of life at the front, but it has to be remembered that each man has his own story to tell. Whilst I was sitting in my little corner of the front, hundreds of other men were engaged in their own private battles all the way from Tobruk to the frontier. In tanks, behind guns, on foot or in the air, whether they were fighting with the Axis or with the Allies, they were all men sharing a similar experience. We all huddled against the same wind and felt the same rain driving into our faces. We all knew fear and we all felt sadness at the loss of our friends. My own exploits were of no significance other than that they serve to illustrate some of the things that were common to us all.*]

* * *

They had told us at the beginning that the battle would last for three days; in fact it lasted for two whole weeks, by which time the German Army had started to fall back towards Derna and the west. The first troops to enter Tobruk were New Zealanders, and we were delighted to see them. I can well recall my own feelings of joy and relief when we realised that for the first time in nine months we were no longer under siege and that we were once again linked up with our own army. We were now ready to sit back on our laurels and have a well-earned rest because our guns were no longer serviceable and what was left of our transport was in no condition for further active service. Imagine our dismay when orders were given for us to hand over our worn-out equipment to a New Zealand Artillery Regiment and to take over their brand-new guns and transport. The transfer took place at night and I found myself in a brand-new gun-tower of a make I had never seen before. The driver had no idea how to start the engine and we sat there in the darkness pushing levers and pulling various knobs in our attempts to get it going. At one stage we turned on the headlights and that caused a furore.

By morning we had left Tobruk and were in hot pursuit of the retreating Germans. We went through Bomba and on to Tmimi, where we had to stop because of a shortage of fuel. In this place there must have been an Italian camp because someone found an abandoned barrel of Chianti. The officers had all disappeared and the lads started on the Chianti with a vengeance, drinking it by the mugful. Everyone was in high spirits and there was much backslapping and friendly banter as the wine started to take effect.

It suddenly occurred to me that the whole troop was well on the way to becoming paralytic with drink and so I called Frank Birkinshaw to one side, told him of my fears, and warned him not to drink any more. From then on we both went through the motions of drinking along with everybody else but it was merely pretence. What an amazing sight it was to see the progressive stages of intoxication overcoming the whole troop. First there was a lot of laughing and shouting, then this gradually changed as one by one they fell into a state of maudlin sentimentality. Tears then began to flow as mothers, wives and sweethearts were remembered and then, without any warning, each man fell as if he had been pole-axed. It was not surprising really because they had been drinking the wine as if it were water. It was not long before Frank and I were the only two men capable of standing and we spent the next half-hour collecting blankets from where they were stowed in the gun-towers and lorries. We then went round and wrapped each snoring body in a couple of blankets, for the night was bitterly cold. When this was done, we too had a couple of drinks and climbed under our own blankets, praying that the regiment would not be called upon to move into action during the night.

We remained at Tmimi for about a week, including Christmas Day. The weather continued to be bitterly cold, with continuous rain, and we had no cover at all. There was also some trouble with the rations and we were short of food until someone discovered an abandoned Italian food dump, and after this we were issued with Italian rations. It was a miserable period but at least we were out of range of the enemy artillery for the first time in nine months. At last we were moved back into the desert in the region of Tobruk and it was decided that a group of men should be sent back to Cairo on leave. The battery commander told me that the leave party was to be selected from the men who had held the most dangerous positions during the siege and that I was to be included amongst them. After hurriedly drawing some money from RHQ, we threw our kit into the back of a three-ton truck and were soon making our way along the Trigh Capuzzo for what was to be a three-day journey across the desert.

Although the main body of German troops was now in full retreat many miles to the west, fighting was still going on around Bardia, Sollum and Halfaya Pass, and we could hear the sounds of battle over by the coast. We drove through the recent battlefields and passed the burnt-out hulks of scores of tanks and lorries that littered the desert for miles and miles. In order to skirt the fighting we turned south in the direction of Sidi Omar, where we spent the first night sleeping beside the truck. The following day we reached the railhead, which had now advanced to a point south of Sidi Barani, and after a long wait we were allowed to travel as far as Mersa Matruh in some empty box wagons. We spent the second night at Mersa Matruh and the following day we climbed aboard another train that was to take us to our destination in Cairo. By chance it was New Year's Eve, exactly a year to the day since I had been travelling on the same line to start my previous leave. I had been twelve months without leave.

We arrived late in the evening, very tired, dirty and unshaven and still wearing the same filthy ragged clothing that had served us for so long. On my arrival at the hotel my first priority was to run a hot bath and to lie there and soak. This was the first time my body had been properly washed since we had left Tahag nine months previously to make our way in the direction of Tobruk.

## Chapter 10

# In the Nile Delta

Having arrived in Cairo, my first objective was to find Gennia, but a whole year had passed since my previous leave and many things had changed. The Bardia was now reserved for 'Officers only' so I could no longer gain admission, and when I enquired from the staff I was unable to learn anything other than that she no longer danced there. I next tried to find her flat, but this meant straying into parts of Cairo that were out of bounds for British troops. It was dangerous to loiter in such areas and it also made me liable to arrest by the local police. In spite of this I did go searching and I found many wrought-iron gates with gardens and fountains, but they all looked the same and Cairo is a very big city. In the end I had to give up my search and I was never to see Gennia again.

It had been the intention that we should spend four days in Cairo: eight days had been allowed for travelling there and back, which meant a total of twelve days' absence from the regiment. On the morning of the third day I met Major Birkin for a drink at the Kursall. He and I had spent hundreds of hours together at the OP and had shared a great many dangers and hardships during the siege, so that within the limits of rank we had become good friends. Now he told me that he had news that the regiment was being pulled out of the line. It had been decided that as the South Notts. Hussars had been in continuous action for over nine months, they should be brought back for a rest and a refit. We were to remain on leave in Cairo for another week.

We rejoined the regiment at El Tahag and it was pleasant to be able to enjoy the simple pleasures of life once again. New uniforms were issued and there were hot showers, decent food, tented accommodation and, best of all, no gunfire. What a great delight it was to have a trestle bed and to be able to sleep peacefully all through the night.

At El Tahag we were issued with new guns and vehicles, and our equipment was all brought up to standard. During the final days in Tobruk I had named my gun 'The Saint', after a character in the books by Leslie Charteris. This idea became popular in 425 Battery and soon all the guns bore names chosen by their sergeants. Sammy Hall, one of the signallers, had been a signwriter in civilian life and he enjoyed painting the names on the gun shields for us. For me he painted the characteristic matchstick man with a halo and below it the words 'The Saint', in the regimental colours of red, blue and gold. Training in this camp was kept to an essential minimum and it was generally a quiet and restful time. We were content to spend our evening in the sergeants' mess, writing letters and drinking, sometimes very heavily, until the early hours of the morning. Occasionally a visit would be made to Moascar on the Suez Canal, but for the most part we were happy to lie in our tents and relax.

Our next move was to Sidi Bishr, which was within easy reach of Alexandria. This was by far the best camp we had ever seen. There were many palm trees and green vegetation, hedges and flowers, and the city was only a short distance away by tramcar. It was beyond our belief to be free every evening to hop on a tram and to spend time in busy streets, or to walk along the waterfront before dropping into a bar for a drink. My favourite place was the Petty Officers' Club, a comfortable place where the food was excellent. I still dream of the mixed grill they used to serve in the Petty Officers' Club in Alexandria. It was in Sidi Bishr that I became a full sergeant, which meant that I wore three stripes surmounted by a gun. It was here also that we began to get busy again as we became attached to the 22nd Armoured Brigade of the 1st Armoured Division. Training was resumed and we filled our days with gun drill, schemes, lectures and all the normal functions of an artillery regiment preparing for battle.

It was during this period that I was despatched to the Royal Artillery base depot near Cairo to attend an anti-tank course. When I arrived there it was discovered that a mistake had been made as this particular course was for officers only. After some discussion, the colonel in charge decided that it was too late to make changes and that I should be allowed to remain and take part. It was a somewhat unique experience to be the only non-commissioned rank in a group of about thirty officers, the majority of whom were either captains or majors. To be fair, they were all extremely kind and friendly towards me and there was never a single occasion when I was made to feel conscious of my inferior rank.

Apart from the usual lectures that formed part of the course, most of the time was spent in actually manning the guns in practice situations. As I had far more experience of this than anybody else on that course, I found it oddly amusing to watch a group of officers doing gun drill and doing it rather badly because it was strange to them. There was one occasion when the officer acting as Number One (normally a sergeant) failed to notice a mistake by the gun layer (Number Three). It was the rule when engaging tanks for the sergeant to call out the range and this had to be continually repeated by the gun layer until it was changed. In this case the range of three thousand five hundred yards was not repeated. The colonel took the officer acting as Number One to task for his negligence. After giving him a brisk dressing-down, the colonel bellowed: 'You should have shouted "Three, five hundred you stupid bastard".' Soon after this I found myself acting as Number One and the same thing happened. I shouted the estimated range and to my consternation the gun layer who was a major forgot to repeat it back to me. With the colonel standing just behind me, I had no option but to bellow, 'Two, seven hundred, you stupid bastard … Sir!' At this the whole acting gun team fell about laughing and even the colonel allowed himself a little smile.

I quite enjoyed this anti-tank course which, amongst other things, brought home the fact that whilst the twenty-five-pounder was an excellent field gun, it certainly had its limitations when used as an anti-tank weapon. This was not to be wondered at because it had not been designed for such a role. It was completely out of its class when attempting to compete with fast-moving tracked and armoured vehicles equipped with guns of equal calibre plus heavy automatic weapons. The twenty-five-pounder was, by comparison, slow to traverse and immobile, which made it an easy target; worse, the crew was completely exposed and therefore vulnerable to small arms fire.

My return to Sidi Bishr found the regiment once more in preparation for a move and within the space of a few days we were limbered up and ready for the road. We were sorry to leave Sidi Bishr, but the next camp, Beni Yusef, although close to the open desert, was pleasantly situated not too far from Cairo. It was in the region of Memphis and close to the very ancient step pyramid of Saqqara and not very far from the Great Pyramids themselves. Here we started training in earnest and it was apparent that the division was preparing to go into action. We did many drill orders out in the desert beyond Mena, but they were easy – mere temporary hardships with civilisation just beyond the horizon.

It was after one of these exercises that I became disenchanted with the whole concept of war. It was probably the thought of moving back into the wilderness in the sure knowledge that it meant more battles, more danger, more hunger and thirst, and the risk of serious wounds or death. Whatever the reason, I was sick and tired of everything concerned with warfare. I was weary of military discipline, of striving to become more efficient in the art of killing and I was tired of the corporate life that is the thief of solitude. I longed to find some place where I could be alone and at peace. In this frame of mind I slipped away one afternoon and walked several miles until I found a friendly group of palm trees just below the brow of a hill and there I settled down to think. There must have been an Arab village just on the other side of the slope because I could hear the shrill, excited voices of children at play.

The sound of children's voices when they are playing together is almost exactly the same the world over: it transcends language. As I listened I became aware that it was a special kind of music, bringing waves of delight in its passage.

It told of purity and innocence and trust and wonderment, and it filled me with contentment. It was what I had been seeking. I resolved that afternoon that if I were spared to live beyond the war I would always strive to guide and protect that trusting innocence found only in childhood. I felt that those children on the other side of the hill represented children everywhere; they were like an oasis of godliness in a desert of aggression and greed, selfishness and cruelty. They had been so little time on earth that they were still close to the angels and to be in their company would be as close as one could ever get to heaven in our sad, old world.

I walked back to the camp engrossed in my thoughts and mentally refreshed. It had not occurred to me to look over the hill and so I never saw those children, but they were to have a profound effect upon my future life. As I write these words I am still of the same opinion: that to be in the company of children is to be very close to the angels, but at that time I felt that I was very close to becoming an angel myself.

Several of my old friends had recently left us to go to an Officer Cadet Training Unit (OCTU). Bob Foulds, Charles Westlake, Ian Sinclair, Bill Brameld and David Boe had all been selected and were now in training in Cairo. I had been sorry to see them go, but Major Birkin had already told me that I was amongst those earmarked for the next batch to be sent for officer training and I was well content. It seemed that if I could survive, the future would be both interesting and rewarding. It was by this time over two-and-a-half years since the war had started and I was no longer the shy and reticent lad who had lost his rifle outside the Western Tennis Club. Eighteen months of almost continuous active service had removed all traces of naivety.

Whilst we were at Beni Yusef I had two motorcycle accidents, one on the road to Cairo, where I narrowly missed hitting a tram standard with my head, and the other when I skidded down the bank of an irrigation canal. In the second of these accidents the bike fell across my legs and, as I was wearing only shorts, I sustained severe burns where the hot cylinder dropped onto the inside of my thigh. The medical officer treated the wound and bandaged my leg.

Stan Keeton and I had made friends with a couple of young Egyptian girls in Cairo. Our interest at first had been purely (or impurely) carnal, but it quickly developed into a friendly, social relationship and we used to visit them most days. When we arrived they would make tea and they sometimes bought cakes for us to share. When I arrived one afternoon with my leg bandaged, one of the girls insisted on examining my injuries. When the bandages were removed she said, 'Your doctor, he is no good. He has treated this wound as a graze and it is a very bad burn. Do not worry; I will treat it for you.' With this, she sent a boy out to buy various salves and ointments and when he returned she treated and rebound my injured leg. This meant that I dared not to return to the MO for treatment and instead I went each day into Cairo to meet the girl, who tended my injuries with much greater compassion than the doctor.

The day at last arrived when we received our orders to move up into the line once again. There was the usual last-minute hectic rushing around, collecting gun stores and ammunition, and making sure that everything was up to scratch. The members of my gun crew were all men freshly out from England, all older than me, all strangers and not a single man from the original 425 Battery. For them it was all strange and exciting to be preparing for battle for the first time and I found myself recalling the day two years previously when we had first moved up to Mersa Matruh in the same excitable frame of mind. Now I was the old and seasoned soldier: I was twenty-two.

## Chapter 11

# The Battle of Knightsbridge

On 21 April 1942 the 107th Regiment (SNH) RHA was ready once more to move into action. There were now three batteries, making twenty-four guns. It was quite an impressive sight to see the whole regiment in line abreast, pulling off one at a time until the whole convoy of over one hundred and fifty vehicles was on the move. We wound our way out of the camp at Beni Yusef, turned along the Mena Road, watched the Great Pyramids disappear away to our left and then set off along the desert road in the direction of Alexandria. The first night we halted at Amariya, and the following day saw us back on the old familiar desert road heading in the direction of El Alamein and Mersa Matruh.

As we made our way further westwards into the desert, it became prudent to sit on the roof of the gun-tower hugging a loaded Bren gun in case of a sudden attack from the air. We were fortunate in having a relatively uneventful journey and after three days of travel we were able to meet up with other elements of the 22nd Armoured Brigade in the vicinity of Fort Capuzzo. We then moved more deeply into the desert.

We began to operate very far inland in close support of the 3rd County of London Yeomanry ('The Sharpshooters') and the conditions were extremely harsh. It was stiflingly hot, there was no shade whatsoever and the parched land reflected back the dazzling glare of the sun so that the desert shimmered in the intense heat. To make matters worse, we were very, very short of water and constantly thirsty, which was most distressing under such conditions. It was also irritating because the lack of water was solely due to negligence. The British Army, after two years of campaigning in the desert, had yet to provide suitable containers for transporting water to the forward troops. The Germans had solved this problem by using strong, purpose-built containers that we called 'jerrycans'. We still used tins that were so thin that they regularly burst in transit with the result that when our water ration arrived many of the containers were empty. We took to sucking pebbles in an attempt to alleviate the tormenting and ever-abiding thirst, but the effect was more psychological than practical.

The temperature range in the desert is quite remarkable. A blistering heat can accompany the daylight hours, but during the hours of darkness the temperature often falls almost to freezing point. We were not equipped to deal with either of these extremes of heat and cold and as a result we roasted by day and shivered by night. Although by now most of us were well used to such privations, it was something of a trial for the reinforcements for whom this was an entirely new experience. It is very often the case that soldiers in combat are exasperated by the fact that their equipment does not match up to the conditions under which they are expected to serve.

We were not made any happier at this particular time by a strategy worked out by our brigadier. He had brought forward a scheme whereby the guns were to be used as decoys. The idea was that we should be placed in situations that put us at a disadvantage in order to tempt the enemy tanks to attack us and so lure them out into the open desert. When they did so, our own tanks would sally forth, charge into action and engage them. This may have sounded very fine in theory, but as we very well knew, the theory was not substantiated by fact. The twenty-five-pounder gun was not designed as an anti-tank weapon, and in any case we were only supplied with eight armour-piercing shells in every hundred rounds of ammunition. Our guns were only properly effective against tanks at a range of about a thousand yards or less; given that the German tanks could cover that distance in less than two minutes, this left little margin for error. We were also very conscious of the fact that the gun crews were completely open to small arms fire and therefore very vulnerable when in action against tanks. The shield on the gun was merely there to protect the crew from the blast of the gun itself; it afforded no protection whatsoever against enemy fire. The truth of the matter, as we all well knew, lay in the fact that at that time we had no effective anti-tank guns and the twenty-five-pounders were being pressed into service as a substitute.

We moved about the desert like ships at sea, with the brigade split up into regimental groups known as 'boxes'. The twenty-five-pounder guns flanked each box and the armoured regiments brought up the rear. When on the move, which was most of the time, the vehicles really did look like ships; the dust clouds that flowed out behind each truck were like the wake of a vessel forging ahead in a calm sea. Needless to say, a large concentration of vehicles such as this was very conspicuous from the air and for this reason we were widely dispersed, again like a flotilla of ships. The enemy still had air superiority that enabled them to roam the skies at will, and as a result of this we suffered continually from air attack. When night fell all the vehicles drew close together in what was called 'close laager' and this made a perfect target for the bombers who were always watching our movements.

In order to escape their attentions during the hours of darkness it was necessary for us to keep on the move for several hours after the sun had set. In this way we were able to lose ourselves in the vastness of the desert. All through the night the enemy bombers droned about the sky dropping flares in the hope of finding a concentration of troops and vehicles. Often we would go on travelling for three or four hours after dark until we arrived at some pre-determined spot to meet our 'B' Echelon, which had brought replenishments of fuel, ammunition, water, food and spares. All these essentials then had to be unloaded in the darkness and transferred to our own vehicles. When all this was finished there was little time left for sleep because it was necessary for us to be up and away before dawn in order to be well dispersed when the first rays of the sun appeared to disclose our position. It was not possible to sleep during the day because of the intense heat, the accursed flies and the fact that we were continually on the move. As day followed day we became increasingly weary and this began to show itself as we became more edgy, irritable and quarrelsome.

During an enemy air attack I received a wound on my left hand that I chose to ignore. This proved to be a mistake, however, because it quickly turned septic and within a couple of days I had to report to the medical officer, who lanced the wound several times over a period of days, using a local anaesthetic and the brandy bottle to deaden the pain, but the wound refused to heal.

It was a miserable time for everybody. There were so many things to contend with: the heat, a raging thirst that was never quenched, the weariness, the continual attacks from the air and, very often, the hot, stifling wind of the Khamsin. Such a combination made life all but unbearable. All these things, together with my injured leg and a poisoned hand that caused me excruciating pain as we bumped along for hours at a time, brought me to a very low ebb. I was very thankful when, after lancing the wound again, the MO had me transferred to a first field dressing station for proper attention. I remained at the FFDS for only a couple of days before they sent me to the hospital at Tobruk. Within a couple of hours of my arrival I was in the operating theatre, where they gave me a general anaesthetic.

I woke up in a ward, the end of which had been blown away by shellfire, and was astonished to see a nurse standing at the foot of my bed. It was a complete surprise to me to find that English nurses were stationed so close to the front. These girls were extremely kind and considerate; they worked for very long hours and were obviously under great stress, but they were always patient and gentle. I remember them with both gratitude and sadness, because just before the fall of Tobruk they were evacuated by boat and the ship on which they were sailing was torpedoed. They were all lost at sea.

From Tobruk hospital I was sent by ambulance to a field hospital situated in a wadi near the coast, not far from the bottom of Hellfire Pass. It was a tented hospital and I remained there for several days before being transferred to an emergency underground hospital at Mersa Matruh. By this time I was beginning to feel much better. Both my leg and my hand were healing nicely, although both were still sore and tender, and I had to keep my arm in a sling. It was whilst lying in this hospital that I began to have feelings of guilt. It preyed on my mind that my friends were up at the front and I was lying on a bunk in Mersa Matruh with very little wrong with me. Instead of taking advantage of the situation, which would have been the sensible thing to do, I decided that it was my duty to make some effort to return to my unit.

Climbing from my bunk, I removed the sling, put on my uniform and packed my kit. When the medical officer came along on his daily rounds I informed him that I was better and ready for discharge. To my amazement he went red with anger and told me to get back on my bunk and obey orders. He would decide when I was ready to be discharged. 'Who did I think I was? He had never seen anything like it in his life. What were things coming to?' He stomped away in disgust.

The following morning I repeated the procedure, insisting that I no longer warranted a place in the hospital. Never have I seen a man as angry as that doctor. I thought he would burst with rage. He stormed and ranted, striding up and down between the bunks as he went on and on about lack of respect and insubordination. Then he ordered me to leave the hospital. He just kicked me out, refusing to give me any discharge papers, rations or means of transport, and this left me completely stranded.

In the army it was not normal to leave one establishment without being formally posted to another: you had to be on the ration strength for one thing, and for another, any man without documents could be taken for a deserter. The doctor's attitude would probably have been understandable had I been trying to feign illness to avoid being sent to the front, but I was doing the very opposite. As it was, I found myself standing in the desert with nothing but my small kit. As there was no transport for me, I just started walking in the direction of a tented camp that I could see in the distance.

Fortunately this turned out to be a transit camp, but when I asked for transport back up the line (the front at this time was over a hundred miles from Mersa Matruh) I received no cooperation at all. Without the proper documentation they were not disposed to transport me anywhere and what was more, to my immediate concern, they were not prepared to give me food either. Looking back, it is hard to believe that a British soldier in the Western Desert should have been refused rations in a British camp simply because he lacked the necessary papers, but such was the case. I could not even get a tin of bully and a couple of army biscuits.

This called for some action. Whilst wandering round the camp I made contact with a captain in the Royal Army Service Corps and he told me that he was in the process of leading a large convoy of one hundred three-ton trucks carrying reinforcements to the front. They had come up from Alexandria and had stopped for the night on their way to the next transit camp at Fort Capuzzo in Libya. We discussed the dangers attendant upon such a large convoy during the next stage of its journey, which would take two days, and he agreed that the trucks would present a wonderful target for any enemy planes that might spot them. I explained my position to him and after some further discussion we struck a bargain. If he would take me as far as Fort Capuzzo and arrange for me to get something to eat, I would take charge of half the convoy for him. I would leave with my fifty trucks several hours after his departure and in this way the convoy would be less vulnerable to air attack. He was delighted to shed half the convoy and lost no time in having the necessary documents prepared for me to sign. In this way I became, temporarily at least, a bona fide member of our armed forces and I was now permitted to draw rations from the sergeants' mess.

The following morning he left at dawn and by early afternoon I was leading my fifty trucks up the now familiar road in the direction of Sidi Barani, Sollum and the Libyan border. We stopped for the night in the desert in the region of Buq Buq and I clearly remember walking round and showing the men, who were newly out from Britain, how to select a suitable spot for sleeping: always on hard, exposed rock, never on soft sand because that is where scorpions lurk.

We arrived at Fort Capuzzo the next day in the middle of a terrible sandstorm. The Khamsin was blowing with great force and the visibility was down to just a few yards. Having handed my convoy over to the RASC captain, who had been awaiting our arrival, I made my way into the Sergeants' Mess, which was in a marquee. The tent was full of dust and the heat was intense, but it provided some shelter from the sandstorm. The place was practically deserted but I joined a sergeant from the Sharpshooters, a tank commander, who, like me, was on his way to rejoin his unit.

The struggle I had to rejoin my unit was beyond belief and I began to feel like a stateless person. I had to plead to be taken each step of the way and very often I had to beg for my food. It was as if I was trying to desert, rather than the other way round. At last, after a long and weary journey, I managed to make contact with our 'B' Echelon, which was laagered way out in the desert somewhere to the south of Tobruk. It was good to be back with the regiment again and to catch up with the news. I collected some mail that had arrived during my absence: the usual welcome letters from Mother and Binkie. I had now been overseas for two and a half years and they were the only people who wrote to me regularly.

I moved up that same night with the 'B' Echelon lorries as they went to make their nightly rendezvous. It was an ominous journey with the sky ahead illuminated by flashes, and the rumble and crash of artillery growing ever nearer as we approached the front. I arrived at battery HQ in the middle of the night and the guns were in action as I reported my return to Captain Slinn. He shook me by the hand and said, 'Thank God you're back.' He was not inferring that I was in any way indispensable, merely underlining the fact that every man was needed, but those few words made it all worthwhile.

* * *

The next few days were to see the end of the 107th Regiment RHA (South Notts. Hussars) because after the battle of Knightsbridge the regiment ceased to exist. It was an epic battle that has earned its place in the annals of the Royal Regiment of Artillery. The story of the battle is told elsewhere, very inaccurately, I believe, in the Regimental History, and in an account written soon after the battle by the second in command. This account rests with my other papers. What follows is merely my own view of the battle as I saw it at the time and without the benefit of knowing anything about the general strategy or the deployment of troops anywhere other than the sector in which I was fighting. As with everything else I have written, I shall endeavour to tell the true story without any heroics or glorification. The story of that battle doesn't need any such appendages: it stands well enough on its own.

There is, of course, no such place as Knightsbridge in the Western Desert, and the battle of that name was fought in the open desert some miles southwest of Tobruk. It was the custom of the British Army to give familiar names to trench systems, strong points, redoubts, etc. and in this case the name Knightsbridge had been given to a spot in the desert where two tracks crossed. There was a wide, circular depression nearby and this was later known as 'the cauldron' because of the ferocity of the battle that was fought within its confines.

\* \* \*

It was a clear night with a full moon and the visibility was very good. The guns had been hurriedly dug in earlier in the evening and I hurried over to my gun to resume command from the lance sergeant who had taken over during my absence. How I missed the old 'B' Troop. These lads were comparative strangers and although they expressed pleasure to see me back, there was not the same warmth; it was not to be expected, as we had only known each other for a few weeks.

We managed to snatch a few hours' sleep, fully dressed and wrapped in a blanket, but as dawn broke we heard heavy firing somewhere over to the south and we were not surprised when the order came 'Prepare to Move'. Within minutes we were on the way, bumping and bouncing over the rocky ground as we proceeded with all speed in the direction of the gunfire that was growing in intensity all the time. Suddenly shells started falling ahead of us, but as we received no orders to the contrary we drove straight into the barrage. It was a hair-raising experience, but we were fortunate to suffer only light casualties before we emerged on the other side.

A short time later we dropped into action and engaged an enemy concentration of tanks and vehicles that could be seen about a mile away. It was a confused situation, for as we were throwing shells at the tanks and vehicles ahead of us, shells started to fall around our gun position, and they were coming

Charles Westlake, Ray Ellis, Bob Foulds and
David Boe, photographed in Wragby,
Lincolnshire, 1939.

Binkie: the girl in church.

The gun team: Clifford Smedley, Reg ('Tansey')
Leigh, Ray Ellis, Jim Radford and Jim Martin,
photographed in Palestine in 1940.

Captain P.L. Birkin, commander of 425 Battery.

The gun-tower passing through an Egyptian town on the way to Tobruk.

A wrecked Italian truck, with Tobruk in the background.

Sergeant Jim Hardy, later BSM of 425 Battery, who was killed in action on 6 June 1942 at Knightsbridge.

Bob Foulds and Ray Ellis in a gun-pit during the siege of Tobruk.

The shield of my gun, which I christened 'The Saint'.

My gun-tower, limber and gun, prior to moving up for the battle of Knightsbridge.

A Panzer IV of the Deutsches Afrika Korps.

George Ellis and Fred Lamb on leave in Cairo shortly before Fred was killed when B Troop was overrun in the vicinity of Knightsbridge.

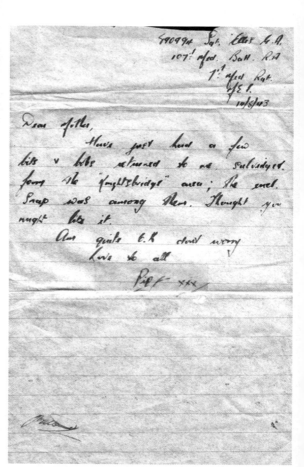

This photo of me at Mersa Matruh was blown up with my kit when my gun took a direct hit during the battle of Knightsbridge. It lay on the battlefield for many months until it was picked up by members of the regiment who visited the site while advancing through Libya after the battle of El Alamein.

A copy of the letter accompanying the lost photograph, sent home by my brother George who was always known in the family as 'Pip'. (Note that the letter had been censored, and the remnants of the SNH were serving with the 7th Medium Regiment, Royal Artillery.)

Concentration Camp 53. This photograph was taken a few years after the war. By this time the buildings were being used as warehouses. The high wall was still there and its shadow can be seen on the left. Six thousand prisoners were held here.

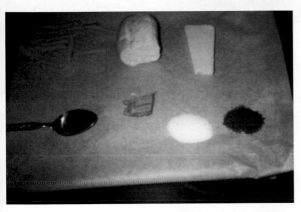

The official daily ration of food for a prisoner in Camp 53 at Sforzacosta.

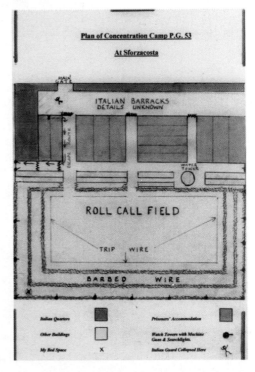

A plan showing the layout of the camp.

This is where I made my escape. The original gate, watchtowers, machine guns, barbed wire and high wall have all gone, but the water tower remains, and the hill that obsessed me can be seen in the background.

Ray and Igino standing at the spot where we first met in 1943.

The house at Massa Fermana.

Ivo, Davidi, Nichola, Igino and Aurelio.

The wayside Madonna between Monte Vedon Corrado and Falerone.

Mamma and Babbo: Paola and Alessandro as I remember them.

Ray and Harry Day at the barn in Monastero which had been our bedroom fifty years before.

The Minicucci family.

Elena: the girl in Italy.

from behind. It was obvious that we were in danger of becoming encircled and I was not sorry when the order came to cease firing. We quickly limbered up and started to move rapidly towards the east.

Whilst on the move we picked up some stragglers from 'D' Troop, which had been in action against tanks and had suffered heavily. We also heard from them the devastating news that 'B' Troop had been annihilated during the morning's fighting. There was no time to learn more because of the need to move quickly out of what looked like an encircling movement. This terrible news left me with an enormous sense of loss and I was desperately worried about the fate of my brother, and my dear old pals in 'B' Troop. It was hard for me to comprehend that 'B' Troop no longer existed and they were very much on my mind as we bumped and bounced our way at speed, first to the east and then to the north.

We swung into action again facing south near the track crossing known as Knightsbridge and within a few minutes of establishing ourselves we could see what looked like hundreds of tanks advancing towards us. As we opened fire on them I saw what I believed to be 426 Battery dropping into action behind us, but to my astonishment and dismay they were facing the other way. We had no idea at all what was going on and no knowledge of troop dispositions. We had enough to worry about protecting our own positions: there was no time to concern ourselves with the wider issues.

We beat off the first attack, the German tanks wheeling off to the flank as a second wave took their place, but they received the same treatment and also wheeled off. The enemy artillery opened up and soon the air was alive with bursting shells and the whine of small arms fire. As the day progressed, German dive-bombers also joined in the attack, screaming down, one after another, to jettison their bombs among us. It was like hell let loose as the battle raged on into the afternoon. In between the bursts of firing we gathered bits of rock and tried desperately to build some sort of protection around the guns. It was terrible ground on which to fight because the surface was composed of huge slabs of rock. This meant that not only were we unable to dig any sort of gun pit, but also that every shell burst immediately on impact with deadly results.

As the day wore on the news filtered through that we were engaging the 22nd German Panzer Division, which was making desperate attempts to break through our line in an effort to open the way for an advance into Egypt. We also learned that 'B' and 'D' Troops had been attacked by no fewer than one hundred and fifty tanks. The first wave had charged the guns and then swept behind them as a second wave made its frontal attack. With tanks coming at them from both directions, they had been shot to pieces. Some of 'D' Troop had survived but 'B' Troop had been wiped out.

I was greatly relieved to be told that George had not taken part in the battle. He had been taken ill a few days before and had been sent down the line, but all my old pals had gone, including my oldest army pal, Fred Lamb. I remembered how we had joined the South Notts. Hussars on the same day and how we had gone for a drink together at the Borlace Warren pub at the top of Derby road. Pat Bland, another friend from the earliest days, had also been killed. In fact they had all gone.

Jack Tomlinson, 'Tommo' as we used to call him, had died most stubbornly. With both his legs shattered, this brave lad had remained in the layer's seat and fired a last shell point-blank at a charging tank, which was so close that the shell had taken its turret clean off. The tank burst into flames and carried on out of control to crash into the gun, and Jack had died beneath its tracks. There was little time for grieving as the battle raged on fiercely. As well as repeated tank attacks, there was artillery fire to contend with, while the Stukas, with no opposition, had a field day, making attack after attack along the front and creating havoc everywhere.

It went on like this for three whole days. Apart from the danger, there was also the exhaustion factor, which began to have an effect on us because of the heavy work and the lack of sleep. There was no opportunity for rest, for even during the hours of darkness there was harassing fire from both sides, and of course stores, ammunition, food and water had to be unloaded from the vehicles of the 'B' Echelon. We slept in short snatches, just lying near the gun wrapped in greatcoats and blankets. Food was reduced to the eternal bully beef and biscuits, but we still managed to brew tea for ourselves on fires made from petrol-drenched sand. Hot, sweet tea was our salvation and we used to say that the motto of the Eighth Army was 'When in doubt, brew up!'

After three days of constant fighting the enemy called off the attack and withdrew to the south; the shelling stopped and there was no more small arms fire to contend with, but the air raids continued and gave us little rest. We used this period to bury the dead and also to recover some of the equipment we had lost at the start of the battle. A party was sent off in search of water, which was in very short supply. They set off in the middle of a blinding sandstorm and were never seen again. To this day I do not know what happened to those men: they were probably lost in the desert and died of thirst.

I think it was on the second day of this lull in the fighting that I was called to the command post, along with the other sergeants, and we were told that we were going over to the attack. It seemed that our section of the brigade was to attempt to break through the German line and then advance as far as Derna. We were told to throw away all unessential equipment in order to lighten the vehicles, and to do so as quickly as possible. The battle would start with a barrage and we were to be ready to open fire at three-thirty the following morning.

The gun-towers were brought up to the gun position and I set to work pretending to throw away equipment. I had been far too long at this game to throw anything away on the advice of some general who was, most probably, sipping cool drinks in a hotel in Cairo. Instead I had the driver check the engine and set the gun crew to work cleaning and maintaining the gun. I checked the reserve of food and water that I had secretly stored in the vehicle. We frequently had to stop whatever we were doing and dive for cover as the enemy kept up the incessant air attacks along our section of the front all through the day. It was late at night before everything was finished and all the shells necessary for the barrage were stacked conveniently behind the gun. The crew slept rough as usual near the gun, wearing their greatcoats and rolled in their blankets.

I was very tired and became lost in my thoughts. I wished that it were possible to postpone the war, just for a little while, so that I could get some sleep … the front had gone quiet…. How quiet the desert could be – quiet enough for men's bones to whiten in the silence of interminable ages, until they, in their turn, changed to form the particles of dust which the wind swept quietly along, or let them rest as best befitted its particular mood.

Three o'clock in the morning, cold and still. An air of excitement and expectancy … the barrage due to start in half an hour and then the advance. If only I had not been so tired. I was not frightened any more, that had passed long months ago, nor was I homesick, that too had passed, I was just weary – cold and weary. I wished the gun would never fire again – that no gun would ever fire again. Soon it would come, that vivid yellow flame and the horrible crash and then the clang of the breech as another shell took its place in the chamber … men were walking about like shadows, moving kit and asking my advice, which I gave automatically. I didn't have to think, I had done it all so many times before. Poor devils, this was their first battle – they had done very well up to now, but they were afraid – I could sense their fear – and they were homesick. It was only a matter of months since they had been in England with their wives and sweethearts, and home was still fresh in their minds. Not like we old soldiers, for us home was in the far distant past … *old soldiers?* – I was twenty-two.

Everything was ready so I sat on a pile of sandbags, took out my watch and counted the minutes. Someone was going to die very soon … maybe it would be me. I could feel the familiar stiffening of my body as I thought of hot steel tearing through my flesh … I kicked the sandbags, looked up at the stars – and waited.

\* \* \*

When a barrage opens up on a quiet night it has a startling effect, and this night was no exception. One moment everything was still, with the desert bathed in that eerie white light of a moon just passed the full, and then, in a second, it all changed in a blinding, shattering roar as the guns discharged their screaming missiles into the protesting night sky. We worked to a prearranged plan as round after round was hurled in the direction of the enemy troops. As soon as we had finished firing the barrage, we prepared to move forward. In a matter of minutes

I was standing in my gun-tower, with my head out of the roof hatch, helping my driver to keep his place in the medley of guns and vehicles moving forward in the misty light of early dawn.

Strangely, there was no response from the enemy as we approached the rim of the wide, circular depression that had to be crossed during our line of advance. Then, as we topped the rise, it was as if the sky had exploded all around us. The Germans had obviously been wise to our intentions and early the previous night had quietly withdrawn their forces beyond the far edge of the depression. Our barrage had been fired onto empty ground and had been of no avail at all. Now, they were ready and waiting for us and we ran straight into a hail of deadly and accurate fire.

It was unbelievable that the movement forwards continued. Some vehicles were hit and burst into flames, but apart from those there was no faltering at all. Then, as dawn broke, it became obvious that this senseless advance could not continue and we were brought to a halt. We brought the guns into action just where we had stopped, right in the middle of this great saucer in the ground that was the 'Knightsbridge cauldron'. We had been lured into a deadly trap from which we were never to escape. The guns of the 107th Regiment, South Notts. Hussars, had reached their last positions. We replied to the enemy fire and managed to silence some of their guns, but we were in a very exposed and precarious position and our armoured regiments were still behind us.

I was very relieved when our tanks came rumbling and rattling from the rear to pass between the guns as they made their way to hold the rim of the depression, a mile or so away to our front. There was not a moment's respite and we remained constantly in action so that the guns glowed red. As the day wore on the tanks kept returning in relays to refuel, and each carried a load of wounded men from the infantry who were fighting desperately to hold the line along the edge of the depression. We were also suffering casualties from shellfire and from persistent attacks by both high-altitude aircraft and dive-bombers.

When darkness fell, things quietened down a little and from time to time it was almost peaceful. The only sound was the crackle of fires from the many burning vehicles that were scattered around us. This peace was then broken by the sound of approaching armour: it was our tanks, coming back from the direction of the front. To our dismay, they passed through the gun positions and out of the battle area.

The word was passed around that the Eighth Army was in retreat and that we were to be left behind to fight a rearguard action from the Knightsbridge cauldron. It was a crazy idea and at first we could not credit the truth of it. More tanks passed through and gunners could be heard calling to them, asking them to remain and help, but they carried on into the darkness. They were only obeying orders, of course, and we could see that each tank was carrying a load of infantrymen. These men were not wounded. Then columns of men on foot started to pass silently through on their way to the rear. Gradually it began to dawn upon us that there was now nothing but the open desert between the 22nd German Panzer Division and us.

We were ordered to remain fully dressed and alert. Alert?! We were all just about worn out. I rolled myself in my blanket and went to sleep. A fussy little officer who had joined us during the last days in Tobruk awakened me. I have forgotten his name, but he was a silly little upstart who had no battle experience and I had already had several brushes with him. He told me to stay awake and I replied with a very rude word and promptly went to sleep again. I had long since learned the importance of snatching sleep whenever possible.

Before dawn broke I was awake and standing beside my gun, when out of the half-light I saw two figures approaching. As they drew nearer I recognised Captain Slinn and Lieutenant Timms. We discussed the situation for a few moments and then Captain Slinn told me that it was true, we had been left to hold the line. He said that we had been ordered 'to fight to the last man and the last round of ammunition' – there was to be no retreat for us. He warned me that it was going to be absolute carnage. As we spoke the sun tipped the horizon. He said, 'The sun is rising, sergeant, but very few of us will live to see it set.' Then we all three shook hands and wished each other well – but within a few short hours both these splendid men were to be killed in action.

As the daylight strengthened the German tanks crept cautiously forward, probing to find our first line of defence. We could see them in the near distance, crawling over the rim of the depression and down the slope as they approached us. Then, as they realised that there was no opposition, they came on boldly in open formation and we received the order from the command post, 'Engage tanks'. We loaded with armour-piercing shot and waited for them to come within effective range. No one in my gun crew spoke as the tanks came bouncing towards us, each leaving a huge cloud of dust in its wake. I chose my first target and swung the gun roughly into line. I indicated the tank I had selected to the gun layer, who picked it up on the open sight. I shouted the estimated range, which he kept repeating until I gave the order, 'FIRE'. As if by magic, every gun sergeant along the line seemed to have chosen the same second to open fire and the battle started with the familiar roar of gunfire. Several tanks in the leading line were stricken and lurched to a halt, some of them bursting into flames, but we were already reloaded and selecting the next target.

The German attack soon faltered in the face of such relentless fire and the tanks swung away to left and right before hurriedly making their retreat. After this there was break in the fighting, which we used to clear away the spent cartridge cases. We also tried to build some protection for ourselves by piling rocks in front of the gun, all the time cursing the nature of the ground upon which we had to fight and the exposed position into which we had been lured. The surface of the ground was solid rock with only a light covering of sand and it was not possible for us to dig ourselves in. The men of my gun crew were as yet unharmed, but we could see several stretchers being carried away somewhere to the rear, where the medical officer and Harry Day, the medical orderly, would be waiting to care for the wounded.

After a short time the German tanks came again, charging towards us with their guns blazing, but only suffered the same fate, and as they withdrew they left more burning hulks as testament to their inability to overcome our fire. After this there was another pause in the fighting, and we soon realised why. They had been bringing up more artillery and summoning help from the Luftwaffe. The German guns now opened up with a mighty roar and soon the air was filled with the sound of screaming shells that fell amongst us with devastating effect. We tried to find what shelter we could, but the inhospitable ground made it almost impossible for us to scrape a hole more than a few inches deep. Whilst we were hugging the ground, the main German force started to edge its way forwards. The artillery remained behind the rim of the crater, but we knew that the advancing infantry were now well into the depression.

The Germans indicated the position of their forward troops by means of purple smoke signals. These signals were for the benefit of their aircraft. They did not have to consider the danger of any attack from our aircraft because in those days we did not have enough for them to worry about. Even as the shells were crashing down upon us, we could hear and see the dive-bombers wheeling above as they prepared to attack and soon the ground was heaving under the explosions as their bombs came crashing down amongst the already exploding shells.

When the next attack was launched it came with the full support of their artillery; in order to resist it, we had to man the guns despite the shells dropping all around us. It was during this stage of the battle, about ten o'clock in the morning, that disaster struck my gun team. We had just made a direct hit on a German Mark IV tank when the whole world exploded around me. I felt myself being propelled into the air and then I hit the ground again with a thud. I was dazed and my ears were ringing as I tried to stagger to my feet, but before I was able to do so there was a second devastating detonation and again I was whirled up into the air to fall heavily amongst a cloud of smoke and dust. I lay there for some time – I have no idea how long – but gradually I came to my senses, coughing and retching, and at last I got onto my knees. Everything was covered in black smoke and shells were falling in every direction. I could hear the whoosh of small arms fire and slowly came to realise that the tank action was still taking place.

When I looked around I could see that my gun was upside down and that the bodies of the gun crew were draped around it. I thought that I must be wounded, but I couldn't feel anything. My whole body was black with the blast, and my arms and legs were bleeding. My shirt was torn and covered with blood.

I wasn't afraid, more surprised than anything else, and I was certainly not thinking clearly because I just remained there on my knees for some considerable time, just shaking my head from side to side. Eventually it became clear to my fuddled mind that the noise had subsided somewhat, which meant that another attack had been beaten off. I crawled over to see if I could help any of my gun crew, but some were most obviously dead and as I went from one to another it became apparent that I was the only survivor. We had taken two direct hits within seconds of each other: probably both shells had been fired from the same gun.

With my gun out of action, there seemed little else that I could do except find the safest-looking hole in the vicinity and hide there until the battle was over. I crawled over to a spot nearby and found a shallow depression into which I pressed my body and then I set about trying to build a little wall of rocks around the edge. From this dubious refuge I had an excellent view of the gun positions and the sight that met my eyes appalled me. The ground was littered with the bodies of the dead and dying, and even as I watched, an airburst high-explosive shell from a German 88mm burst bang on target, just above number one gun. I saw the whole gun crew hurled to the ground by the force of the explosion and they all lay very still where they had fallen.

This meant that we had lost two guns within a matter of minutes. Half the firepower of the troop had gone, and even in my befuddled state of mind, I realised the implications of the situation. With only two guns left in action, the next German assault could be successful. This brought me back to reality with a vengeance, and so, with a somewhat heavy heart, I dragged myself out of my little hole and made my way over to the crewless gun. It was in a battered state: the tyres were both flat and the shield was in ribbons, but it was still workable.

The trouble was there were no gunners left. I looked around for help and gazed upon a scene of complete devastation: scores of vehicles were on fire to the rear, each sending up columns of black smoke, the ground was littered with bodies and to the front were the blazing hulks of tanks destroyed by our guns. Thank God I was not the only one to appreciate the situation: the old spirit prevailed. They came without bidding: drivers, cooks, signallers, specialists and orderlies all crawled forward to offer their help in manning the guns. These men had little or no experience of gunnery, but so long as there was one gunner present to show them what to do, it was possible to keep the guns in action.

By now it was afternoon and practically all the original gun crews had been killed, but by some miracle some of our guns were still capable of firing. Most of the gun shields were riddled and torn, many of the tyres were flat and ammunition was running short. The armour-piercing shells had been expended hours before. Still the dive-bombers came and went, and God knows how many trips they made that day. Still the massed guns of the 22nd Panzer Division continued to blast us and by now their heavy machine guns were close enough to sweep our positions with a withering fire.

As the lads came up to take their places on the guns, so were they killed, but there was always someone else to creep forwards to fill the gaps that were left. By now, many of these men were strangers and I well remember one young fellow who was not from our regiment at all – I think he was from the Royal Corps of Signals. He took a burst of machine-gun fire in the lower part of his body and leapt high in the air before crashing down over the trail of the gun. I went over to pull his body clear and as I did so he looked up at me with such frightened eyes that I felt the need to stay with him. I knelt and put my arms under his shoulders and tried to help him. I knew that he was dying but I told him not to worry, as his wounds were not severe. I promised that we would soon have him out of it and in a nice clean hospital and then he would be sent home. It was like being in some corner of hell and talking about heaven. The continuous explosions and the scream of ricocheting bullets punctuated my words. Then, after a while, whilst I was talking to him in this fashion, I noticed that the dust was settling on his eyes and I knew that he had just died there in my arms.

Nobody should have escaped alive from that bloody shambles. The guns themselves should have been destroyed within the first hour. I still do not know how they managed to survive the continual barrage of bombs and shells that was thrown at them, but survive they did. The colonel had by now been killed as he bravely roamed among the forefront of the battle in his lightly protected Honey tank. The battery commander, Major P.L. Birkin, remained near the gun line in a similar vehicle and during the late afternoon he drove up to my gun and shouted above the shattering noise, 'We're not finished yet, are we, Sergeant?'

'No, Sir', I replied and I received a forlorn wave from Jim Hardy, who was with him in the tank. They drove on, but before they had gone twenty yards the tank took a direct hit from an armour-piercing shell. It killed the driver, passed between the major's legs and sliced into Jim Hardy, cutting his body into two pieces.

It was at about this time that my gun came under fire from a German tank firing from a hull-down position over to our left rear, and I realised that we were gradually being surrounded. With great difficulty I managed to swing the gun round so that I could engage him, but he was difficult to hit because only the top of his turret was visible. This meant lobbing shells high and with a short range in an effort to drop them onto him, howitzer-fashion. Unknown to me he had positioned himself at the side of our regimental aid post, which meant that some of my shells landed amongst our own wounded, but I did not learn of this until later. It is impossible to describe the fury of the battle at this stage, the ear-splitting noise, the scream of shells, the deafening explosions, the smoke and dust and flames. The gun position was being blasted from all directions and chaos reigned.

The second in command now had control of the regiment and I think he must have lost his head because he gave the order for the guns to form a British square. Even the lowliest recruit could surely have seen that such a deployment in those circumstances was suicidal. It meant that the troop of guns further along the line from us had to try to hitch onto their gun-towers and move to new positions whilst surrounded by enemy tanks. They obeyed the order and, needless to say, they were shot to pieces. I saw my old pal, Jim Martin, who had once been Cliff Smedley's driver and had helped me fetch in the guns at Tobruk. His truck had been hit and set on fire, and as he tried to get clear he was hit. He fell from the vehicle, and landed under the petrol tank, but that was also hit with incendiary bullets. The blazing petrol poured over him and he was incinerated.

After this episode the second in command of the regiment loaded his truck with food and water and drove away from the battlefield. He was the only man to escape from the carnage. Everyone else was either killed or taken prisoner. We had known before the battle had started what the outcome was going to be, and from the beginning it had only been a matter of time. But time was the essential factor: the whole purpose of our fight had been to give the remainder of the army enough time to withdraw and to establish themselves in new defensive positions further back. Ammunition was now in very short supply. I noticed that there were some Italian tanks among the German Mark IIIs and Mark IVs and that the dive-bombers had ceased to attack in case their bombs fell amongst their own troops, but the small arms fire had increased in volume as the infantry edged ever nearer.

One by one the guns had fallen silent until at last ours was the only one left in action. There were only two of us left on my gun and the man with me was not a gunner but a complete stranger. Our rate of fire was very slow, but we were still managing to engage the tanks that were almost upon us. Then I heard the loud rattle of a machine gun that appeared to be almost in my ears and the man who was so bravely helping me was reduced to a bloody mass as he was hurled spinning into the gun shield. I turned to see a Mark IV tank only a few yards behind us with his machine gun still aimed and smoking. I tensed myself for the inevitable, but he held his fire. Whether he was distracted, or whether it was an act of compassion, I shall never know. I prefer to think it was the latter, but whatever the reason, he released the trigger and I lived to tell the tale.

It was over. The enemy tanks swept through the position and for the first time in thirteen hours the sound of gunfire ceased. All that could be heard was the rumble of tanks and the crack and crackle of fire and exploding ammunition from the scores of burning tanks and vehicles that littered the desert. I was dazed and disorientated, as yet not properly realising that we had been overrun and were therefore, prisoners of war.

I walked over to the tank where Jim Hardy's twisted body lay. His water bottle was still attached to his webbing equipment and I took my knife and cut it free because I was desperately thirsty. I drank the tepid water and then, as I looked down at my old friend's lifeless face, the tears ran down my face. All my friends had been killed. Then I made my way over to my own gun, where my gun crew lay as they had fallen. I could still make out the name painted on the shield in the regimental colours, but the little figure with the halo was upside down. 'The Saint' had fought its last battle and it would fight no more. Most of my kit had gone, blown up with the limber on which it had rested, but I did find my haversack containing the essentials, and I also rescued my greatcoat.

There was still no sign of the German infantry and so I just stood there beside my old gun and surveyed the sad scene. It was too early to reflect upon the miracle of my own survival, but I did know that the regiment in which I had so proudly served was gone for ever. It was six o'clock in the evening of 6 June 1942, and for the previous thirteen hours the regiment had held at bay the entire 22nd Panzer Division. The men who had been such loyal comrades, and with whom I had shared so much, had nearly all perished. They were all my brothers and they had fallen bravely, refusing to surrender in the face of overwhelming opposition; they had obeyed without question the order to fight to the last man and the last round of ammunition. The tears that rolled down my cheeks have never dried.

As I turned away, a German tank stopped beside me. Its commander, a sergeant, looked down and beckoned me to climb aboard. I did so and pulled myself up to stand beside the turret. We stood for a moment eye to eye, two men who had fought each other hard and long, and then we both raised our eyes to heaven and inclined our heads in mutual agreement as to the futility of it all. He picked up the microphone of his intercom and spoke into it, and the tank lurched forward. We drove away from the battlefield together, two enemies who felt no hatred for each other, only a shared sense of loss and bitterness.

## Chapter 12

# First Days as a Prisoner of War

Until this point it has been quite easy to recall the incidents that happened, but the next stages are much more difficult to bring to mind. The weeks that were to follow my capture held nothing but suffering. It was a constant battle not only against exposure, hunger, thirst and disease, but also, despite my increasing weakness, to continue the struggle to maintain pride and dignity when surrounded by men who had lost both these virtues. Those weeks held the most terrible experiences of my whole life, and either my mind was dulled by the acute misery of it all, or it is reluctant to let the memory of it resurface. It is most probably the latter because a month has elapsed since I completed the section dealing with the Battle of Knightsbridge, and since that time I have made several attempts to continue writing, but the mind plays strange tricks and each time I have found some excuse for delay. It is only with extreme reluctance that I am now making the effort to record the events of those terrible days that were spent travelling across Libya to the port of Tripoli.

I think it was a period of eight weeks, but I am not exactly sure. I will do my best to give a true record of that journey, but places, periods of time and the sequence of events are blurred and confused in my mind, and only certain incidents stand out starkly in my memory. I do not have the skill to reveal the horror of it all, nor can I properly plumb the depths of misery endured by the hapless men who lived, and sometimes died, between Tobruk and Tripoli. If I have made it appear dreadful beyond belief, then I have only half succeeded in my task; double my effort and you will still be far short of any understanding of the misery of those days.

\* \* \*

The fact of being a prisoner of war requires a complete readjustment of thought and attitude, and the acceptance that whilst previously one's life may have been held cheaply by the army, it now had no value at all. To the enemy, a prisoner of war is just an expendable nuisance. My own period of readjustment was very abrupt, spurred on by an incident that occurred within a few moments of leaping from the German tank that had brought me several hundred yards from the gun position.

Here the Germans were collecting together all the prisoners taken in the vicinity. Amongst them was an officer, still carrying his field glasses on a leather strap over his shoulders. A German officer walked up to him and demanded that he should hand over the glasses. The officer refused, whereupon, without further ado, the German drew his revolver and shot him point-blank in the chest. The stricken man staggered back and fell to the ground, and as he lay there kicking out his life, the German coolly stooped down, took the glasses and swaggered away without so much as a backward glance.

I had just witnessed at close hand the callous disregard for human life that was displayed by a certain class of Germans during the period when they were victorious and confident of their invincibility. It was my first real encounter with the overweening arrogance and brutality of the Nazi regime under whose domination so many people were suffering and which had made the war such a necessity. This arrogance was strangely lacking after their ultimate defeat, when it was difficult to find a single Nazi, but that was to come much later. In my present situation it was a sobering foretaste of what was to lie ahead.

Amongst the prisoners being herded together I looked for some time for a friendly face that I could recognise. Most of the men seemed to be stragglers from other regiments who had been lying low during the battle, or who had been picked up in the rear of our lines. At last I caught sight of Stanley Keeton, the signal sergeant who had won the Military Medal in Tobruk and had become a close friend of mine. We were both thankful to be alive and glad that we were able to face this new situation together. (Stan Keeton was never known as anything but 'Buster', a nickname derived from the 1920s film star Buster Keaton. I always refer to him as 'Buster', because I never called him anything else.)

Eventually there must have been several hundred prisoners at this collecting point and we were all pushed and driven to stand in a tight circle that measured about twenty-five to thirty yards in diameter. Spaced around this group of prisoners, and some distance away, stood about twenty German infantrymen, each armed with a light machine gun. It was at this moment that a British fighter plane roared into view.

Ironically, it was the first British plane we had seen that day. It was a Hurricane and we could clearly see that it was one of those that had been adapted to carry a bomb. When the pilot spotted us he zoomed around and came down very low to investigate, and the bomb was plainly visible below the fuselage. We were in no doubt as to his intentions and we all waved madly to warn him away, but the pilot of that plane must have been of scant intelligence. It should have been obvious to him that such a press of waving men just behind the front line could be nothing other than prisoners, particularly as they were surrounded by guards and were making no attempt to scatter. But the pilot disregarded all the evidence as he climbed to prepare for his attack. Some of the prisoners, realising the danger, attempted to run to safety and were promptly shot down by the guards. As they fell, the plane came swooping down with all eight machine guns blazing to cut a swathe through the press of bodies, and then released its bomb with such accuracy that it exploded right in the middle of us. The centre of the explosion was but a few yards away from where Buster and I were standing. Thank God, we were on the outer edge of the circle and the force of the blast was absorbed by all the bodies pressed so closely together, so that we were among the fortunate few to escape injury.

It was a shambles. Many men had been blown to pieces, others lay in bloody piles, some dead, others horribly wounded, and the screams and groans were pitiful to hear. There was little we could do to help them and the Germans showed very little concern – after all, a British pilot had done the damage. The badly wounded men had no chance of survival; no doctors arrived, no ambulances, no stretchers – they just lay there and many of them bled to death before nightfall. It was a fitting end to a horrific day.

Night comes rapidly in the desert; there is no twilight. As the sun cast its last rays across the darkening scene, we huddled under our blankets and my greatcoat and tried to find escape in sleep from all the horror, the cold night air, our thoughts and the groans of the dying men who lay around us. We kept falling asleep from sheer exhaustion only to wake again to the cries of the wounded. Staggering about in the darkness, we tried to give comfort to those poor wretches who were moaning in agony. It was a hideous situation because we were so helpless and reeling with fatigue yet unable to sleep.

The shattered men were begging for water, but we were thirsty ourselves and we did not have a drop of water between us. By the morning most of the wounded men had died, speeded to their end by the relentless cold and the complete lack of care. The battlefield presented an eerie sight as the first rays of light filtered across the burnt-out tanks and lorries. There, in the near distance, we could see our guns as the German tank crews must have seen them on the previous day. Then they had been spitting fire, but now they were still and silent and twisted at crazy angles. Gradually the sun made its reappearance and we dreaded the heat that was to come because we were thirsty and we had no water.

Sometimes we would see a convoy of trucks passing in the distance and during the morning several lorries arrived at our position. They had been sent to collect the wounded men who still lived. Whilst they were being loaded, amid much groaning and shouting, Buster and I walked over to a smaller lorry where the driver was tinkering with the engine. The guards had been less belligerent since the bombing incident the previous evening and they made no move to stop us as we made our way across. I can remember that the truck was an Opal Blitz.

We had little German and he no English, but we went through the motions of asking for food and water and he made negative gestures indicating that he only had enough for himself. As we turned away he had a change of heart and started to pull out the seat cushions of his lorry. Underneath he found a loaf of bread that must have been lying there for weeks. It was as hard as rock and green with mildew, but we accepted it with gratitude. Then he fetched a jerrycan that contained water for the radiator. This can had most obviously held petrol at one time because the water was heavily tainted, but again we eagerly took advantage of his generosity and filled our water bottles most carefully. I believe that we both owed our eventual survival to the kindness of this unknown German soldier. How ironic that in the short time since our capture, our lives had nearly been taken by an Englishman and saved by a German.

As the lorries drove slowly away, Buster and I began to take stock of our position. We had one old loaf, a bottle of petrol-tainted water each, a blanket each, my greatcoat, a pair of socks each, shaving soap, razor and razor blades each, a few personal things like photographs, and also the clothes we were wearing: shorts, a shirt, desert boots and a pair of socks. Buster had a gold wristwatch that he was keeping carefully hidden and in my haversack was something much more precious: a tin of sardines. These things comprised the sum total of our worldly possessions.

Later in the day we were informed that there was no water and no transport available and that our only hope of survival was to walk towards Gazala. That was forty miles away! For a trained soldier a march of forty miles is no great hardship, but this was a trudge across the desert in the blazing heat of June. Furthermore we had not eaten for two days, but more importantly we had only the water we carried in our bottles and this varied from man to man. Buster and I had half a bottle each, and there was the ever-present temptation to drink this in one glorious draught.

We set off in a column. I do not remember and probably never knew how many men set off on that dreadful march. It was probably seventy or a hundred men plus the German guards who travelled on two small lorries, one at the front and the other at the rear of the column. The lorry at the front moved on about a quarter of a mile at a time and we just walked endlessly towards it, and the lorry at the rear followed the same pattern. There was no hope or thought of escape as we were surrounded by empty desert, and the only thing that filled our minds was 'water'.

My recollections of that march are very indistinct, but I do remember on the first day being passed by a number of German vehicles, one of them being an open staff car with a man standing behind the windscreen. The word was passed down that it was General Rommel; it may have been, I shall never know. From time to time we rested, just lying face down in the sand under the pitiless sun, but the longer we rested, the less chance there was of reaching some place where there was water. Even after dark we staggered on for what seemed to be hours before we each rolled ourselves in a blanket to sleep. Before dawn broke we were on the way again; we needed no urging as we were desperate to cover as much ground as possible before the sun regained its power.

Each man had only what he carried at that time. Buster and I had been fortunate to be able to fill our bottles with the petrol-flavoured water given to us by the German driver, but some of the men had started the march with their water bottles almost empty and their water had run out the previous day. There was no question of sharing; it was every man for himself. We drank the last of our water during the morning of the second day and after that life became a torment of thirst and heat and dust and absolute weariness as we dragged our feet, a step at a time, through the burning sand.

It was at some time during that second day that the first man collapsed and we trudged past him as he lay on the sand. Some minutes later we heard the crack of a pistol shot and realised that the guards in the rear truck had despatched him. This was not an act of cruelty, rather the reverse – better to go quickly than to be left to die of thirst – but the knowledge of it gave me fresh resolve to keep my legs moving. By late afternoon my lips were cracked and my tongue was dry and swollen. Conversation had ceased earlier in the day and the pace had become very slow. I watched my boots as they plodded forward, one at a time, one at a time, one at a time, for hours and hours and hours and hours. As the day progressed more men fell until it became a steady stream and each time I waited to hear the crack of the pistol shot that gave me the will to carry on.

I cannot remember anything at all about the second night, but during the morning of the third day another lorry joined us and then drove on ahead. When we reached the point where it had stopped, I could see several German officers and amongst them a British officer wearing the insignia of a brigadier. They had a jerrycan of water and the brigadier was carrying a revolver, which seemed rather strange until he shouted down the line of half-crazed men that there was only a small amount of water for each man and that he would personally shoot any man who broke ranks. We started to file past and as we did so each man was allowed to drink his share from a small metal can. It amounted to no more than a mouthful as far as I can remember, but no doubt it provided vital moisture for dry and swollen tongues.

My own memory of that episode is the agony of awaiting my turn and the screaming desire I had to push everybody aside and to drink my fill from the jerrycan. This must have been true of every other man in the column. It was only the drawn revolver, and the sure knowledge that it would be used if we made the smallest hostile move, that gave us all the will to move on.

After that I have no clear memory of anything but heat and dust and sand and the weary plodding of aching feet and thirst – thirst that gave me the strength to go on, sometimes stumbling, towards some unknown place where precious, life-giving water could be found. I cannot remember the end of that march. I have searched my memory hard and long, but there is no trace at all. I have no recollection of reaching a water point, or of how the water was issued, or how much I drank – nothing at all: it has all gone. Neither have I any recollection of how many men survived or how many perished in the desert during that dreadful march for water. I can only assume that I must have become delirious during the final stages.

The next thing I can remember is a rough and ready prisoner of war cage somewhere between Gazala and Derna. It consisted of nothing more than an area of desert in the shape of a rectangle enclosed by barbed wire. By the time we arrived there it had obviously been in use for some considerable time, or, at least, a good many prisoners had been there before us. This was evident by the state of the ground, which was covered in human excrement. There was no place in that vile patch which was not soiled, no place to stand and certainly no clean spot to lie. Outside the barbed wire was a water bowser, but for us it might as well have been two hundred miles away. The prisoners were all crowding together at that spot and calling to an Italian soldier who was standing beside the bowser. They were begging for water and I was appalled to see them demeaning themselves in this way.

At last, the Italian filled a bucket with the water and walked towards the barbed wire and the thirst-crazed, pleading men. When he was within a few yards of them, he slowly tilted the bucket and let the water pour into the sand. He laughed heartily at the groans of dismay his action had caused and then he repeated the pantomime. As he approached the wire with a third bucket of water he suddenly leapt into the air, propelled by the boot of a German officer who had walked up behind him and delivered a mighty kick into the seat of his pants. After this, the officer shouted commands that brought many Italian soldiers running to the scene. The bucket-carrier was marched away and others made a start on bringing water into the compound.

Six days had now passed since our last proper meal; we had received no food on the final day of the battle and the only food we had tasted since then had been the stale bread and the tin of sardines we had shared on the day following our capture. We were ravenous! We were also dirty and unshaven and very, very tired, and as the sun began to sink we looked around for a clean place to lie. It was impossible to find a clean square yard of ground and even as we watched, men were squatting to empty their bowels wherever they happened to be. It was unbelievable: the stink, the filth and the way so many men had become so demoralised in so short a time. We had no alternative but to spread our blankets in this stinking midden and to sleep amidst its squalor.

The following day we were taken to Derna by lorry, and it was here that we received our first issue of food: it consisted of a tiny tin of meat and a piece of bread the size of a finger roll. To ravenously hungry men it was little more than an appetiser, and after we had eaten it we felt hungrier than before. It was the start of a continuing hunger that was never to be satisfied during the whole of the time that I remained in captivity. There was a limited supply of water in this camp, sufficient, if one was very careful, to produce enough lather for a shave. It was a wonderful feeling to be clean once again, but I am sad to say that the large majority of prisoners did not take the trouble; they just sat huddled in little groups hardly bothering even to waft away the flies that beset them.

There were millions of flies, which was not surprising considering the heat and the complete lack of sanitation that prevailed. This camp was an improvement on the previous noxious compound, but even here there were no latrines, just holes in the ground that had filled to overflowing. Although we were now near a fairly large town, which was also a supply base, there was no provision to house or feed prisoners of war. During the recent German advance thousands of prisoners had been taken and now the Italian Army was overwhelmed with the immensity of the task of moving them all to Italy. As we had been taken prisoner in Libya, which was an Italian colony, the Germans handed us over to the Italians and so we came under their jurisdiction. There was a complete lack of organisation, insufficient food and water, no sanitation of any kind and no transport available to move all these men quickly and efficiently into reasonable accommodation.

The heat and the dirt and the millions of flies quickly began to have an effect upon the prisoners, who were already weak from lack of food and water. The first cases of dysentery were reported in this camp but there was no medication available. Whilst we were at the Derna camp I received treatment for the wounds I had suffered during the battle. They were not serious, but in the course of being blown up, and during the bombing and the shelling, I had collected several bits of metal that had embedded themselves in various parts of my body. Although only superficial wounds, they were now beginning to turn septic and I was relieved to join a queue of men in similar condition who were waiting for treatment from an Italian doctor.

He was sitting out in the open at a trestle table and was assisted by two orderlies. At last my time came and I stepped forward for treatment. It was the most rudimentary surgery imaginable. The doctor just scraped off the scabs that had formed, delved in with forceps, extracted the bits and pieces, dabbed the wounds with antiseptic and that was that. No bandages, no dressings, not even a bowl of water to wash away the dirt and sweat.

I rejoined Buster on the patch of ground we had commandeered, and which we were guarding jealously after our experience in the previous compound. Fortunately the injuries I had sustained before the battle were in the process of healing. I had lost a fingernail on the hand that had been poisoned and it was very tender, and my leg was also very sore, but they had both formed a protective layer of skin that kept out further infection. I just had to hope that the new wounds would begin to heal now that the bits of metal had been removed.

It was not a very happy situation to be in, but everything is relative. At least I was still alive. It was a time for positive thinking: to indulge in self-sympathy in such a place was a waste of vital energies. Every thought had to be aimed towards survival. A complaining body had to be disciplined by a mind that refused to accept its complaints. I decided in that camp that no matter how long I remained a prisoner, I would never beg, nor plead, nor demean myself in any way, and that I would maintain my dignity no matter how appalling the conditions became. I resolved to keep as clean as possible, to exercise whenever I could and one day, if it became humanly possible, to escape.

## Chapter 13

# A Nightmare Journey

The disparity between commissioned and non-commissioned ranks in the British Army had originally aroused in me some feelings of resentment during the early part of the Second World War. This, I believe, was because in many cases the officers had attained their rank not through ability, military or otherwise, but solely because of their social connections. This wide gulf became far less prevalent during battle conditions and a much more friendly relationship prevailed in the latter years. However, if the gulf between the two classes was wide in the British Army, it was as nothing when compared with that prevailing in the Italian Army. Italian soldiers were treated as illiterate peasants by their officers, who themselves enjoyed every privilege imaginable.

With such a view prevailing amongst our captors, it was not surprising that our own officers disappeared from view within hours of their capture. Not for them the long trudge through burning sand in search of water. They had no experiences of filthy, insanitary conditions; they suffered little from thirst and hunger; and they received priority treatment in the matter of movement and transport to Italy. For the other ranks it was a very different matter: as prisoners of war they were treated as if they were low-grade animals – and to be a low-grade animal in the hands of a people who are not noted for their kindness to even high-grade animals was a sorry experience.

From Derna to the port of Tripoli is a road journey of approximately a thousand miles, and this is what lay before us. It was to be carried out in stages over a period of several weeks, and many men were to lose their lives in the lorries and in the camps along the way. We knew that we were about to move from the camp at Derna when a convoy of lorries, each towing a large trailer, was seen in the vicinity of the camp. We were herded like cattle and pushed at bayonet point up ramps into these lorries and packed so tightly together that it was difficult to breathe. Sitting down was out of the question and to turn around was quite impossible: we were jammed together more tightly than sardines in a tin. There was no shade from the sun and we carried neither water nor food.

It took what seemed an age to load all the lorries and trailers, and then we continued to stand there, baking in the blinding heat, whilst overdressed and self-important little officers strutted up and down making last-minute arrangements for the journey. At last, the first truck moved off and one by one the others followed. It was the start of a nightmare journey that was to make a mockery of civilisation, and bring nothing but shame on the Italian authorities who were responsible for such inhuman treatment of the helpless men who had fallen into their hands.

During our incarceration in the camp at Derna, there had been a rapid deterioration in both the health and the morale of the prisoners. Food was virtually non-existent, comprising nothing more than a small amount of rice each day – just rice and water, with no additions of any kind, and there was no other food at all. Water was also in short supply, quite unnecessarily, and the sanitary conditions went from bad to worse. Gradually the dreaded dysentery began to take hold and the number of cases grew from day to day. Before we left this camp the first man had died, and some of the men herded aboard the lorries were in acute distress and should have been hospitalised. They were almost too weak to stagger up the ramps and were in no condition to stand all day in the hot sunshine. As a result of such exposure some of them died during the day as we moved along the endless road, but as we were so tightly packed together, their bodies remained upright until the end of the day's journey.

It is impossible to properly describe the misery of those tightly packed lorries as day by day we made our way through Cyrenaica and into Tripolitania. Sometimes we spent eight or nine hours standing, unable even to turn; we were thirsty and hungry and our bodies and clothes were in a filthy condition. We were given no opportunities to perform the normal bodily functions so that our condition at the end of each day is best imagined, especially as most of us were now suffering from dysentery or some milder form of stomach complaint. Sometimes we remained for several days in a variety of camps along the way. One such camp was at Benghazi; it was a misery of hunger and filth, but again there was no excuse for such conditions as the camp was situated on the outskirts of quite a large city, which contained all the amenities necessary for feeding and housing men in sanitary conditions.

At the end of another series of long, blazing-hot days we reached a place called Tarhuna, where we were housed in a small barracks which had been designed to cater for about two hundred men. It already contained over a thousand prisoners when we arrived, and it was extremely difficult to find a place to lie down on account of the overcrowding. At the end of each of the four or five barrack blocks were ablutions and toilet facilities, but the water had been turned off and it was impossible to wash. More seriously, the toilets had long since ceased to function. Even if they had been in good order, with an abundance of water to flush them, they would still have been inadequate because in all there were no more than fifteen toilets for over a thousand men. The result almost defies description: the floors were awash with raw sewage, the heat was suffocating, and demoralised men were lying about on the filthy floors and making no effort to improve their conditions. They were completely apathetic and I found it difficult to believe that these same men, only a few weeks before, had been proud, smart, disciplined soldiers of the British Army.

I realised then, for the first time in my life, that the veneer of civilisation is very thin and any society that is to survive must have strict laws and rules of conduct. A permissive society must inevitably lead to a lowering of vital standards. When starry-eyed sociologists prate on about the sanctity of human life and the rights of the individual, they are talking dangerous nonsense. The average man is not capable of overcoming the animal instincts that are so lightly covered; he needs to be strictly conditioned by a framework of laws and these laws must be rigidly upheld. There is nothing new in such ideas: wise men discovered these facts thousands of years ago. The great civilisations of the past only continued to thrive whilst such rigid rules were strictly enforced. When discipline failed and anarchy prevailed, men were left to their own inadequate resources and civilisation collapsed. We should be warned!

I decided that something had to be done to clear up the cesspool in which we had to exist. My first move was to find the interpreter, who turned out to be an Italian soldier who had spent some time in the USA and spoke English with a strong American accent. I told him a frightening story about disease and epidemics, and explained to him that he and his colleagues would be just as much at risk as the prisoners if there were an epidemic as a result of the conditions within the camp. I remember saying that typhus and dysentery had no respect for barbed wire and could not recognise uniforms. I asked him to speak to the camp commandant and to explain to him that disease did not defer to rank either – *everyone* would be at risk. My request was for an immediate supply of water to the ablution blocks and the provision of shovels so that we could dig our own latrines.

I could see that I had really put the wind up him and he hurried away into the Italian lines. Within a couple of hours my mission began to bear fruit. A handcart containing shovels was trundled into the compound, and the first trickles of water began to emerge from the taps in the foul-smelling ablution areas. I called for volunteers to make a start with the digging, but not one single man came forwards. In despair, I walked around, trying to persuade someone to help me, but it was of no use; I merely received blank stares or filthy remarks. Then I came across a sergeant from the Scot's Guards, who offered to help me. We discussed the situation together and decided that we should adopt a different strategy: we would ignore the fact that we were prisoners and instead of asking, we would command.

Together we walked into the barrack block and in parade ground voices hustled a group of men off their backs: 'You, you and you, fall in outside for digging fatigues and bloody well look sharp about it. –CAN YOU HEAR ME, MAN? Get off your lazy arse and let's have you moving.'

It worked. They responded to their military training and within a short time a start was made in digging the latrines and clearing the filth that had accumulated. The men were very weak and could only work for a short time, but we made sure that there were other men there to replace them when they tired. It was a disagreeable task, like the fifth labour of Hercules, but we had no rivers Alpheus and Peneus to assist us in the cleaning of our Augean Stables – only an inadequate supply of water and a group of debilitated and unwilling workers. In spite of this, we gradually cleared the repulsive, stinking midden and restored some degree of salubrity in this indescribable dunghill that posed as a prisoner of war camp.

After several days of supervising this noxious task in the blazing-hot sunshine, my stomach rebelled. Although I was weak from hunger, I could no longer face the rice and water that was our only food. The ration was very small, but I could not bring myself to swallow even a spoonful. This meant only one thing in those conditions: certain death. Buster did everything in his power to persuade me to eat my portion of rice, but my stomach was soured and I just pushed the bowl away.

What followed could not possibly be appreciated by anyone who has not had the misfortune to experience such a situation. Buster walked over to the barbed wire fence and attracted the attention of one of the sentries. By means of signs and gestures, he negotiated the exchange of his gold watch for a piece of bread smaller than my fist, and then, showing tremendous will-power, he somehow managed to carry it back intact and place it in my hands. It was one of the greatest acts of comradeship that I was ever to witness in the whole of my life. He had sacrificed his gold watch, but that was nothing to the self-denial he had displayed in carrying that bread to me without eating it himself. He was starving, but he resisted what must have been an unimaginable temptation in order that I could start eating again. Stanley Harry Keeton MM was indeed a very gallant gentleman.

I ate the bread, which settled my stomach and then I was able to take the rice so that the crisis was over. Dear old Buster – in the middle of all the dirt and misery his kindness and selflessness shone like a beacon of hope, and I lay down to sleep that night very conscious of the fact that he had saved my life. Just before dropping off I called, 'Buster?'

'Yes?'

'What time is it?'

His reply was unprintable ... and I think we were still laughing when we fell asleep.

Eventually the time came for us to continue our nightmare journey through Libya – long, hot, dusty days packed into the backs of lorries and trailers with the ever-present stink of ordure and diesel fumes. On one of these days my hat was carried away by the wind, and I remember watching it gradually disappear into the distance. I was sad about its loss because I had worn that old cap through a good many battles. I was also concerned because its loss meant that I had no protection against the pitiless sun. Having mounted the truck early in the morning, we were never allowed to dismount again until we reached our destination at the end of the day. It was a weary business standing tightly packed for hours and hours in the blazing heat, hungry and thirsty and often buckling at the knees, but without the room to fall.

Some days one would be unfortunate enough to be somewhere along the edge or the back of the vehicle and when this was the case there was the added discomfort of being pressed against the hard, chafing metal. The horror of spending long hours in such close contact with dirty, sweaty, unshaven men who had no option but to perform their bodily functions as the day progressed is hard to describe. We just had to tolerate each other. For some, these were to be their last hours; they just died as we went along, for dysentery was taking its daily toll.

We stayed for several days near an old Roman town. I believe it had been known originally as Lepcis Magna, but it now rejoiced in the name of Homs. Here again we saw nothing of the town, Roman or otherwise, but were driven into the courtyard of what appeared to be either large warehouses or huge garages. There were several of these structures, rectangular in shape and about fifty feet high, each one covering a floor space of something like three hundred square metres. They were completely empty and the floors were of concrete. We were herded inside and made to lie on the floor and when there was no space left, the doors were closed and locked.

Inside it was almost dark, as the only light filtered in through three small windows set high in the walls about forty feet above the ground. Soon after our arrival the sun set and we were plunged into stygian darkness. There was nothing more to do than lie down on the hard, concrete floor and try to sleep. At some time during the night there must have been a sudden, strong wind, because one of the windows was blown open with some force and the frame swung down and hit the wall. The glass was shattered and a small piece came spiralling down to hit me on the left of my temple. It was not particularly painful, but when I lifted my hand I could feel blood spurting from the small wound. I called to Buster to tell him that I was bleeding, but he thought that I was dreaming and he just ignored me. Then a voice from the darkness called: 'By God! He is bleeding; I can hear it splashing.'

There was suddenly a great deal of activity, with people milling around in the darkness as the blood continued to pour from the severed artery in my head.

There was a call for matches – a very precious commodity – but they began to arrive. Then, in the intermittent light of many matches, the men who had been lying nearby struggled to stop the bleeding, but without any success. I began to despair as the blood poured over my face and I heard someone call out: 'What are we going to do? He's bleeding to death.'

It began to look hopeless until some unknown man in the semi-darkness stripped off his singlet, rolled it into a sausage shape and pressed it against the wound. Then two men knelt and held it down with all their strength. It seemed an age before I heard someone say that it was working. After a long time they were able to gently remove the sodden vest and the bleeding had stopped, but by this time I was feeling very weak and dizzy. This loss of blood on top of all the other privations had brought me very close to the end of my resilience and everything seemed to be far away and unreal. Buster and the men around were convinced that I was dying and they made me as comfortable as possible on the concrete floor.

Buster and I had shared everything during this traumatic journey and our most precious possession at that time was our one remaining cigarette. There had been no tobacco issue since our capture and we had kept this one treasured cigarette, reluctant to smoke it and so leave ourselves without any tobacco at all. Now he said: 'Would you like to smoke our last cigarette, Mate?' He took out the cherished cigarette, placed it between my lips and held out a match to light what we both thought was to be my last smoke.

It was fortunate that we were destined to remain at Homs for several days and this gave me the opportunity to build up some strength before the next leg of the journey. I must have lost a considerable amount of blood because the concrete floor was stained for an area of over two square metres. In spite of this I was able to totter about weakly, but spent most of my time lying on the floor being plagued by thousands of flies that came to feast upon the blood-stained floor. As I lay there feeling sorry for myself, Buster cheered me up with a few sympathetic words: 'You old bastard,' he said. 'You smoked our last fag, and lived!'

Our final camp in Africa was called Trigh Tarhuna and it was situated near the port of Tripoli. It was a wired compound attached to an old fort that had all the trapping of a story from the past, with its whitewashed wall, turrets and courtyards. We were held outside its walls in a barbed-wire enclosure in the desert. There were rows of small bivouac tents made from Italian groundsheets fastened together to provide some shade from the heat of the sun. At the end of this enclosure, and under the walls of the fort itself, was a strip of concrete and I used this hard surface to try to get some exercise. It was still part of my routine to keep as clean as I was able, and to shave whenever it was possible to do so, and I also endeavoured to keep myself in some sort of shape – hence the walking.

Whilst I was striding up and down I must have caught the eye of an Italian officer. He beckoned and called me over to the gate of the compound, which was opened to let me through. I could not speak a word of Italian so we were unable to converse, but he signalled me to follow him and he led me into the fort where we met an Italian sergeant who was an interpreter. From this very unpleasant man I learned that I was to be placed in charge of the cookhouse.

This was indeed a lucky break. It gave me an interest, some responsibility, a measure of freedom and, best of all, access to a reasonable amount of food. My knowledge of cookhouse routine could not have been less, but it was a simple affair consisting of nothing more than some open, wood fires, over each of which stood a large container in the shape of a dustbin. The bins were filled with water, the remainder of the ration was added and then it was all brought to the boil, and that was the meal. The rations in this camp were superior to anything we had previously received, but the amount of food per man was still pitifully small. The skilly we made in that cookhouse contained rice, a few vegetable leaves and sometimes a minute quantity of meat. This, supplemented by a tiny piece of bread the size of an orange, comprised a whole day's ration of food.

The food for the Italian soldiers was prepared in the same place. Their staple diet was risotto – again the basic ingredient was rice, but in greater quantity, and with tomatoes, beans, other vegetables and a generous amount of meat. It also contained herbs and when it was served it was thick and very tasty. To us it was like ambrosia, and because of my exalted position as 'boss' of the cookhouse I was allowed to fill my mess tin with this nutritious food. It was a great temptation to keep it all for myself, but instead I used to carry it back into the compound at the end of the day, to share it with Buster. He saved his food too and we mixed the two together to make a welcome meal before settling down to sleep.

The sergeant interpreter was an abominable man. His name was Lezzi, and he had spent most of his life in the back streets of New York, hence his English had a broad, Bronx accent. His sadistic nature was illustrated by the fact that he had a small dog which he kept locked up in a small room behind the cookhouse. At intervals during the day he would visit the room with the sole purpose of thrashing this unfortunate little dog with the stick that he always carried. When it heard his footsteps approaching, the poor little creature screamed in terror. Lezzi also took pleasure in using his stick on the prisoners and everyone tried to keep well out of his way. One day he caught a man from the Northumberland Fusiliers carving a piece of wood with a bit of tin (knives were not allowed). He was carving the letter 'V' because his regiment was known as the 'Fifth of Foot' in the British Army. Lezzi, of course, knew nothing of this and assumed that he was carving a 'V' for Victory. This made him very angry. 'I'll give you "V" for Victory, you English bastard,' he screamed, and then, wielding his heavy stick, he set about the defenceless man. Being already weak, the poor fellow fell to the ground as the sadistic monster rained blow after blow along the whole length of his body. He had obviously lost control of himself and was foaming at the mouth by the time a group of prisoners managed to drag him away. He shambled out of the compound, but his victim did not move. He had been beaten to death.

It was the custom in the Italian Army for soldiers to be brought to attention before being issued with their evening meal. A non-commissioned officer would then give the Fascist salute and call out, 'Viva il Duce,' after which the food would be doled out. Sergeant Lezzi, in his twisted mind, thought it would be a good joke to make the British prisoners follow this procedure and he ordered me to go through the ritual as the NCO. I refused point-blank and told him he could go to hell and back, but under no circumstances would I give the hated Fascist salute and I would certainly never express any wish for the good of Mussolini's health.

Lezzi danced about in a furious rage and threatened to tip all the prisoners' food into the sand if I did not obey him, but I was resolute in my refusal. Nothing could have moved me. I was so angry that I believe I would have seen everybody starve rather than cower before that dancing upstart. At last, he screamed some orders and a group of soldiers came running over and manhandled me out of the cookhouse and through the big gates into the fort with Lezzi bringing up the rear and mouthing obscenities at the top of his voice. They bundled me down several flights of stone steps and along a dimly lit corridor under the fort. A huge wooden door with studded iron hinges was swung open and I was pitched inside. The door closed with a bang and I heard a key turn in the lock. I was in a dungeon. It was pitch dark, not a glimmer of light, and I sat there bewildered. After a short time I felt my way around the wall and called to see if anyone replied, but I was all alone.

It was a shattering experience – sudden darkness after the bright sunlight, silence and loneliness after the noise and bustle of the cookhouse – and the realisation that I was at the mercy of a half-crazed sadist did little to reassure me. I half-expected to be released after a short time when his anger had subsided, but the hours dragged on until at last I must have fallen asleep.

The time that followed has become a confused memory. Even immediately after my release from this stinking hole I found difficulty in relating the experience to Buster. Being kept in solitary confinement in pitch darkness causes one to lose all sense of time. There is neither day nor night, just complete silence, and no contact with any living thing; time just stretches out. At intervals the door would open, there was a glimpse of light as food and water were pushed in and the empty mess tin removed, but no conversation. Then came a careful feel for the mess tin and spoon, a grope for the piece of bread. The water was in the lid of the mess tin – take care not to spill any! A tasteless meal of something unseen but known to be the inevitable rice skilly. When necessary a careful crawl to the corner that had become the toilet, taking extreme care to keep as clean as possible. Stubble on the chin growing longer. Thinking, dozing, measuring the wall in hand spans. It was dry, thank God, and there was ventilation from somewhere – I could not touch the roof ... time just dragged on and on. I was convinced that I had been imprisoned there for six months, but I was to learn on my release that I had been confined in this cell for two weeks.

Lezzi had to let me out because all the prisoners in the camp were to be embarked for Italy. When I was brought back into the daylight I had to keep my eyes covered for a time, as they could not bear the glare of the bright sunshine. I was also a bit unsteady on my feet as I was led back into the compound. Here I was able to clean myself up a bit and it was a wonderful feeling to wash. Even a blunt razor blade did not take the pleasure out of that first shave. Buster was glad to have me back again. No explanation had been given for my sudden disappearance and he had begun to wonder if I had been killed.

We boarded a very old vessel in Tripoli harbour, walking up a long, wooden ramp to reach the deck, then down a series of ladders to the bottom of the hold. It was a dirty, rusty old ship and a thin skim of water covered the iron plates at the bottom so that there was no dry place to sit. It took a long time to load as more and more prisoners arrived from other camps scattered around Tripoli, and the hold became more and more congested until we were packed almost to suffocation. When everyone was finally aboard, they started to batten down the hatches and we felt a sense of dread as the sky was gradually obscured. The news circulated that the Royal Navy had already sunk several transports such as this one, unaware that they were packed with prisoners of war, and that there were never any survivors. (This turned out to be true. Several such ships were sunk with complete loss of life.)

The voyage across the Mediterranean was the most terrifying journey I have ever made. It was agonisingly slow, taking over a week to travel from Tripoli to Naples. We were all apprehensive and very jumpy, and every loud noise had us wide-eyed and scared because we knew that if the ship was sunk, we would all be drowned like rats in a trap; there could be no possible hope of escape. At one point in the crossing the Royal Air Force attacked us. I have no idea what kind of planes they were because we could see nothing but the battens high above us. We heard the roar of aircraft engines and the sound of machine-gun fire and we prayed that the aircraft were not equipped with torpedoes. The noise of screaming engines and chattering machine guns kept us all on tiptoe for what seemed an age and then it all went quiet. We assumed that the attack was over, as indeed it was, but the episode left us even more fearful than we had been before. Our new fear was that our position was now known and that it would be passed on to the Royal Navy.

Most of the voyage was spent in queuing. The queue took the form of a long spiral that eventually led to the foot of the series of ladders; it then continued up and up to a trapdoor leading onto the deck. From there it made its way to a series of latrines suspended on planks high above the water. Having used the latrines, one joined the queue again, this time to descend into the bottom of the hold. The whole process took about three hours, so, having returned, it was politic to join the queue again unless it happened to be the time for the issue of food and water. This necessitated joining another queue to pass through a barrier that was moved slowly along the hold to prevent any man from receiving two rations. Food and water were only issued once each day and the food ration was one biscuit and a tiny tin of meat.

I think that I aged ten years on that crossing and I still find myself imagining what it must have been like in the holds of those transports that were sunk. What a dreadful death it must have been. I was not alone in my uneasiness. I remember one man who spent almost the entire voyage tapping the side of the ship and asking anyone who would listen if they thought the plates would be strong enough to stop a torpedo. It was a journey full of foreboding, of hunger, of acute discomfort, with the ever-present stink of excrement as dysentery and other less serious stomach disorders were still rife amongst the prisoners.

There was little conversation as everyone was constantly listening for any sound that might herald an attack. Buster and I tried to remain calm, but we were more intent on listening than speaking, and even sleep was hard to find as we moved slowly across the Mediterranean towards Italy and the coast of Africa slipped away behind us. Somewhere on that journey we must have crossed the path of our previous voyage when in the troopship *Devonshire* we had made our way towards Haifa in Palestine. That had been more than three and a half years before, when the food had been excellent and plentiful and we had yet to learn the realities of war. Now we were tired and disillusioned, hungry, dirty and in the hands of the enemy, but Buster and I still had our sense of humour and a bond of friendship that helped us to survive the horrors of that ghastly journey across the Mediterranean.

The first intimation that we were approaching a harbour was the closing of the hatch above us. This meant that there were to be no more visits to the latrine to grab a breath of fresh air and to escape for a few moments from the death trap within the hold.

We saw nothing of the approach to Naples, nor of the docking of the ship, but at last, after some bumping and shouting, the engines stopped, and I had a feeling of profound relief, knowing that we had reached the port in safety. It had been the most dangerous journey I had ever made.

It was a sorry band of men who trooped ashore in Naples harbour, filthy, stinking, weak and absolutely crawling with body lice. We were taken to a compound where we were made to strip and place our ragged garments inside a stoving machine. Then we were taken into a building which was equipped with showers and what a blessed relief it was to wash away all the grime and sweat. There were no towels – we just dried in the sunshine. Then each man was issued with one large army biscuit and a small piece of cheese.

Dressed once more in our de-loused, but still filthy clothes, we were marched to a nearby railway siding, where there was a long train of cattle trucks into which we had to climb. As usual we were packed in so tightly that there was no room to move and there was hardly any light, apart from that which came from the ventilation grille. At last the train started to move, but after a very short time it became obvious that we had been shunted into a siding, and there we remained until eventually even the light from the grille began to fade, and I realised that it was getting dark.

It suddenly became obvious to me that we were to remain packed in this iron cell for the whole night. I knew from experience that they would never move prisoners about in the dark, and the thought of standing in this cramped position for all those hours prompted me into action. I slid my body down, threading myself between countless legs until I was in a prone position on the floor of the wagon. It turned out to be the worst move I could possibly have made, because everyone else in the cattle truck copied my example, with the result that I found myself lying on the steel floor with a mass of heavy bodies piled on top of me.

The air was full of shouts and groans and curses, as people at the bottom of the pile, like me, tried to fight their way up to the top. It was a melée of thrashing legs and flaying arms, and the pain was excruciating as the twisting bodies ground my hip bones and elbows into the rough metal floor, but more terrifying was the difficulty I found in breathing. The sheer weight of all the bodies above me was squeezing the air out of my lungs, and at times my mouth and nose were closed for a few seconds by the pressure of someone's body against my face, as I struggled to wrench my head clear. It was a nightmare that went on for hours and hours, and it must have been well after midnight before the last man was able to regain his feet. After this, we spent the remainder of the night standing. Before morning we had become well aware that the stoving machines had not done their job very efficiently: we were all still lousy and the lice were having a banquet at our expense.

Although we did not know it at the time, we had been brought to Capua, a town just outside Naples, where there was a transit camp for prisoners of war. At some time during the morning the doors of the trucks were opened and we tumbled out to stand by the track. What a ghastly sight! Yesterday's shower might never have been because we were all filthy again, our clothes were in rags, most of us were covered in bruises from the previous night's debacle, and some, including myself, had black eyes and cut lips. We were also very thin, hollow-eyed and very, very, very hungry. In this state we were made to march through the town to the prison camp, whilst all the locals lined the streets to watch us pass. It was, of course, good propaganda for the Italian cause:

'Look! These are the British soldiers.'

'What a poor lot they are!'

We were not really marching, just shuffling along. It was a very degrading experience, and one that I shall never forget.

It is a strange fact, however, that life constantly presents us with paradoxical situations that leave us puzzling about the rights and wrongs of things. Here, for me, the world was cruel; I was being starved of food, deprived of even the basic necessities of life, humiliated and surrounded by crowds of mocking enemies. I was burning with hate. Then, out of the throng of jeering onlookers, a young girl appeared. She paused for a second, and then ran out into the road to press a huge peach into my hand, before disappearing back into the crowd.

No fruit was ever sweeter than that peach, and no lesson ever better learned. That unknown girl taught me the folly of blind hatred, and the stupidity of labelling whole nations with mass characteristics. She made me realise that behind every howling mob that claims the headlines and ranges itself within the camera's focus there are girls with peaches – people who take a different and more enlightened view. She made me wonder how many other Italians, or Germans for that matter, were in fact kindly and sympathetic people. I have never forgotten that girl; she brightened not only that morning, but also hundreds of other mornings all through my life.

The prison camp at Capua was known as 'Concentration Camp No. 66'. It was a sizeable place with a few permanent buildings and rows and rows of tents that had been made by fastening together a number of Italian groundsheets. For purposes of counting (to make sure that no one had escaped) we were put into groups of about ninety men and each group was subdivided into three sections of thirty. I was put in charge of one of these sections and we were in Group 18. There were no clearly defined responsibilities, but in practice it meant keeping an eye on cleanliness, general discipline (as far as it reflected on the well-being of all the prisoners), and the fair distribution of the meagre food allowance.

I still have before me, as I write, the piece of card on which I wrote the nominal roll all those years ago. I have no idea why I saved it. It must have travelled with me for fifty years. That well-worn piece of card, which bears the names of all the men in the group, is a pitiful reminder of the privations we suffered in those times. The scratched-out names bear testimony to the number who died during our short stay of only a few weeks in this camp. From our small group of eighty-eight men, all of them in their early twenties, nine were to perish before we left Capua.

Doling out the food ration was my most important and most difficult job. I had to be scrupulous in this regard because we were all ravenously hungry, and there was precious little to share. Our meagre ration of food was issued twice daily. During the morning there was a tiny piece of cheese and a small bread roll, then, at about six o'clock in the evening, a bowl of thin soup. There was no possibility of obtaining more food: there was no little shop, no canteen, no money, no way out and, for some, no hope.

In such circumstances it was necessary not only to be fair, but also to be seen to be fair, and to achieve this I had to evolve a system that left no room for doubt. I made the thirty men in my section line up and then allocated them all a place in the line, my own place being at the back. When the bread and cheese was issued, I first divided it up into thirty rations and then the men filed past in line, each man choosing his own ration. Obviously the men at the front got the largest pieces and those at the end the smallest. In fact, there was really very little to choose between them.

The same system was used when sharing out the skilly in the evening. This I served from a tin can fastened to the end of a stick. I had two men stirring all the time; otherwise the first men would have got nothing but water. Then each man was given a tinful, carefully filled to the brim. At the end, if anything was left, the men who had been first in the queue came back for 'seconds'. Each day the man who had been first in the queue the previous day went to the back of the line. I had my own place in the queue and filled my own bowl, which was carried by Buster, at the appropriate time. In this way each man could see that he was getting his fair share. Such was our hunger that every crumb and every morsel of food was measured by famished eyes, and often I would have to dip again into the pot because I hadn't gone deep enough, or because some hungry wretch didn't think the tin can was quite full.

When the time came for us to leave Capua, we had to march back to the station to find the familiar line of cattle trucks, but by some quirk in the organisation a passenger coach had been placed amongst them. It was my good fortune to be among the group of men who were loaded into that coach and instead of standing in a cattle truck for the journey I had the pleasure of sitting in a carriage. Needless to say, it was no luxury coach – the seats were wooden benches – but it was a vast improvement on what had gone before. As we pulled away from Capua and out into the country, I was able to look out of the window and watch the passing scenery, and gain my first impressions of 'Bel'Italia'.

I was fascinated to see so many trees and cultivated fields, houses, villages and ordinary people wearing civilian clothes, girls in pretty dresses, women holding little children by the hand – all the everyday things that I had not witnessed for so long. There was no sand, no palm trees, no blazing, pitiless sun, no shellfire; it was almost like a return to normality, and for a little while it seemed that the only thing left to remind me that I was still a prisoner was the ever-present, gnawing hunger.

We reached Rome during the late afternoon and remained there, parked in a siding, for several hours. A group of girls collected to bandy remarks with the Italian soldiers guarding the train, and it was pleasant to watch all the fun even though we took no part in it. As we set off again it started to get dark and I climbed up onto the luggage rack and wrapped myself in my groundsheet. The rack was perilously narrow, but I was soon asleep and did not awake until the following morning. By this time we were in the mountains, and as we turned a long curve in the line I could see that there were two huge engines pulling our train.

Later that morning we arrived at a station that I now know to be Sforzacosta, and this was our destination. Amid the usual shouting and confusion that seemed to attend all Italian Army functions, we were gradually sorted out and formed up ready to march towards our next camp.

Sforzacosta was a small town and the camp was only a few hundred metres from the railway station. As we approached I could see the big solid gate of the camp with two sentry boxes high above on either side. I was in the leading file and so as we swung round to enter the camp, I had the dubious honour of being the first to pass through its portals. The fact that I was the first prisoner to enter that prison camp was probably portentous, because in the course of time I was certainly to be the first man to leave it on the way to freedom.

# Chapter 14

# The Winter at Camp 53

There is a certain thrill about entering new accommodation, whether it be a house, a hotel or even a caravan, taking a quick look around, opening doors, peeping into cupboards, wondering which rooms will catch the sun, or which will be the cosiest room on a winter's night. No such little pleasures attended our entry into a new prison camp, and it was obvious from the start that there were to be no rooms flooded with sunshine in this camp, and precious few cosy corners when the cold winds began to blow.

Campo Concentramento 53 was anything but cosy. It had, until recently, been a group of four or five large warehouses, high, brick-built, windowless structures with concrete floors. Now all the floor space in these soulless buildings was covered with three-tiered wooden bunks. These had been laid out in long rows so close together that the passages between them were too narrow for two men to pass without standing sideways. (Many years after the war I visited the concentration camp at Dachau, near Munich, part of which had been converted into a museum that contained bunks of an identical pattern to those we used at Camp 53.)

After a documentation check and a strip-search to make sure we were carrying nothing that could be used as a weapon, I was allocated a bed space in a section of a warehouse that had been selected for sergeants and warrant officers. Mine was a middle bunk halfway down the right-hand alleyway. I was dismayed to find that there were no mattresses of any kind, just two old army blankets to each bunk. The bed itself was nothing more than a series of wooden slats about two inches wide with a piece of solid board tilted to form a pillow.

I find that many people imagine a prisoner of war camp to be something along the lines of a normal army camp, with rows of huts equipped with beds, and a slow combustion stove to provide heat during the winter months. This may have been the case in England but nothing could have been further from the truth as far as we were concerned. The section of the warehouse in which we were held was about seventy feet long and thirty-five feet wide, and in this space three hundred men both lived and slept. The use of three-tiered bunks placed in double lines meant that six men could be accommodated on little more than four square yards of floor space, equating to less than one square yard per man. There was absolutely no privacy, and even during the night hours there was no possibility of finding some solitude in darkness as the lights were kept burning for twenty-four hours each day. This overcrowding, the inability to find a secluded corner and the constant noise all combined to make us irritable and quick-tempered, and as the time wore on quarrels, and sometimes fights, became more and more frequent.

At least the sanitation was generally adequate, and it was possible to keep clean if one made the effort, but it was no easy thing, and to get a wash and shave, or to launder a few articles of clothing, could sometimes take a whole day or even longer. The washing facilities were somewhat basic. There was a long pipe about two inches in diameter into which small holes (about the thickness of a matchstick) had been drilled and from these holes jets of water spouted. The water was only turned on for short intervals during the day, and there was no set time for this to happen. In consequence, this usually meant sitting in a queue waiting for the water to appear. It was quite normal to sit in this very slow-moving queue for hours, and then, just as your turn was approaching, there would be a roll call. After this had finished it could mean starting again at the back of another newly formed queue. I once spent four whole days in this fashion, just to get a wash and shave.

Within the camp there was some freedom of movement, and this included the use of a large area where we had to muster for roll call, sometimes several times each day. We called this area 'The Field' but it was a misnomer if such a name should conjure up visions of a grassy meadow. In dry weather it was a dust bowl and if it rained it became a sea of mud, but at least it gave us somewhere to walk about and in fine weather a place to lie in the sun.

Surrounding the field was a high fence of tangled barbed wire that, at its base, was six feet thick. Some yards to the front of this there was a trip wire about eight inches above the ground. We were informed that the sentries had been ordered to shoot any man who put so much as one foot over this wire. The stretch of ground between the trip wire and the fence was undisturbed and therefore covered in green grass, but this was rarely seen because the prohibited area made a good, clean, drying place and was usually covered by articles of clothing that had just been washed. During the time that I was in this camp a couple of prisoners were shot because in reaching over for their clothes they either forgot or stumbled, and placed a foot over the wire.

The main topic of conversation was food. We dreamed of the halcyon days when food had been plentiful, and men told the most outrageous stories of meals they claimed to have consumed in the past. I recently found amongst my papers a copy of the official food ration for Italian prisoners of war, which I had scribbled down in those far-off days. I have no recollection of my original source of information, but when I weighed out these items the quantities were exactly as I remember them. The list reads as follows:

| | |
|---|---|
| Bread | 30 grams |
| Cheese | 48 grams |
| Meat | 11 grams |
| Macaroni or Rice | 66 grams |
| Olive Oil | 15 grams |
| Coffee (substitute) | 11 grams |
| Sugar | 15 grams |

It was little enough to satisfy the hunger of young men; in fact it was barely enough to keep us alive.

The substitute coffee was issued each morning around ten o'clock. It was a bitter, black liquid and we were told that it was made from acorns. I have no means of knowing if that was the truth but one thing is certain: it had nothing to do with coffee beans. I never saw or tasted any sugar: if that was part of the ration it must have been diverted onto the black market long before it reached the camp. The bread and cheese were handed out at midday and the macaroni or rice, together with the minuscule ration of meat, was cooked in huge cauldrons in a communal outdoor kitchen and it was served as a thin soup during the early evening. Sometimes this soup would contain fragments of cabbage stalks, traces of tomato, onion or scraps of swede. I never saw or tasted any olive oil. There was no way of supplementing this ration, and it had to suffice for twenty-four hours.

In Germany I believe it was the natural thing for prisoners to be sent out in working parties to labour on the land or in factories or wherever they were needed. This was not normally the case in Italy. On the diet that I have just outlined, it would have been impossible for any man to do any work at all. It was just sufficient to sustain life, and whenever there was a long interval between the distribution of Red Cross food parcels, we became so weak that we could walk only a few paces without falling to the ground in a temporary blackout. How we longed to be able to walk down to a NAAFI canteen for a plate of eggs and chips to be washed down with a mug of hot, sweet tea, but there was no canteen and no possible way of supplementing our meagre diet.

Without any doubt, the brightest star in our dark sky was the arrival of a batch of Red Cross food parcels. They contained vitaminised food and they saved the lives of thousands of prisoners, my own included. English parcels came from various centres and each parcel bore the name of the town where it was packed. We were grateful beyond measure to those good souls who were responsible for the collection, packaging and despatch of those parcels, particularly considering the fact that food was rationed in England at this time. The best parcels of all came from Canada. The Canadian parcels were bigger and contained things like butter, powdered milk, jam, meat and even chocolate. Our bodies were starved of sugar and because of this deficiency in our diet our fingers and toes would often become swollen and painful. When parcels were issued the sweet things were always the first to be consumed and it was surprising how quickly our bodies responded. Within hours all the swellings disappeared.

As time wore on and autumn gave way to the approaching winter, it became more and more difficult to keep warm and survive on our sparse allowance of food.

Previously I had always imagined that the climate of Italy was a continuation of cloudless blue skies and warm sunshine. In common with many other Englishmen at that time, who held similar ideas, I was in for a big shock. We were to learn that the sunshine disappears behind thick, grey clouds, and there is heavy and continuous rain. The warmth is replaced by bitter winds, and frost and snow are frequent visitors in central and northern Italy.

In our draughty prison, with its concrete floors and high asbestos roof, we became increasingly aware of the approaching winter, and the steadily falling temperature made the differences in the personal kit carried by each man more apparent. There was a tremendous variety in personal possessions amongst the prisoners. Not all prisoners of war are taken in battle; large numbers of men are taken as a result of being rounded up in the rear areas after the front has broken. Men such as these had been employed in dumps or workshops or in some other work along the lines of communication. Being captured in this way meant that they had both the time and the opportunity to pack their kitbags, and consequently they were well equipped. (The South Africans who surrendered in Tobruk were in this category.) Such men were now in a position to delve in their kit bags to find extra clothing to protect themselves against the cold. Once again it turned out that the most unfortunate man was the poor old front-line soldier; all he had was the uniform he had been wearing at the time of his capture.

All the men in our little group had been captured in the heat of battle and none of us had anything but the clothes we stood up in. As we had been taken in the desert during the summer, these clothes were nothing more than shirts, shorts, boots and stockings. They had been in constant use since that time, and had never been washed. There was no soap available for washing clothes. Our socks had disappeared altogether, and our shirts and shorts were hanging in ribbons.

In this near-naked condition we were in poor shape to combat the cold and once again the grim reaper came to call. The death toll started to rise again, but this time the dreaded duo of pneumonia and nephritis replaced the old enemy dysentery. It took a remarkably short time for a man to die. He would start to shiver, show the symptoms of a cold, then a cough that quickly developed into pneumonia, and in a trice he would be dead. Sometimes the cold affected a man's kidneys and when this happened he became incontinent before he died. This was particularly unpleasant in a situation where we were using three-tiered wooden-slatted bunks!

Eventually, the Italians issued us with warmer clothing. It came in the form of a rough serge army uniform from one of the Balkan countries, probably Yugoslavia. The uniforms were blue in colour but large red diamonds had been sewn into them in the middle of the back, on the seat of the trousers, and at the knees. This was to make the wearer conspicuous in the event of an escape. It was a relief to have this thicker clothing, particularly when going out for roll call.

By this time the camp was full to overflowing and there were over six thousand men packed into the converted warehouses at Sforzacosta. For roll call we had to form groups in the field to be counted by an Italian officer. It was a ridiculous system because these officers invariably made mistakes that meant they had to start all over again. Sometimes we would stand there for hours at a time as they checked and rechecked the numbers.

If after three counts there was still a discrepancy, we had to wait whilst all the sleeping quarters were searched. When this was the case, the missing man, or men, would invariably be found either dead or dying in their bunks. Standing out there in the rain, or in a cold, driving wind, with an empty stomach and few clothes, was a miserable experience and must have been the cause of many deaths.

Under the Geneva Convention we were allowed to send and receive mail from home. Our outward letters were on a printed form and were heavily censored, but mail from home was pretty well unrestricted. Gradually my mail link with home, which had fallen into a pattern prior to my capture, was re-established. The same old faithful few kept up a steady supply of letters which, in their way, were as important to my survival as the food that kept me alive. Mother and Binkie were the mainstays, with occasional letters from other members of the family and friends, although these were now rather thin on the ground after so long an absence. It was now well over three years since I had left home.

I hated being a prisoner, and not merely because of the hunger and other privations; the mere fact of being kept in a pen with absolutely no freedom was abhorrent to my nature. I longed to be free to wander about at will without any restrictions, and I vowed that if ever I regained my freedom I would never allow anybody or anything to put a curb on my movements again. One of my favourite occupations was to sit and look at a hill that was quite close to the camp. It was not a high hill, merely a field that sloped up high enough to block the view. My game was to imagine what lay on the other side. I spent many hours day-dreaming in this way, and conjuring up the most romantic scenarios, until it became almost an obsession for me to find out what really did lie on the other side of that tantalising hill.

I had great feelings of anger and frustration at being restricted, of not being able even to climb to the top of the hill. The boredom and all the petty annoyances that went with being kept in an overcrowded prison without proper food or clothing started to come together in the germ of a new idea – escape! I started to consider the possibilities of escape and from that moment onwards my thinking took on a new slant, and my whole attitude became more positive. I had something for which to strive, an improbable goal maybe, but at least it was something to aim for. It took but little thought to conclude that any escape plan must fall under two main headings: first, how the actual escape was to be accomplished, and secondly, having escaped, what route would have to be followed in order to reach a place of sanctuary.

After a very careful appraisal of the general layout and security of the camp, I came to the doleful conclusion that escape from Camp 53 was virtually impossible. The digging of tunnels was a non-starter from the beginning as all the floors in the living quarters were of solid concrete, and the only implements we had amounted to one aluminium spoon per man. Outside these quarters, every inch of the ground was under constant surveillance for twenty hours each day. Also to be taken into account was the fact that on the diet provided, we were almost too weak to walk, let alone dig, and there was absolutely nothing with which to shore up tunnels even if it had been possible to dig them.

The trip wire and its thick barbed-wire fence, mentioned earlier, was only the first of such barriers to freedom. Some thirty feet beyond that obstacle was a second fence, and beyond that again was a high wall surrounded by a formidable array of spikes and yet more barbed wire to a height of about thirty feet. At regular intervals along the wall were observation towers. These wooden structures were quite large and sturdily built, and they were roofed to protect the sentries from the worst of the weather. Three men, equipped with a powerful searchlight and a machine gun, manned each tower. The sentries in these towers had a complete and unrestricted view of the whole camp both by day and by night because the whole camp was illuminated after dark. In addition to this there was a continual patrol of armed prowler guards within every section of the camp.

Having established the fact that escape from the camp was not really within the bounds of possibility, I next turned my attention to the second problem: how to proceed having once escaped. Today, Italy and England are within easy reach of each other – two hours by plane from Luton or Heathrow, and even by road it is only a couple of days' journey in a good car. In 1942, to a prisoner in an Italian concentration camp, England was as far away as the moon. Any attempt to reach England would have entailed a journey of well over a thousand miles through enemy-occupied territory, to say nothing of crossing either the North Sea or the English Channel.

The nearest neutral country was Switzerland, but this was hundreds of miles to the north, and how did one get through the alpine passes and over the mountainous border without being spotted. Then there was the question of language. There could be little hope of surviving for long as an escaped prisoner without a reasonably good command of the language and my knowledge of Italian amounted to about ten words. It was a daunting prospect and as far as I could see no amount of ingenuity would be sufficient to overcome all the obstacles. In fact, there was only one of the many problems that I could do anything about: at least I could make some attempt to learn the language. There was a man in my section who for some reason had a book of Italian grammar in his kit. He had no desire to learn the language and after a little bargaining, I was able to buy this book with some cigarettes.

I walked back to my bunk the proud possessor of *Russos's Italian Grammar*. I had never previously attempted to learn a foreign language. It meant, in the first place, trying to recall what I had been taught about the structures of a modern language such as English. I had to search my mind for half-forgotten facts about the rules of grammar, and dredge up knowledge about verbs, the rules of conjugation, moods and tenses, and such things as imperatives and subjunctives, and double conjunctive pronouns. It was going to be a hard slog without a teacher to help me sort things out, but a start had to be made somewhere and so I opened the book at the first page and embarked upon my daunting task. It soon became obvious to me that whilst my own knowledge of modern languages was woefully inadequate, the compiler of the book had even less understanding of my present needs. The first things I found myself learning were the Italian words for student, exercise book, blackboard and chalk.

The task of learning the language was doubly difficult because of the constant hunger, and the conditions under which I was trying to study. To get one's mind to concentrate on lists of nouns, or to ponder the present indicative of regular verbs, when it keeps straying away to thoughts of bread and cheese is an extremely difficult task. There was a scarcity of paper on which to write, and the continuous noise from hundreds of men all confined in the same room did not produce an atmosphere conducive to quiet thought and learning.

During these miserable winter months of close confinement we became more and more infested with lice and bed bugs so that several hours of each day had to be spent searching for lice in the linings and folds of our clothes. Impetigo was also quite common and at one period the whole of my face was covered in horrible running sores and scabs. I also developed a crop of huge boils on the back of my neck, which were extremely painful. There was no treatment available for any form of sickness; things just had to take their natural course and one either recovered or died. I well remember the day when one of the boils on my neck burst. There was absolutely nothing with which to clean up the mess, not even a chance to wash. A regimental sergeant major from an infantry regiment tried to help me by finding a small square of paper and tying it in place over the wound with a piece of string.

Some men grew so demoralised that they ceased to make any effort to keep clean. They remained in their bunks, dirty, unkempt and unshaven; they made no attempt to converse but just lay in a state of listless apathy. As sergeants, we felt some responsibility for the men in the other blocks, and when such occurrences were reported to us we sometimes had to take drastic action. There were several incidents when we over-rode the normal queue to the ablutions and had the man in question carried in and forcibly scrubbed in cold water. His hair was roughly cut and then he was made to shave himself. Often such men just quietly died in their bunks and this caused us to have a long wait in the cold at roll call whilst the sleeping quarters were searched and their bodies found.

There was a building near the front entrance to the camp that bore the name 'INFIRMERIA', painted in large red letters on the whitewashed wall. This was the most dreaded building in the camp for it was here that the very sick were taken. The name Infirmeria really means hospital, but this was no hospital. There were no doctors, no nurses, no medicines and no attention; just rows of camp beds in an unheated building with the same bleak, concrete floor. It was in this building that so many men spent their last hours, cold, dirty and unattended.

The winter of 1942/3 has been etched on my mind as a period of cold and misery. We had no news of the progress of the war; there seemed little hope of release, small chance of escape and nothing in the future but dirt, disease, hunger and cold. The only thing worth living for was the slender link with home through letters and the parcels that provided some nourishment for our thin, pinched bodies, and helped to keep us clear of the dreaded Infirmeria. Camp 53 was an evil place that I remember with horror, and I still shudder when I think of that bleak and dreadful building which masqueraded as a hospital.

The infestation of fleas, lice and bugs eventually became so serious that the Italians made the decision that the camp was to be fumigated. We were told to leave all our blankets and clothes, other than those being worn, in the sleeping quarters while the fumigation took place. The warehouses would then be sealed before being filled with gas that would kill all the offending vermin. This process was to take three days, during which time we were to remain in the field without cover or blankets.

It was February and the weather was atrocious, with icy winds and frequent showers of sleet and snow. We were all convinced that this would be the end of us, and that as the microbes died from gassing, so we would be perishing at the same time from exposure. Then a miracle happened. At least we were all convinced it was a miracle. The day before the fumigation was to commence, the weather changed. The clouds rolled away, the sun came out and the winds dropped. For the three days that we spent out in the open the weather was glorious: warm sunshine during the day, while at night the temperature was sufficiently high for us to survive if we huddled together in groups.

As soon as we moved back into our fumigated quarters the weather reverted back to what it had been before. Since that time I have taken particular notice of the weather in February and it is a surprising thing that almost every year the same change occurs. At some period during the middle of the month there is a short spell of warm, sunny weather. It has occurred countless times over the years, so perhaps it was not a miracle after all!

At long last the days began to lengthen, we were able to feel once more the warmth of the sun, and the rooms started to lose their icy chill. It was a gradual change but we appreciated every upward movement of the thermometer until we were able to say with some degree of certainty that the worst of the weather was behind us. When the middle of March arrived, I was able to celebrate not only my twenty-third birthday, but also the fact that I had survived the rigours of that dreadful winter.

# Chapter 15

# A Bid for Freedom

With the coming of summer our life became much easier. Whilst there was no increase in the food issue, and we were always hungry almost to the point of starvation, we were relieved of the constant necessity to fight the cold, and this meant that we had a little extra energy. There was also the psychological effect of the bright sunshine, which gave us lighter hearts and greater hope. What a pleasure it was to soak up the warmth of the sunshine after those long, cold days of the winter. We did just that, day after day, lying on the dusty field, dreaming of home, thinking about food, and willing the time to pass. I also had my share of that but most of my time was spent in studying Italian, committing to memory hundreds of words, and coming to grips with the general structure of the language. My vocabulary was becoming quite extensive, and I was acquiring a very good working knowledge of the various forms of both regular and irregular verbs.

A prisoner of war is totally different from a criminal serving a sentence in a normal gaol. The latter is well fed and housed, and he knows the length of his sentence. The POW has none of these privileges. We had no idea how long our captivity was to endure. At that time there was no surety that we were going to win the war; in fact, at times, it looked very much the other way.

Whilst most of my time was spent in studying, I did have another asset that helped me to pass away the boring hours of captivity. It was that habit of slipping away into my imagination, which had so infuriated my teachers when I was a boy. The ability to daydream came to my rescue many times whilst I was a prisoner, and I spent many an hour lost in dreams that took me far beyond the barbed wire that held my body captive. I also watched my favourite hill change with the seasons, saw one crop grow to a dazzling yellow before it was harvested, and watched the farmer with his white oxen turning the ground from a misty white to a rich golden brown as he ploughed the long furrows, and I wondered again what lay beyond that tantalising hill. It became a beautiful fantasy world of my own making.

Daydreaming is a pleasant way of escaping from reality, but it can be dangerous if overindulged. There were other things that had to be dealt with practically and sensibly. The first of these was very basic: to remain alive. It was also necessary to keep an active brain, and to be ever watchful for any sign of slackness on the part of the guards, never failing to keep a look out for any possible way of escape. Physical fitness was also important to a man contemplating escape, but this was very difficult to attain on the prison diet and in such an overcrowded camp. Then I met a man who was to change all that. Billy Angus was a Scotsman, who prior to the war had been a professional wrestler of some repute. In fact he had been a world champion in the featherweight class.

We started to talk about forming a group of men within the camp who would become a team of wrestlers. He said that if I could find about a dozen men who were prepared to learn, he would teach us all the skills we needed to know. I set about this task with relish, for here was the opportunity I had been seeking as a way of getting into good physical shape.

It was not an easy task. Men who are living on the verge of starvation are not likely to look with any relish on a pastime that involves intense physical effort. It was only after much persuasion, and in some cases, a little gentle bullying, that I managed to get enough volunteers for us to make a start, and it is a significant fact that all the volunteers were sergeants.

Before learning anything about wrestling, we had to make some effort to improve our general fitness, and it was decided that we should start by trying to run round the roll call field. The first day we all set off in grand style, only to fall flat on our faces with exhaustion after no more than twenty paces. The following day we managed about thirty paces, and so it went on, day after day, always managing to run those few extra steps, until at last we were able to make a complete circuit of the field without resting. Then we were able to begin learning the arts and skills of Cumberland-style wrestling, and to make a start with more strenuous exercises. It was at this stage in our endeavours that a group of Italian officers began to take an interest in our efforts. We assumed that they must have been sportsmen of some kind, but they offered no explanation for their unusual behaviour. Whatever the reason for their interest, it was most fortunate for us because they started to make things available, including a padded mat that was absolutely invaluable.

As time went on we became more and more proficient until at last we were able to stage a little show in the camp one Sunday evening. It turned out to be a huge success and our interested Italian officers had chairs brought in so that they could sit and watch. When it was over there was a bonus for us in the form of a bowl of food from the Italian soldiers' kitchen and this made a delicious change from our meagre and monotonous diet.

With Billy Angus providing the basic knowledge, our training went from strength to strength, and once we had mastered the main skills of wrestling, it became possible to add a bit of stagecraft. All the grimaces, the moans and the feats of strength that go to make all-in wrestling so entertaining to watch became part of our daily training routine.

It was decided that a proper ring should be constructed in the middle of the roll call field, and again this was at the instigation of the Italian officers, who provided most of the materials. The making of the ropes for this ring, however, was the result of much work among the prisoners and it was a marvellous achievement. A camp of six thousand men contains representatives of practically every trade under the sun, and not surprisingly there was a roper among the prisoners, and he took charge of this operation.

Hundreds of men became involved in sorting out bits of string that had been taken from Red Cross parcels and dumped somewhere beyond the wire. This huge pile of string was now brought back into the camp, and the work began. It took several weeks for it all to be sorted out into pieces that then had to be knotted together to make long lengths. There were literally thousands of these strands and when they were ready the roper constructed a ropewalk so that the task of making the actual ropes could begin. It was fascinating to see it happen.

The ring itself was of standard size, and was raised about two metres above ground level. In all respects it was identical to a professional wrestling ring: the ropes were fitted and padded, and the floor was padded. When everything was ready we gave our first full show. From that time onwards, all-in wrestling became the standard entertainment every Sunday evening.

These shows were highly popular and were attended by almost every man in the camp, as well as by all the Italian officers who were not on duty. We wrestlers, all good friends, had adopted nicknames by which we became very well known within the camp. There was Darkie Scovelli, Digger Lumsden, Ginger Derby, and an extremely nice fellow from the Scots Guards who had volunteered to be the villain of the piece. He was the one who played all the dirty tricks, and fouled his opponents behind the referee's back; he was known as Bully McGee and he attracted all the hisses and boos from the crowd. I went under the name of Bob Ellis of Nottingham, and most of the men in the camp thought my real name was Bob.

It was amazing really that we were able to perform in this way. The majority of the prisoners were still too weak to do more than totter about, whilst we were training each day and fighting four or five rounds in the ring each week for their amusement. True, we were given a bowl of decent food after each bout, but it says much for the power of mind over matter that we had managed to achieve this degree of fitness.

Having watched us throw each other about the ring each Sunday evening, the men in the camp began to view us with a special respect. They thought that we were some species of supermen, and I found as I walked about the camp that complete strangers would nod in a friendly way as they said, 'Hello, Bob'. We found this very amusing because we were well aware that most of our marvellous feats of strength and endurance were merely the result of showmanship. The wrestling itself, without all the make-believe, is a fine sport and a skill which I enjoyed learning. I fought in a great many contests and I must admit that I found pleasure in being known as 'Bob Ellis the wrestler', and receiving the applause of several thousand men when I won a bout. The real pay-off, however, was not the acclaim of my fellow prisoners, but the fact that I was now as fit as it was possible to be in such conditions. This, together with my rapidly increasing knowledge of the Italian language, was to be of prime importance in any attempt that I was to make to escape, and then to remain free.

During the summer months we had been gleaning new information about the course of the war. New prisoners, as they arrived, brought news of the great Allied victories in Africa, and then, to our great delight, we heard that Africa had been cleared of the enemy. Things began to look more hopeful and our spirits began to rise. When the news broke of the Allied invasion of Sicily, it seemed as if the end was in sight, and we all began to talk about our release, and how long it would be before we returned home. We began to notice a difference also in the attitude of our guards; the cockiness was beginning to subside, they were becoming less self-assured in their manner, and there was a furtiveness about them which had not been there before. It was obvious that something was causing great consternation among the Italian troops. Rumours abounded, as we watched our enemies collecting in little groups, talking and gesticulating excitedly.

Then there was an ominous incident that gave credence to all the rumours, but at the same time filled us all with trepidation. A large German bomber aircraft circled the camp at very low altitude, the black crosses on its wings plainly visible. Then it landed in a nearby field, and shortly afterwards German officers were seen within the camp conferring with the Italians. After some hours the bomber took off again and circled the camp several times before finally flying away.

Suddenly all our dreams of freedom were dispelled. Hopes of release at the hands of advancing British or American troops were replaced by the dreaded certainty that we were going to be transferred to Germany. The idea of such a move filled me with horror, and I realised that if I were going to escape at all, it would have to be in the very near future. I sat down to do some very hard thinking.

At that time I was involved in an incident that was to have a direct bearing on the way my plans would evolve. I had been fetched by an Italian sentry to perform some duty in the area of the camp where the Italian soldiers had their quarters. It was the first time I had ever been in this part of the prison camp, and I was most interested to learn all I could whilst I was there. As we walked across what was obviously their parade ground, I could see the main entrance to the camp. It was a wide archway, and as the gates were open, I had a good view of the two sentries standing guard outside. The lower half of the Italian flag was visible below the arch and I could see the stone fascia, the symbol of the Italian Fascist regime, which was erected at the main entrance to all military establishments.

We were about halfway across the parade ground when suddenly my accompanying sentry fell to the ground, kicking and jerking convulsively. It was obvious that the poor fellow was having some form of a fit. He was still clutching his loaded rifle, which was fitted with a bayonet, and it was apparent that he was in imminent danger either of shooting himself or of being impaled upon his own bayonet. Whilst it was difficult in those days to have any regard for the life of an Italian soldier, I found it quite impossible to just stand there and leave him to his fate. I made a dive to wrestle the rifle from his grasp, which was a very foolish thing to do because it gave every impression that we were fighting. It was some seconds before I was able to wrench the weapon from his frenzied grip, and then I had to struggle to get the rifle strap over his shoulder. All this time I was terrified lest some soldier be tempted to put a bullet between my shoulder blades. It seemed an eternity before it finally came free and I was able to hurl both rifle and bayonet away with all my might. This done, I stood well back from the afflicted man.

By this time there was an almighty din of shouted orders, and soldiers came rushing up from all directions. I was promptly marched back into the camp, my original errand, whatever it was, completely forgotten, but I had an entirely new train of thought. I knew immediately that I had been inexcusably stupid and that the Italian guards had been grossly inefficient. On seeing one of their colleagues struggling with an enemy soldier who was trying to grab his rifle, they should have opened fire instantly. Whilst I was cursing myself for being so foolish, I kept seeing that open gate and the road beyond; it kept flashing before me. Then suddenly a brand-new idea came flooding into my mind ... this was the way! It was the normal way out of the compound. Why had I never considered it before? Why think of digging tunnels or scaling impassable barriers of barbed wire when there was a gate that had only to be opened.

On reflection, such an idea was verging on the ridiculous, but it gave me food for further thought. Then there was the Italian sentry. He was obviously an epileptic and therefore a man of low medical category. A little further reasoning led me to the conclusion that all our guards were most probably men who were unfit for normal active service. No general would be stupid enough to use battle-hardened troops to guard prisoners. The more I thought about it, the clearer it became. The soldiers guarding our camp were most likely chosen for the role because they were unfit for active service. Whilst they were capable of guarding defenceless prisoners, they had neither the training nor the experience of seasoned troops. Moreover, they were becoming even less efficient as a result of the demoralising news that the Allied armies had invaded, or were about to invade, their country.

The more I thought about it, the more I became convinced that now was the time to make a bid for freedom, and gradually my plan began to unfold. It was to involve no heroic or frantic attempts to break through barbed-wire entanglements or to scale heavily defended walls, but rather a quiet and stealthy exit through the gate by which I had entered the camp so many months before. This was not the main gate that I had recently seen – that was beyond reach – but rather the entrance through which the mule carts came when delivering supplies into the camp.

This gate became the object of my close attention. It was approached by a path some ten metres wide and fifty metres long, which was flanked by windowless buildings. Two removable fences that were constructed from a framework of crossed timbers and liberally draped with barbed wire protected the path. The first of these fences was placed near the start of the path, and the other midway between that and the gate. When the carts entered or left the camp, these fences were pulled aside to allow them to pass.

The gate itself appeared to be made of oak, or some similar hard wood. It was thick and sound and fitted with huge, strutted, hinge brackets. It was twice the height of a man and surmounted by an archway of deadly looking steel spikes. When closed, it was locked in position by a stout piece of timber that swung into a strong metal bracket set in the gatepost.

On either side of the gate were platforms from which the sentries kept watch. These platforms followed the same pattern as all the others situated at intervals on the outer boundaries of the camp. They were high enough to give a commanding view and were manned by either two or three men equipped with rifles, a machine gun and a searchlight. I had no way of finding out if further sentries were posted on foot beyond the gate.

There could be no question of breaking through such a formidable barrier by force – that did not warrant consideration – but I was thinking along other lines. I had convinced myself that our sentries were untried and unseasoned soldiers and probably of low mentality. They were, moreover, in a state of uncertainty, knowing their country was likely to be invaded. They would, I argued, be slow to shoot English soldiers knowing that the British Army was just beyond the horizon. I reasoned that if I walked quietly and purposefully towards the gate, moving the barriers as I reached them, my whole demeanour would give the impression that I was on some legitimate exercise, probably under the orders of their own officers. The guards would be so surprised by my behaviour that they would be thrown off-balance, and this would cause them to hesitate.

The success or failure of the whole exercise would depend solely upon the first impression gained by the sentries. Only a casual, unhurried, seemingly innocent manner would cause them to question whether or not to fire. Any suggestion of fear or furtiveness on my part would signal my intentions, and that would be disastrous. Having once hesitated, I believed that they would find it doubly difficult to open fire; instead they would begin to shout and demand to know the purpose of my errand. This would allow me the opportunity to reach the gate, where I would deliver a prepared speech. This would be to the effect that any attack on my person would be avenged by the British troops on their early arrival at the camp. Then I would have the gate open and be across the road and away before they had time to collect their thoughts. The whole thing would take no more than three or four minutes.

Whilst formulating this skeleton plan, I spent many hours studying the route from the camp to the gate, and also the gate itself. I was fairly sure that I would not be in any great danger from any of the other watchtowers until I was clear of the gate, and then only for a matter of seconds. I realised that I would have to travel light, with nothing more than a small haversack containing a few essentials. To be laden with a greatcoat and blankets would immediately destroy any element of doubt in the minds of the guards as to the reason for my movements.

At last I reached the point where there was no more thinking to be done. It was a simple plan and I couldn't find any more excuses for delay. No one knew what I had in mind – it was not the type of thing one discussed – but now that I had arrived at the point of action, I was filled with trepidation. It is one thing to think glibly about outwitting a stupid enemy, but quite another thing when it comes to putting such ideas into practice. Suddenly I began to have doubts: the guards didn't look quite so stupid as before, and I began to think that even an idiot should be treated with some respect when he is armed with a machine gun. The truth of the matter was that I had begun to get cold feet. I was no hero from an Alistair MacLean novel, and the thought of walking up to that gate under the muzzles of two machine guns filled me with terror.

I also began to consider what it would be like if by some miracle I was successful in breaking out of the camp. What then? I would find myself all alone in an enemy country, over a thousand miles from home. I lay on my bunk and sweated, not with the heat but from fear of what I was proposing to do. I began to question my own resources. Did I have the courage to walk nonchalantly towards those loaded guns? Would I lose my nerve and bring about my own execution? I tossed about for hours trying to come to a conclusion, whether to say nothing to anybody and let events take their course, or whether to go ahead and make an attempt to be free. In the end I made a compromise with myself. If I could find somebody to go with me, I would put my plan into operation; if not, I would forget the whole thing and remain a prisoner.

The following morning I took Buster into my confidence, outlined my plan of escape and asked him to join me. He was aghast! He said he had never heard of such a foolhardy escapade in his life. It would be courting disaster, he said, to walk up and move the barriers. We discussed it for a long time, but he remained adamant in his opinion that I would be shot dead before I reached the first fence. He became very upset, pointing out that we had survived all those desert battles, the bombing in Mersa Matruh, the siege of Tobruk, the disaster at Knightsbridge, the horror and disease of the African prison camps and the cold and hunger of the past winter. To throw away our lives at this juncture on such a hare-brained scheme would be nothing short of sinful. Of course, he was absolutely right, and I should have listened to him.

Instead, I continued in my efforts to find a willing companion from among my little circle of friends, swearing them to secrecy as I did so, but the answer was always the same. It was not only a stupid idea, but suicidal. It had no chance of success. Then at last I found a man who was willing to take the risk. He was an Irishman, known to us all as Paddy Perrin, and he was a sergeant in the Royal Armoured Corps. We discussed all the details at length and he finally agreed to accompany me on one condition: that we both had to be completely ruthless. He stipulated that we must have a firm agreement to kill any person who threatened us in any way. I was content to agree with this, but only up to a point. I refused to commit myself to the murder of women or children. Under no circumstances could I imagine myself killing a child. This was no good to Paddy: he wanted a full committal and when I refused to bend, he withdrew his support.

I was secretly pleased, because he was not a man whose company I particularly enjoyed. It also occurred to me that a man who would not hesitate to kill a child would have few scruples about turning on me if it suited his purpose. I have to state that another reason for my pleasure in his refusal was that it gave me a wonderful excuse for opting out.

I am well aware that all this sounds very melodramatic and divorced from reality, but that was the dreadful thing: it was real. It was not some story of fiction, or an exciting film with a cast of handsome, intrepid heroes. We were real people; the guards and the barbed wire and the machine guns, they were all real too. We were not stalwarts of indomitable courage either, but just ordinary men. I was not really the wrestler Bob Ellis of Nottingham, but Ray Ellis from Arnold, who as a child had been afraid of the dark. Small wonder that I was pleased to have found an excuse not to go ahead with it.

Then, just as I was heaving a great sigh of relief, one of my wrestling pals changed his mind. Bill Sumner, a sergeant in the Rifle Brigade, came to me during the evening to say that he was willing to take the chance and make the break with me. I was secretly horrified, and cursed myself for thinking up such a stupid project in the first place. But Bill's offer left me with no alternative; I either had to go on with my plan, or be dubbed a boasting coward, and carry this ignominy for the rest of my life. Feigning great satisfaction, I accepted his offer, and we shook hands on the deal. Then we settled down to discuss the finer details. There was no point in further delay and before turning in for the night we agreed to make our attempt the following afternoon.

That night must have been the longest on record. I was convinced that all the men sleeping in the vicinity of my bunk were aware of the fact that I was lying awake in a blue funk, tossing about, dreading the morrow. It was much worse than waiting for a battle to commence. When the morning came we set about packing our haversacks. I took a few precious papers and letters, some photographs, a pipe, some tobacco and cigarettes, my shaving kit and a small towel. Whereas the night had passed on leaden feet, the morning started to slip away at an alarming rate. My confidence was draining away at a similar speed, and with every minute that passed I became more certain that I was about to be the architect of my own destruction. The low-grade soldiers of my original thoughts were replaced, in my imagination, by highly skilled troops, intelligent and highly trained. When I told myself that this was nonsense, I merely replaced this fear with another. I found myself reasoning that unseasoned soldiers were highly likely to panic in any emergency and so be trigger-happy. All these thoughts were chasing each other around in my poor old brain until by midday I was as taut as a violin string.

The last thing we wanted was a crowd of gaping prisoners giving the game away, and so the few men who were in the know had agreed to saunter into the area near the approach to the gate, but not to give the impression that anything was about to happen. These friends now came to shake our hands and say their farewells, and I felt like a condemned man on death row about to receive the last rites. Dear old Buster came last of all to shake my hand. We had become as close as brothers, and shared so many hardships and dangers; now this was to be the end of all our adventures together.

'I'm not coming to watch, mate,' he said, shaking his head. 'I will stay here and pray for you'.

I shook his hand firmly, and then it was time to go. I looked at Bill. 'Are you ready?' He nodded and swallowed hard. Then we picked up our gear and with a last wave to my old pal, I made my way out of the room that had been my prison for so long. (I little realised that forty years later I would return to stand in the very same spot.)

As we walked down to the compound, I was trying desperately hard to act naturally, but my every gesture seemed to be exaggerated, my mouth had gone dry, and I felt that everybody was aware of the fact that I was walking stiff-legged, and stiff-armed. I took a deep breath as we reached the end of the buildings, and then we turned the corner and made our way towards the first of the barriers. Immediately, there was a shout from the gate towers, and I saw the machine-gun barrels being turned swiftly to cover our approach. As planned, I lifted my arm in a sort of friendly salute towards the sentries, and then, with my heart beating like a trip-hammer, I lifted the barrier and moved it slightly to one side to enable us to pass. This was the crucial moment, and I tensed my body in the way that only soldiers who have been in close combat know how.

There was no shot. Instead the sentries began calling to each other and there was a lot of arm waving, but still no shooting. We moved slowly forward. It seemed like two miles between those barriers and I had to fight down the mad impulse to run as fast as I could. My mouth was as dry as tinder and I found myself swallowing and trying hard not to lose control of my voice, which was going to be so vital if ever we got to the gate. The second barrier was reached, and as we pushed it aside I could hear the guards shouting: 'Che fai? Che fai? Do vai? Do vai?' – 'What are you doing? Where are you going?'

As we drew nearer to the gate I could plainly see the angry faces of the sentries as they leaned over, gesticulating wildly, shouting all the time. Then we were at the gate staring up into the muzzles of their guns. A quick glance behind us and I could see that a crowd was quickly gathering in the compound. I took a deep breath and shouted my rehearsed speech, to the effect that if they shot us in full view of all those prisoners, the English would hang them from the highest tree they could find as soon as they arrived. Whilst I was making these dire threats, Bill was busy pushing back the retaining bars on the gate and pulling it open on its hinges.

We gave them no time to reflect. In a flash we were through and racing across the road and into the cover of a wood on the opposite side of the road. Without pausing for breath we ran obliquely to our left until we were well clear of the camp, then left again, parallel to the western perimeter. We were quickly out of sight of the watchtowers and it was significant that at this stage only the gate guards were aware of our escape. In a matter of minutes, we had left the camp behind us and were racing towards another belt of trees that lined the banks of a river. Fortunately it was a snow-melt river which in the early spring would have been a raging torrent, but at this time of the year it presented us with little difficulty.

Having crossed the river in record time, we were soon scampering up the far bank and making our way towards the foot of the hill that had been the inspiration of so many of my daydreams. This foolish obsession of mine about the hill nearly cost us our lives. We should have made our way directly towards the north, but I insisted on doubling back in order to climb the hill for the sole purpose of seeing what lay beyond. It was just as we were starting to climb that we heard the first sounds of firing: first one machine gun, and then several, all firing together. Between the bursts we also recognised rifle fire.

We learned later that our departure had initiated something of a breakout. It had been some minutes before the Italian officers had been able to establish control of their troops, and by this time the prisoners were flooding into the road. As soon as the officers took command of the situation, the guards opened fire, and a troop of armoured cars was brought in to assist in the round-up.

Much later we were told that there were several casualties, but most of the escapees were herded safely back into the camp.

Out on the hill we knew nothing of all this, but as we started to climb we put ourselves in full view of the machine gunners and the crews of the armoured cars, which had been ranged along the road adjoining the camp. This was something I had neglected to foresee, and it could easily have been our undoing. It was very fortunate for us that we were now some distance from the camp. Even so, it soon became obvious that we had been spotted, and the old familiar buzz and whine of passing bullets put wings on our heels and spurred us on to mighty efforts. I cursed my own stupidity as we stumbled and gasped in our bid to reach the safety that lay beyond the summit.

As we threw ourselves gratefully over the brow of the hill, I had time to fulfil my dream of finding out what lay beyond: of course, it was just another valley identical to the one we had just escaped from.

We kept on running and running and running, until I could see nothing beyond a red mist, and eventually I fell to the ground in an agony of breathlessness, choking and croaking as my body screamed for oxygen and adrenalin. It was several minutes before I found the strength to roll over onto my back and open my eyes – only to see, hanging above my face, a huge bunch of cool, green grapes. We had run blindly into a vineyard, and I could hear Bill's laboured breathing somewhere close by. I reached up to pick a bunch of grapes; they weren't yet ripe because it was still only the middle of August, but I revelled in their cool, thirst-quenching tartness.

Lying there in the shade of the vines I felt a great elation. I was alive; my plan had worked and I had escaped. I couldn't believe it. I was free!

## Chapter 16

# Running Free

'Everyone suddenly burst out singing;
And I was filled with such delight
As prisoned birds must find in freedom
Winging wildly across the white
Orchards and dark green fields; on; on;
and out of sight.'

These lines by Siegfried Sassoon, written at the cessation of hostilities at the end of the First World War, express my feelings exactly as they were on that afternoon when I realised that I had regained my freedom. It was a heart-bursting joy to have escaped from the barbed-wire cage and all the miseries that go with confinement and lack of liberty. I too felt the urge to go winging wildly over the white orchards and dark green fields, on, on and out of sight.

Never in my life, either before or since, have I experienced such a sense of being free and untrammelled, and I cannot find the words to describe the irrepressible delight that filled me, and gave to those Italian hills an enchantment that still lures me back. Sassoon captured the mood perfectly, the sheer ecstasy of being free is exemplified in his lines, and his voice says it better than a thousand words of mine ever could.

We rested long enough to regain our breath before making our way, without any proper sense of direction, through the countryside. At this stage the only direction that concerned us was one that took us as far away as possible from the prison camp, and any pursuit that may have been set in motion. It was not long before we hit a country road; this we followed for a short distance before deciding that this was sheer lunacy, and we struck off into the country again, seeking cover from trees whenever this was possible.

It was always to be a problem for us that the Italians cultivated every inch of available ground. Unlike England, there were no hedgerows or convenient ditches; tree-lined cart tracks and hidden lanes were not to be found; there was not even a grass verge along the loneliest track. It was extremely difficult to move without being seen at least by the local farmers and peasants, and at first we found this very disconcerting. What made matters worse was the fact that we were wearing distinctive blue uniforms complete with scarlet diamonds sewn into the knees, chest, back and seat, which proclaimed to the world at large that we were escaped prisoners.

After several anxious hours of dodging from cover to cover, we turned a corner in the track we were following, only to find ourselves almost on the doorstep of a little cottage. It was too late to turn back because we were almost within touching distance of the two occupants, an elderly couple who were just as startled by our sudden appearance as we were to confront them. After a moment's hesitation I bade them a good afternoon, and they responded with some degree of civility, and then after a further long silence the woman disappeared into the cottage to reappear a few moments later with a flask of wine and two glasses. We drank the wine and I thanked them warmly for their hospitality. They seemed to understand my Italian and I found that I was able to converse with them, at least to some extent.

Several glasses of wine later we were on quite good terms. The man had informed me that he had no love for Mussolini, and for some reason – I cannot think why – I told him that Mussolini was dead, which was quite untrue. This false news filled him with delight and so I took the opportunity to ask him for some old clothes. He looked to his wife and I saw her run her shrewd peasant eyes over our serge uniforms before she nodded in assent. Within minutes our uniforms had disappeared and we were clad in thin old cotton clothes several sizes too small, for we were both six foot tall. I had a shirt, trousers and a straw hat; the trousers ended just below my knees and the shirt was too short to tuck into the trousers. Bill was similarly clad, but we were thankful to be rid of those conspicuous uniforms. The old couple gave us a small loaf of bread and a bottle of wine, and we went on our way rejoicing. It was a promising start.

By the time the shadows were beginning to lengthen we had put several miles between the camp and ourselves and we began to look for some sheltered spot for the night. Without blankets, we needed some kind of shelter, and we decided that a haystack would be the ideal place. Unfortunately, it seemed that these were always built close beside the little farms that dotted the countryside, and we had no desire to make our presence known. Accordingly, we waited until it was almost dark before making a stealthy approach across an open field towards the stacks behind an isolated farm. Then, just as we thought we had arrived undetected, the farm dogs began to bark incessantly and it was only a matter of seconds before we were under the scrutiny of several men and women and two young children.

They demanded to know who we were and what we were doing, and my shaky Italian had to come to the rescue once again. I told them we meant no harm and that we were travellers seeking a warm place to sleep. They chattered excitedly in some strange dialect, and there was some disagreement amongst them before one of the women beckoned us to follow her, saying, 'Vieni, vieni.' We followed her through the door and into the house, where, somewhat to our surprise, we found ourselves in a cattle stall where several huge white oxen were contentedly munching their hay. She indicated a corner where the hay was stored, and then made the sleep sign by putting her hands together and resting her cheek upon them. One of the men was obviously protesting about our presence, but she silenced him with a few sharp words and he lurched away grumbling to himself. We were thankful to sink down on the hay, and even more grateful when she appeared a few moments later with two blankets. The family watched whilst we spread the blankets, and then one by one they disappeared into another room in the house.

Some time later the same woman reappeared with a chunk of bread and two basins filled with hot soup made with brown, dried beans. One of the children, a little girl, accompanied her, carrying a small brocker of wine and two glasses. I thanked her most profusely, and then we set about the food with gusto, for we were ravenously hungry. The soup was thick and satisfying, and there was plenty of the most delicious bread I have ever tasted. It was a meal I shall always remember because it left me with a full stomach for the first time in so many months. The wine was an added luxury that completed our sense of well-being. The woman and child watched us devour our meal and then she said 'Buona note,' and after that we were left in peace.

It had been an eventful day. We had made our escape, changed our clothes, had a hot meal and several glasses of wine, and we were lying warm and comfortable in the company of seven or eight oxen. They, like us, were content to lie and ruminate, but I could not help thinking that their problems were far less urgent than our own. We lay in the hay and pondered on our situation. To begin with, we had very little idea of our geographical location, except that we were in Italy, somewhere between the Apennine Mountains and the Adriatic Sea. We knew this because we could see the mountains over to the west. We were in a hostile country, without money, papers or documents, and over a thousand miles from home. With neither map nor compass to guide us, and no clear idea of our eventual destination, the future was shrouded in doubt and uncertainty. There was talk that the Allies had landed in Sicily and were probably in southern Italy, but we had no sure knowledge of such events.

Before going to sleep we agreed that our best policy was to strike south in the hope of meeting up with our own troops. I suggested that we should make for the Adriatic, and then follow the coast to the south. The future looked bleak, but at least we had found warmth and shelter for this night and that had to suffice.

During the days that followed we were to become well acquainted with the landscape of that region of central Italy which lies to the east of the Apennines. I still believe that it contains some of the most beautiful scenery in the world, with its myriad towns and villages perched atop the countless hills that tumble in endless succession from the mountains to the sea. We discovered that there is hardly an inch of level ground to be found in these foothills, where many family groups were to be seen toiling away in fields pitched at all kinds of crazy angles. Often the land the people were working was so steep that it was almost impossible for them to stand upright. Between the hills were many deep, gorge-like valleys through which little streams twisted and turned as if desperate to escape, and we had a natural affinity with such waters. We reasoned that they must, like us, be making in the general direction of the sea, but more immediately important was the natural cover afforded by the trees that often lined their banks.

The going in these narrow valleys was very hard and painfully slow. At times we were able to follow little paths but more often it was a case of breaking through tangled undergrowth, climbing up and down greasy banks and wading in shallow, muddy water. If the valley turned off sharply in the wrong direction, or further passage became impossible, we had to climb up into the hills using one of the precipitous tracks that linked the farms and villages. This invariably meant passing close to groups of men and women working on the land. They always worked together, usually in lines, chattering amongst themselves as they swung their heavy hoes to break the sun-baked clay soil. As we approached they would pause to lean on their tools and watch silently as we strode by. Sometimes they would call a greeting, or some witty remark that caused an outbreak of laughter. Not wishing to advertise my foreign accent, I usually answered with some monosyllabic reply such as 'Giorno' or 'Sera', according to the time of day.

In spite of all our precautions, it soon became obvious that in such a labour-intensive agricultural area it was impossible to move around without the knowledge of the local people. We realised, also, that if we were to remain alive, and have sufficient energy to pursue our present strenuous way of life, it was imperative that we find a source of food and shelter. These two facts pointed only in one direction: we were going to be dependent upon the locals for our very survival.

This meant revising any ideas we might have entertained about making a stealthy journey. Instead we compromised, deciding to keep as low a profile as possible, but trying to establish friendly contact with the people in the immediate vicinity, whenever we were in need of succour. When I began to put this idea into practice, it brought a variety of reactions. Some folk were suspicious or afraid, and offered a grudging morsel to see the back of us, others just sent us packing with shouts of 'Via, via.' One man actually threatened us with a shotgun, and a great deal of shouting and bravado. We could have overpowered him in seconds had we wished, but this would have been to our eventual disadvantage and so we just went quietly away. These people were the exception, however, and most of the time our requests were met with a puzzled curiosity and a kindly generosity.

One thing we did learn during those early days of freedom was that it is most certainly the poor who help the poor. The bigger and the richer the house, the colder and more distant the reception we met, until in the end we confined our approaches to the smaller and more impoverished dwellings. Gradually a pattern of behaviour began to establish itself and we became highly efficient itinerant beggars.

It was our practice to keep out of sight as much as possible, keeping always in the depths of the country. Roads, towns and villages were avoided like the plague, and whenever possible we remained in the wooded valleys, only climbing into the open when the going became impossible. When in need of food, we singled out the most isolated and poorest-looking dwelling in the neighbourhood and asked for help, and it was rarely refused. We were able to supplement our diet also from the fields where it was possible to find tomatoes and little green vegetables like tiny cucumbers that they call zucchini. We also became expert egg stealers. We learned to recognise the special clucking sound made by a hen that has just laid, and having found the egg we quickly made two holes in the shell, sucked out the contents and swallowed them in a single gulp.

Sleeping was always a problem, not from any anxiety, but because of the cold. Our ill-fitting clothes were almost threadbare and we had no blankets or cover of any kind. We slept in a variety of places: little caves, behind log piles – any place that gave a modicum of shelter. Sometimes we were fortunate enough to be offered a place to sleep in the stall of a little farm, and that was a real luxury.

Today, when I look at a map of the region, and realise what a short journey it is by car from Sforzacosta to the coast, I am amazed that we took so long to get there. I still do not know exactly which towns and villages we passed on the way, only that we did eventually come within sight of the beautiful blue waters of the Adriatic Sea. We must have been somewhere in the region of Civitanova Marche, probably to the north or maybe around Cascinare, but I shall never be sure. Neither do I remember the actual date, only that we had escaped from the prison camp some time about the middle of August and that our journey took a great many days.

Looking back, I have to smile, because my real reason for heading east to the Adriatic had been the idea that we could probably laze on the beaches, and go for an occasional swim as we made our way south. I was nothing if not a dreamer. This notion, however, was quickly dispelled. We lay in some undergrowth on the top of a high ridge a couple of miles from the sea, and from this vantage point we had a commanding view of the coastal strip for several miles in each direction. What we saw removed any doubts we may have had about the foolishness of my original intentions.

There was a main road following the coast from north to south, and it was a hive of activity, with long convoys of army vehicles moving in both directions as far as the eye could see. There was also a main line railway complete with locomotives belching out smoke and steam as they hauled long trains of trucks laden with equipment. It was too far away for us to distinguish what they were carrying, but we were able to guess.

We lay there for several hours watching the German and Italian military columns plying back and forth. Marching men were also much in evidence; in fact the whole area was swarming with troops. It became apparent that I had planned to travel south along one of the enemy's main lines of supply. The Adriatic coast was not a healthy place for two Englishmen during the summer of 1943.

There was nothing for it but to turn back and put a good deal of distance between the coast and ourselves. We had neither the intention nor the knowledge to retrace our steps exactly, and could only strike off in a westerly direction. The hillsides were almost devoid of any cover and down below we could see a broad, fertile river valley, which I now believe to be the valley of the River Chienti. This too was intensively farmed and it was virtually treeless. The hillside was so steep that the only way down was to follow a winding cart track that eventually led us to the bottom in safety. Here we had no option but to join a busier road that obviously ran from the coast along the valley bottom. Within minutes we heard the sound of engines and barely had time to dive into the maize field that fringed the road before a couple of buses turned the corner and trundled past. We gave them time to get clear and were just on the point of re-emerging when I caught a glimpse of a uniformed man. In less than a second we were down again among the maize stalks as a body of marching soldiers came into view. We saw at once that they were Germans, and we waited with bated breath as they drew nearer to our very inadequate hiding place. They were 'marching at ease', which is an army expression meaning exactly what it says: they were marching informally, and laughing and holding shouted conversations, as soldiers do the world over.

We could almost have touched their boots as they went swinging past, and there was no possible chance that they could fail to see us – but fail they did. The last of the boots passed by and the sound of their marching feet grew fainter and fainter. These were the first troops we had seen since our escape and it made us doubly anxious to get back into the heart of the country, and away from roads and towns.

Still shaken from our narrow escape, we continued to follow the road, speedily dodging from corner to corner until at last we found a track that led back up into the hills. For the remainder of that day we conversed with no one but concentrated all our efforts on getting as far away from the coast as possible.

As the days passed, we began to see the mountains looming closer and wondered whether the time had arrived when we should begin to take a more southerly direction. By this time the general exposure, the continued exertions of scrambling up and down steep hills and our inadequate diet had begun to take their toll. We were becoming incredibly weary and dreaded the thought of another night spent shivering in some hole or corner. In spite of the roughness of our wandering life, we had both kept ourselves reasonably clean and we tried to shave every two or three days. Fortunately it was summer time, with glorious sunshine all through every day, although the nights were often very cold. Had it been wintertime, however, we could not have survived for more than a couple of days. As it was, we were coping reasonably well, but we knew that we were rapidly reaching the end of our tether.

One afternoon we were following a stream along the valley bottom, as was our usual custom, when we came upon a woman and a young girl washing clothes in the stream. They were quite alone and obviously afraid as two rough, strange men burst out upon them. The woman stood up and backed away, pushing the girl behind her. I spoke to her in a reassuring voice and told her that they were in no danger from us. We were only passing and wished them no harm. The woman relaxed somewhat, but did not alter her protective stance. I said I thought the girl was very pretty and asked her name. She replied that her name was Nerina, and it was from her that my second daughter gained her name.

Soon after this we decided to leave the valley and do a reconnaissance of the immediate area. This was necessary from time to time, otherwise it would have been all too easy to walk straight into trouble. Having climbed yet another steep hill we rested for a while, and made a little fire by the side of the track. The previous day someone had given us a few slices of salami and these we roasted on a piece of stick as we waited there.

Unbeknown to us, we were being watched from the window of a farm higher up the hill. Two sharp eyes were following our every movement, and as a result of this two men were despatched from the farm to intercept us when we reached the top of the hill. They were waiting there when we arrived, but fortunately they were not hostile. In fact, to our complete astonishment, they invited us into their house for supper. I was immediately suspicious, suspecting some ulterior motive, and because of this I declined the invitation. They insisted, promising that they were having pasta asciuta for the evening meal. I had never heard of pasta asciuta, but I was very hungry and unutterably weary. Tempted by the thought of sitting at a table for a hot meal, I suggested to Bill that we should take the risk, and he agreed.

We walked to the farm about two hundred yards away and sat on a bench by the door in the afternoon sun. A lady, obviously the older man's wife, came out of the house with a besom pretending to sweep, but in fact she was putting us under close scrutiny. Then she stopped in front of us and asked directly who we were and where we had come from. I looked at her for a moment and then I said to her in Italian, 'We are both English, and we are escaped prisoners.' I do not know what reaction I expected to these words, but she merely nodded and said: 'Va bene, va bene. Fra poco mangiamo.' ('All right, all right. We will have a meal shortly').

I had met Paola, whose sharp eyes had recognised our plight, and whose kindly heart had brought us to her home. I had spoken to her husband, Alessandro, who was to show me more kindness than anyone could have the right to expect, and I had met Igino, their youngest son, who remained my friend until his death. It was to be the start of a lifelong association. I was being adopted into the family of Minicucci, of which I am still a close member, although almost a lifetime has passed since our first meeting.

# Chapter 17

# Massa Fermana

Towards evening there was increased activity around the farm as other members of the family returned from their work in the fields. There was much animated conversation, with us as the obvious source of their interest. Most of the workers carried large iron hoes. They were all bare-footed and the women wore headscarves; in fact they were walking replicas of the hundreds of field workers we had seen in our wanderings. The oxen were also very much in evidence. Yoked together in pairs, they were led away down the track and into a steep valley where we could see them drinking from a trough.

When the oxen had been bedded down for the night in their stall, which occupied most of the ground floor of the house, we were beckoned by one of the women to enter the building ourselves. We mounted a flight of stone stairs to find ourselves in a room called the Sala di Pranzo. Here a long table was set for supper, with plates and cutlery all neatly arranged. Despite an absence of table linen, it was very clean. The bread, which had been cut into large chunks, was scattered along the centre of the table, and we had to restrain ourselves from grabbing it by the handful because we were ravenously hungry.

It was a meal that I shall never forget. The food in itself was simple enough by normal standards, but these were not normal times. We devoured an enormous amount of pasta (macaroni without any added sugo or flavouring of any kind) and a small quantity of salami to give savour to the delicious crusty home-made bread, of which there seemed to be no shortage. The wine flowed freely, and the conversation was loud and friendly.

What a delight it was to be amongst a family again. This was the first time since leaving England, four and a half years previously, that I had been privileged to sit at a table, in a house, and to enjoy a meal in company with a family. True, the language was for the most part unintelligible, the situation was fraught with danger, and I had to tax my brain to the limit in order to communicate with my excitable and noisy hosts. None of this seemed to matter; before the meal was half-finished we were already becoming good friends. There was much laughter, and as the evening wore on I began to lose much of my apprehension, glad to relax in the warmth of such hospitality.

At last it was time for bed; they were all tired from their labours, and we were tottering with weariness. The old gentleman led us along the corridor and into a bedroom. I thought at first that he had gone to fetch something, maybe a lantern to light us down to the stall, but I was wrong. He pointed to the bed, indicating that we should sleep there. It was indicative of my state of mind at the time that I said to him, 'Oh no. We do not sleep in beds. We sleep with the oxen in the stall.'

Alessandro looked at me for a moment before replying, 'If Mussolini comes, he can sleep in the stall, but you are going to sleep in this bed.'

It was unbelievable. To be in a bedroom again! We looked at the large double bed with real pillows in spotless pillowcases. Crisp white sheets were folded back invitingly and within seconds we were enjoying the delight of sliding between them. They were cool and the pillows were soft. It was almost like being home again. Never, ever, in my whole life, have I appreciated the luxury of a comfortable bed as much as I did on that first night in the home of Paola and Alessandro. It made a great impression on me and still to this day I rarely climb into bed at night without saying, 'Aah, dear old bed!' I must have said those words thousands of times.

We slept soundly and when we awoke the sheets were still undisturbed. We found ourselves in a darkened room and discovered that this was because the shutters had been closed. Draped across a chair were our clothes, washed, ironed and neatly mended. It was hard to believe. Someone must have crept into the room whilst we were asleep, but how had they had the time to wash, dry, iron and mend our clothes? This question was quickly answered when we made our way down the stone stairs. It was late afternoon: we had slept half the day away.

Before leaving the bedroom, we had made everything tidy and repacked our haversacks, which were now slung over our shoulders. We made our way towards the old lady, preparing to offer our thanks and say our goodbyes, but Paolina was wearing her fiercest expression. She would have none of our thanks and still less of our farewells.

'And where exactly are you going?' she demanded.

We had no real answer to this question. She went on to tell me, speaking slowly so that I could understand, that to go wandering about the countryside in our present condition was to be courting disaster. She said that we needed food and rest, and all but commanded us to remain with them for two or three days. Truth to tell, we needed little persuading, and I was grateful to accept this kindly offer. It was agreed that we should remain for a further three days, during which time it was hoped that we would regain our strength.

During the three days that followed, we came to know the little farm very well. We explored the house and the outbuildings, walked up and down the steep field tracks, accompanied the oxen down to the well that was the source of our water, and watched the women staggering back up the hill with heavy pitchers of water balanced on their heads. We came to learn the names of the little towns perched on the hilltops in the near distance: Massa Fermana, Mont Appone, Monte Vidon Corrado, Monte Giorgio and Mogliano. Of greater importance, we began to recognise the people in the family, and to learn their names.

Apart from Alessandro and Paola, who was always known as Paolina, there was a very old lady who was always referred to as Nonna (grandma), but her name was Giacinta. I also came to recognise Igino, and his wife Nicholina, and then there were Maria and Constantina, two women in their late twenties who obviously had children, but there was no sign of their husbands. There was also a girl of about my own age named Caterina. We were beginning to know these people as personalities, and to address them by name. Then there were the children: Pierino, a boy of about thirteen, and his sister Dehlia, a quiet and shy little girl. I got on very well with Pierino. I also became fond of Benito, who was a jovial, round-faced little chap of about four years. There was a dark, rather strange child called Luciano, who had a small brother named Egidio, and also a baby boy named Aurelio.

Whilst we had been getting to know all these people, they in their turn were coming to recognise us, not so much as escaped English prisoners but more as individuals. In short, we were all becoming fond of one another. Now, when the time came for us to pack our haversacks and leave, it provoked an emotional outburst. They had become involved, and they did not want to see us walking into danger. I had never witnessed such a display of affection: everyone in the family was in tears and for me it was a very moving experience. There seemed to be a great deal more concern for my safety among these strange Italian people than there had been among my own family when I had left for the war. Back then it had fallen to the lot of a kindly girl to see me on my way.

This was a turn of events that I could not have foreseen, but it was certainly deserving of careful thought. Here I had chanced upon a haven, a place of limited security, where I could be sure not only of food and shelter but also of friendship, even affection. To go on, striking south in the hope of meeting up with our own forces, meant a continuation of the doubt and danger we had already encountered. Such a course held every possibility of future capture, or at worst, injury or death.

This, however, was looking at things merely from my own selfish standpoint. What about the risk to these generous people if we accepted their offer of shelter? There was another factor, too, which had to be taken into account: the provision of food for two extra mouths. It had become obvious during our short stay with them that they were very poor. They worked from dawn until dark to provide only the basic essentials of life. They were not starving, but their food was limited to what they could produce for themselves.

All these points I put to them as they implored us to stay, and then at last I sat down with Alessandro and Paolina to discuss the matter sensibly. We went over all the pros and cons until Paolina summed it all up by saying succinctly that if we stayed with them we would remain alive, and if we went on our way, we would be killed. To her it was as simple as that, and there was only one answer. We should remain under their roof as members of their family until the situation resolved itself. These were not her exact words, of course, but the gist of her opinion.

For me it was a very difficult morning because apart from having to make a decision, which could affect not only our very survival but also the well-being and safety of our newfound friends, I was also struggling with the language. It was no easy matter to argue and reason for hours on end in a language that I had only recently taught myself from books. My experience of spoken Italian was practically nil, and my accent must have been appalling.

Under the circumstances there was only one sensible decision that I could take, and so once again I gratefully accepted their offer of help. I did make two provisos, however: that in the event of any danger we would disappear into the countryside, and that we would share in the work of the farm.

I well remember that Alessandro replied by saying that we could work if we so wished, but we would never be asked to do so. He was always true to his word. Never on any occasion was I asked or put under any obligation to work whilst I remained under their roof. Every stroke of work I did on that farm was of my own volition.

To the delight of them all, we established ourselves as members of the family of Minicucci (pronounced 'minni coochi'). It was also a great delight to me. It was as though a great weight had been lifted from my shoulders, but it was more than that. I think my greatest pleasure was derived from the feeling of belonging to a family again.

Alessandro and Paolina, whom I later came to call Babbo and Mama, were never to waiver in their kindness and generosity towards me. They treated me at all times as if I were their own dearly loved son. They fed me and clothed me, tended me when I was sick, gave me what little money I ever had, and even vacated their bedroom so that we could sleep in the comfort of their bed. No kinder people ever lived than Alessandro and Paolina Minicucci. I owe my life to them.

* * *

Since my capture, and the loss of nearly all my friends, I had greatly missed the comradeship that had become my substitute for family life. Buster and I had kept this spirit alive, but he had now disappeared from the scene. The man who had escaped with me was little more than an acquaintance. Bill Sumner and I had never been close friends, and I realise that in writing the details of our first days of freedom Bill has never been more than a shadowy figure in the narrative. This is because that is all he was to me in those early days. The whole idea had been my own, and so naturally I took the lead and made most of the decisions. He had to remain largely in the background in any case for the simple reason that he could not speak a word of Italian.

Bill Sumner was a sergeant in the Rifle Brigade. A Londoner, he spoke with a pronounced cockney accent. Tall, broad and good-looking, with black wavy hair and rather a dark complexion, he could be quite a ladies' man. He certainly appealed to the fairer sex in Italy. He was a good companion in times of danger, never showing signs of panic or cowardice. He had a wife somewhere in London, but he rarely spoke of her. Bill and I lived in close proximity to each other for many months, but I never came to know a great deal about his private life, except that before the war he had been a tailor. During our time with the Minicucci family he used this skill to help provide clothes, which were in very short supply.

As the weeks turned into months, Bill picked up enough Italian to get by, and he became quite popular, particularly with the young women (though not with old Nonna, who never trusted him). We maintained a good relationship for most of the time until the stresses and strains of our situation eventually led to a rift, but that was all in the future. I always remind myself that Bill had been the only man willing to share with me the dangers of our escape; had he not given me his support and backing, I would have spent the next two years languishing in a prison camp.

The morning following our decision to stay, we were up at dawn and soon following the other members of the family as they made their way into the fields. We were all shouldering the iron hoes that were common in Italy at that time. These were very heavy implements with long shafts and we soon discovered that the work was extremely tiring. It was the custom to work in extended lines and the purpose of our labour was to break down the huge clods of earth into a fine tilth. The land had been previously ploughed, and in fact the ploughing was still going on in one of the other fields. The soil was a light-coloured clay, which, when baked in the hot sunshine, was as hard as concrete. The line of workers moved steadily forwards as we chopped and chopped and chopped at the stubborn earth. The women kept up a lively chatter as the hours passed and the sun gained in strength. After what seemed to be an eternity, we spied one of the women who had remained behind making her way towards us, carrying a huge round basket on her head. It was breakfast. We sat down in the dust to receive our share of the meal. It was scrambled eggs and dry bread, washed down with a glass of wine.

After breakfast, the work continued in the blazing sunshine, hour after hour, until my hands were sore and my arms were aching so much that every stroke was a misery of pain. No one seemed to notice that Bill and I were suffering; to them this was just a normal day of hard, grinding toil. Dehlia, the shy young girl, spent her day walking to and from the house with a small pitcher. She went along the line of workers pouring each a glass of water and wine until the pitcher was empty and then she returned to the house to have it refilled. The midday meal eventually arrived in the same large basket that had carried our breakfast. It was nothing more than dry bread and salad made from tomatoes and the leaves of plants that grew wild in the fields. After lunch we all tried to find some shady spot to lie in, to sleep through the worst heat of the day.

It seemed but seconds before the work recommenced and we continued the slow painful process of breaking down the soil. I thought that first day would never end, and by late afternoon I was absolutely exhausted, but still it went on chop, chop, chop, and it was not until the evening that we made our weary way back to the house. There to my dismay, other duties were waiting to be performed: there were oxen to be tended, grass to be scythed, straw to be cut, the cattle stall to be cleaned – all the normal tasks of a working farm. I must confess that on the evening of my first day of work, I did none of these things. I was almost too tired to eat and could hardly wait to throw my aching body down onto my bed and to lose myself in sleep.

Thus began my life as an Italian peasant. These good people shared all they had with me and I shared the hard work with them. Bill was able to escape from much of the fieldwork because it came to light that the family owned an old Singer sewing machine, and Bill offered to take over all the making and sewing of clothes for the household. They were delighted with this arrangement, and so was Bill. From that time onwards he spent most of his time in the house making and mending. He was certainly very skilful with a needle and the womenfolk made good use of his talent.

I found it somewhat difficult to adapt myself to the way of life that was followed by the people who had welcomed us into their society. It was so different from anything I had ever known. I had no knowledge of the cultural background or the political structure that dictated the economic and social conditions of their lifestyle, and it was some time before I properly realised that I was living in a feudal society.

Another adjustment I had to make was to rid myself of the habit of always wanting to know the time. In the modern world we are conditioned by the clock to such an extent that it has become an obsession to be constantly aware of the exact time. At first I was continually demanding to know the time, but gradually the answers I received from my fellow workers put a stop to my enquiries. Not that they were in any way unkind, merely uninformative. They would glance at the sky and say: 'Somewhere between sunrise and midday,' or 'It is evening,' or 'It is after midday.' These people used the sun as their clock: I don't think there was a clock or watch anywhere in the house.

It gradually dawned on me that I was living in a kind of time warp. I was back in the Middle Ages: I was actually living in the pages of my old history books – no sanitation, no clocks, no electricity, no motor vehicles, no radio, no newspapers, no running water. I discovered to my amazement that we actually had a feudal lord. And then, I rubbed my eyes in disbelief, I saw Nichola with a spindle and distaff. She told me that the people on the next farm had a more modern way of spinning their wool: they had a spinning wheel!

The Lord of the Manor was known as the Padrone. He lived in a very large house that could be seen in the distance on the other side of the valley. This wealthy man owned all the land in the district. There were very many farms similar to our own and he claimed one half of everything they produced. In addition to this, each farm had to send at least two members of the family on one day of each week to work on the Padrone's home farm. For this they received no payment of any kind.

It was an iniquitous system. There were, as I remember, three people in the Padrone's house, the Padrone himself, his son and his daughter in law. The little farms all held large families. In our house there were twelve people, excluding Bill and myself. In some houses there were more than twenty folk. In all I estimated that there were some two hundred people involved. I further calculated that the landowner was claiming one hundred shares for himself, plus the total proceeds of the home farm, whilst his serfs had to be content with one half share per person. To put it more simply, the landowner, who did no work at all, received four hundred times more reward than his serfs, who slaved from dawn until dusk in the hot sunshine.

The Padrone had a horse and carriage and made frequent trips with his son to inspect his land. My friends said that he kept a careful watch on everything they did. He calculated how much wine was produced, how much maize or corn had been harvested, how many oxen, sheep and pigs there were – he even seemed to know how many chickens were squawking about and how many eggs they had laid.

One of the side-effects of living in this primitive and rustic backwater was an almost complete isolation from the outside world. We had no knowledge of the progress of the war. We never heard a broadcast or saw a paper. I was naturally anxious to find out if the British and American Armies had landed in Italy, and if they were making progress. It must have been at about this time that the Italian government surrendered, but we heard nothing of it. In any case, in this part of Italy it had little significance: we were still under the heel of the Nazis and the Fascists.

In this situation I was, of course, completely cut off from any contact with my family in England. No longer could I look forward to a letter from my mother, or from Binkie, or from any of my friends; no more tobacco or cigarette parcels from Rupert. It made me feel very lonely and isolated. Yet any feelings of peace and tranquillity engendered by such remoteness were delusory. We always slept with 'one eye open', and at all times kept our few belongings neatly packed so that they could be whisked away at a moment's notice. The wisdom of such a state of readiness was demonstrated one morning when I was out working in one of the fields. There was shouting across the valleys, which was a very effective means of communication. I could not understand the words in dialect, but Nichola and Tina, who were working with me, quickly translated, saying: 'Fascisti, Fascisti, via, via, via!' ('The Fascists are coming, run, run, run'!)

I needed no second bidding and within a matter of minutes I was diving into a refuge that we had built, to be joined a moment later by Bill. He had been in the house but had been similarly warned. Soon we heard gunfire. It was the habit of these search squads to range across the countryside firing bursts of shot into any spot where a man might lie hidden. They also went into every building in the hope of finding some hapless youth who was trying to evade them. They passed within yards of our hiding-place, but we had made a good job of concealing ourselves and we came to no harm. We remained there for several hours until Pierino came down to tell us that the danger had passed.

During the early days of my life among these country people it would have been easy for me to adopt an air of superiority (although I have no recollection of so doing). Because they had received no schooling and could neither read nor write, I wrongly assumed that they were somewhat lacking in intelligence. But the longer I lived amongst them, the more thoroughly this false assumption was dispelled. I soon came to appreciate that many of them were highly intelligent and indeed very well educated in things of which I had no knowledge at all. They were skilled in a wide variety of crafts and they had an ingenuity that often left me spellbound.

Across the shallow valley and atop another hill lived the family of Vita. Our nearest neighbours, they were also very close friends and we often worked together in the fields. We never knew them by the family name of Vita, but always by the name of La Varesi. (Each family had what they called a 'Sopranome', another name by which they were known locally. Our family name was Minicucci but to the locals, it was Vincinella. It was a strange custom that still survives to some extent in the country regions.) I came to know the La Varesi very well. It was a large family of some eighteen or twenty people. There were four brothers, Danielli, Umberto, Armando and Davidi, plus their wives and children. One of Umberto's children was Nerina, the pretty, dark-eyed girl I had chanced upon by the stream as we had wandered through the valley, but it was the daughter of Danielli who now captured my eye.

Her name was Elena and she was about seventeen years of age. Her complexion was flawless; she had long, dark hair, a fantastic figure, a slightly husky voice and a beautiful face with a smile that illuminated the darkest corner of any room. But I think it was her eyes that attracted me more than anything else; they were so warm and kind. Elena and I were good friends from the start, and I would go across to their house on the slightest pretext, either to visit or to work.

One good excuse for meeting with Elena was to go to church on Sunday. This involved an almighty trek, right down to the bottom of the valley, along the streambed for about half a mile, and then a long, precipitous climb up to the village of Massa Fermana. Our two families usually met where two tracks converged at the bottom of the hill, and continued the journey together in a friendly, chattering group. It was a simple matter to find myself in company with this pretty girl as we made our way to and from the village. I thoroughly enjoyed these Sunday outings to church. At first I received many strange looks, but eventually everybody got to know me as Raimondo and I was accepted as one of the family. Massa Fermana was a friendly place where the Minicucci family was well known and respected, particularly Alessandro, and I was as safe there as I was on the farm.

My contact with the local people, my visits to the village of Massa Fermana, and my growing fluency in the language all helped to give me a false confidence. I started to become rather careless in my attitude, and to stray further away from the farm than was prudent under the circumstances. This was why I was walking blithely along the road towards Mogliano one bright morning in late autumn. It was only a minor road that carried very little traffic and I was just enjoying the freedom of strolling along in the sunshine. There was no purpose to my journey. Then I heard the sound of an approaching vehicle and looked round for a place to hide, but I was surrounded by open fields. There was nothing for it but to continue walking in the hope that the vehicle would pass without incident.

It was not to be. I heard a change in the engine note and knew that the vehicle was slowing down. It pulled up beside me and I turned to see a German staff car, an open tourer, with a German officer sitting at the wheel. To my surprise and dismay, he addressed me in perfect English with just two words: 'Get in!'

I shook my head in feigned perplexity, saying, 'Come dice? Non mi capisco'. He simply drew his revolver and repeated the words: 'Get in!'

There was little else to do. I 'got in'. He was friendly enough in his attitude and even gave me a cigarette. As we drove along he spoke critically about the Italians, for whom he had little regard or respect. When I asked him how he had known that I was English, he said that it had been a simple matter. Finding a tall blonde man, with a military bearing, virtually marching along an Italian country road did arouse suspicions. Such a person could not possibly be an Italian peasant. What else could he be? The answer was easy: an escaped English prisoner of war.

We drove on until we came to the outskirts of a fairly large town that I took to be Macerata, and he pulled into the grounds of a large house that had obviously been commandeered. There was a good deal of saluting, and stamping of feet before I was taken into the house, and put into one of the bedrooms at the back. Two soldiers stood at the door until the officer himself arrived, to check on the security, I presumed. I had noticed that a French window led onto a balcony, and that the window was open. He also noted the same thing; he looked at me and then at the window, before he shook his head. 'Don't try it,' he warned. 'There are sentries on patrol.' With that he left me and I never saw him again.

The bedroom was bare of furniture except for a narrow bed with an old mattress. There were several sacks of maize and corn piled at one end, and assorted trivia that had obviously belonged to the former occupants. I ventured to the window and saw that behind the house were several outbuildings around a paved yard, and behind that the ground sloped away sharply and was planted with olive trees. I kept a careful watch all the afternoon and saw that the officer had told the truth about the sentries. It was clear that they were using prowler guards, and as far as I could judge there were two, but walking separately, not in pairs. I also noticed that they were carrying rifles in the slung position. Later in the day a soldier brought me a piece of bread and a hunk of cheese and a mess tin full of water, and apart from that I was left in isolation.

Sitting on the bed, I cursed myself for being so foolish. I was now on my way back into captivity, most likely until the end of the war, and I had brought it on myself through sheer bravado. I knew that the following day I would be taken to a proper prison camp, and that if I was going to make a break, it had to be done at once. There was an open window and a balcony. It was only on the first floor, but high enough to be a deterrent, particularly as I had no clear idea of what lay beneath. Waiting until I could see no sign of the prowler guards I made a quick dash to look over the rails. It looked a long way down and I have always been scared of heights. The important thing was that the ground below was clear. I decided that I would break out during the night.

Lying on the narrow bed, I listened to all the familiar sounds of soldiers in a billet. The same shouting, singing and laughing and banging about, the same smells of wood fires and cooking; apart from the language difference, it could have been a British unit somewhere behind the lines. I waited until all these sounds had subsided and everybody had settled down for the night before I made my way to the window and strained my eyes for the sight of a sentry. It was a dark night with no moon and I found it impossible to discern anything more than vague shapes of the buildings and trees.

Returning to the bed, I decided that this was the moment. I sat there trying to summon up sufficient courage to climb onto the veranda and then to jump over the rail, but there were two very good reasons for doing nothing of the kind: the height of the veranda, and the bullets in the sentries' rifles! How many times I made the journey from the bed to the window I shall never know, but each time I lost my nerve.

It must have been well after midnight when, on one of my sorties towards the window, I actually found myself on the veranda. More in panic than anything else, I jumped over and into the darkness. It was a long drop, but my guardian angel must have been close at hand, for I landed fair and square on both feet on a piece of level ground. Within seconds I was racing across the courtyard, past the outbuildings and away down the slope among the olive tree. As I plunged into the surrounding darkness, I heard some shouting and a couple of shots were fired, but it was wild shooting and I don't think they were dangerously close.

I kept on the move for the remainder of the night, heading in what I hoped was a southerly direction. It was slow going over ploughed land and along country tracks, but as my eyes grew accustomed to the darkness I could see well enough to give a wide berth to any signs of habitation. My main concern was to avoid disturbing any farm dogs that would have advertised my presence to the world at large.

With the first rays of morning light, I was relieved to recognise the silhouette of the town of Mogliano. It stood boldly on its hilltop, away in front of me. Over to the left was Corridonia. I now knew my location almost exactly, and the rest was easy. I crossed the almost dry bed of the Torrente Fiastra, a snow-melt river, and keeping well away from any road, minor or otherwise, I struck on towards Massa Fermana, my lesson well learned.

It was good to be back in the house that I was beginning to regard as home. The roasting they gave me, and the insults they poured on my intelligence when I recounted my story, only went to underline the anxiety they had felt at my disappearance, and their relief at my homecoming. It was a warm and comforting feeling, and to hear them saying 'Stupid, stupid, stupid. Why are you so stupid?' only made me feel that I really was becoming part of their family.

All the time I was learning, and becoming more helpful in the daily work of the farm. I could yoke the oxen and drive them, and the time came when I was proficient enough to try my hand at ploughing. This was not an easy task. The ground was so hard that it needed a team of six oxen to pull the plough. Whilst keeping the oxen under control, it was the task of the ploughman to make sure that the tine was at the correct depth and the proper distance from the previous furrow. I found this extremely difficult. Anxious to plough a reasonably straight furrow, I worked with rapt concentration, keeping my eyes down on the blade of the tine all the time. I was so wrapped up in my work that I forgot the olive trees. These trees are extremely valuable for obvious reasons, but the more so because they are so slow growing. Olive trees live for hundreds of years, and a tree of fifty years' growth is still comparatively young. The trees in this field had been planted in well-spaced rows about fifteen years previously, and they were now healthy young saplings.

Imagine my horror when I noticed the remains of one of these saplings in the furrow I was ploughing. Although I pulled the oxen to a halt as quickly as I could, my inexperience had accounted for three of these valuable trees. They were beyond help and had to be thrown away. I was not the most popular man in Italy that evening, but everybody was very forbearing under the circumstances. If you should ever have the opportunity to visit the old farm, look into the field to the left of the track that leads towards Monte Giorgio. There you will find a field planted with olive trees. You will also find that there is a gap in one of the rows, where three trees are missing. This is where I left my mark in Italy!

At about this time I began to have trouble with the wrist of my right hand. It became swollen and very painful, and after several days I began to feel concerned because it had turned an angry red colour and was obviously infected. There was no chance of seeing a doctor, and so I tried to draw out the poison by bathing it in hot water and applying bread poultices. It was several days before it came to a head and I was very relieved when it eventually burst and released the poison. Then, whilst cleaning the wound, I felt something sharp – and pulled out a small piece of metal that must have been there since the final battle in the desert.

One day Babbo returned from Massa Fermana to say that he had heard a whisper that there was another Englishman hiding in a house along the road to Loro Piceno. It seemed a thing worthy of investigation, and so I set off in the direction of Massa Fermana to see what I could discover. It was true; there was another Englishman hiding there and I found him. To my amazement he was not only from the South Notts. Hussars, but also a personal friend of mind. It was Harry Day, who had been our medical orderly. We had a grand reunion. He told me that he had escaped during the commotion that followed my departure from the camp. He had been sensible enough to get well clear before the Italians had become sufficiently well organised to round up the would-be escapees. The fact that he had found a place to live in hiding so close to my own was sheer coincidence.

Harry and I were to keep close contact from that time onwards. The Italians from both families were very understanding and accommodating, so that we were eventually able to make an arrangement to visit each other, and we became frequent guests in each other's houses.

The backbreaking work in the fields and on the farm continued, and the beautiful autumn days receded in the face of approaching winter. The first noticeable change, apart from the weather itself, was in the food. As we lived almost entirely off the land, this meant an immediate shortage of all those things that could be collected naturally from the fields or from the countryside. The next thing to become very apparent was the lack of warmth and comfort. There were no fires apart from those essential for cooking, and no cosy corners or comfortable chairs in which to curl up on long, cold, winter evenings.

Life during the winter months really was a cheerless affair, but at least there *was* food to eat, and friendly folk, and kindness and a warm bed at night. Like all things in life, it was a matter of degree. Sometimes I would become very homesick and worried about my family. England seemed to be so far away, and of course, there was no opportunity to communicate in any way. At these times old Babbo would notice my expression and say, 'Stai allegro, Raimondo' ('Don't be sad, Raymond').

By this time I had got to know Elena very well; in fact I made my way over to her house on most evenings. Her parents realised that I was in fact paying court to her and so arrangements had to be made for us to be together. Everybody else in the family retired to bed a little earlier than would have been normal, and nobody objected to an early night. However, there was no question of us being left alone: we had to have a chaperone, and Angelina was appointed to this task. Elena and I would sit holding hands and talking in whispers in the corner, whilst Angelina would sit plaiting straw at the other side of the room.

We liked Angelina; she was a merry person, probably in her early thirties. In fact she was the daughter of Alessandro and Paolina, who had married David, from the Vita family. Angelina was never without a smile, and she always had a twinkle in her eye. At some period during each evening she would steal away to make something to eat, although we knew that she was really giving us the opportunity to be alone for a few minutes. It really was another world. She invariably returned with some delicacy: a slice of bread, dipped in wine and sprinkled with sugar, was a favourite.

I never overstayed my welcome because, like everybody else, we were all three tired from a long day of hard work. I have no idea what time I left because there was no clock, but it must have been no later than ten o'clock that I found myself following the narrow track down into the valley and up the other side to our farm. I had contrived a special catch on the door that gave access only to those who knew how it worked. With this I let myself in and climbed the steps in the silent house and fell into bed.

It was a hard winter and there were frequent frosts and falls of snow. It was during this period that the Fascists decided to do a sweep and search of our area, and they came in the dead of night. Fortunately for me they called first at Vita's farm across the little valley, turning everybody out of their beds and thoroughly searching all the rooms and buildings. Elena and Nerina were awakened by all the banging and shouting and quickly realised what was happening. Their first thought was to warn me of the danger, and so without hesitation they climbed through a bedroom window and scrambled along the roof of a barn, from which they were able to jump down into the thick snow. Then in their bare feet, and wearing nothing more than their thin nightdresses, they set off down the track in the direction of our farm to raise the alarm.

It was a very courageous act; quite apart from the bitter cold, they ran the risk of being shot had they been spotted. The Fascists were not noted for their compassion and would not have given a second thought to such an act. The two girls banged on the door of our house to awaken us, and I was able to make my getaway, whilst they were taken indoors and wrapped in blankets. Dear Elena, she was always very kind to me and on this particular night she probably saved my life.

One of the things that began to concern me was the lack of education for the young children. There was no school for them to attend. For a time there had been a young woman known as the Maestra, and she spent a few hours each day at the La Varese farm teaching the local children, but that had only lasted for a short time. There was a complete breakdown of civil administration. After some consideration, I decided to try to do something about it myself, and with help from the family I installed myself in the large false roof area, which was used as a storeroom. I had a blackboard and chalk and some exercise books and pencils, and it was in this way that I began my teaching career. It was the strangest school ever seen. The teacher was completely untrained, and only able to converse in Italian, whilst the pupils were more fluent in their own dialect. Apart from an old atlas, we had hardly any books at all, but in spite of all these difficulties things went very well.

We had no problems of discipline because, for one thing, we were all good friends, but more than this, the children were eager to learn. I taught them the letters and how to write them down, numbers and simple arithmetic, and I was able to tell them stories about the world with the aid of maps drawn on the blackboard. There was nothing formal about this school of mine; there were no regular hours or compulsory attendance. Whenever I had a free moment I would wander upstairs and the children used to follow me. It was only during the winter months, when work on the land was out of the question, that such a thing was possible. I have no idea what good it did for the pupils, but for myself I loved being with them, and I discovered that I had an easy relationship with young children and a special fondness for their company.

After the war I trained to be a teacher and retired in 1985 as a headmaster after many happy and successful years spent working in education.

## Chapter 18

# A Journey to the Mountains

I t was during the worst of the winter weather that I began to feel the need to do something more positive towards the war effort than just remaining in hiding on the farm. For some time now there had been rumours of a band of partisans that had been formed up in the mountains, and I began to think about joining them. Information was very sketchy; nobody knew who they were, or where they were situated, only that they were 'in the mountains'. There were protestations from all the family, and I was accused of being everything from an idiot to a warmonger, but I was adamant and started to prepare myself for the journey.

There was little to pack in my trusty old haversack: my shaving kit and some photographs was all I possessed. Igino gave me a hunting knife, which I pushed under my belt, then, amidst many tears and recriminations, I set off down the track and in the direction of the mountains. When I reached the village of Massa Fermana, I decided to say goodbye to Harry, but when he heard of my intentions he insisted on joining me. This rather surprised me because Harry was not of a warlike nature; he was more concerned with healing. However, he insisted, and so within the space of half an hour the two of us were making our way through the deep snow towards the village of Monte Apone.

It was a hare-brained venture. It was the wrong time of the year, and to leave the shelter of the farm in such bitter weather was nothing short of foolhardiness. At Monte Vidon Corado (always known as Monte Vedoni) we spent our last centissimi on a box of matches, before turning along the road towards Falerone. We had not the slightest idea of where we were going, or of what we would find as we walked barefooted through the snow.

Not surprisingly, the country roads that we were following were deserted; it was hardly travelling weather. We were pleased therefore when passing a fairly large house to see a pretty young girl standing by the gate. We stopped to chat for a while and she told us that her name was Amabile. This word means amiable, or kind and generous, and she lived up to her name by fetching us an apple each from the house.

A little further on, standing all by itself on the right of the road, was a wayside Madonna. We paused for a short time to admire this lonely little figure behind its wire cage. Other passers-by had cast in money that lay on the tiled floor at the foot of the Virgin. The whole structure, though tiny, was in good repair, and the paintwork was all new and colourful.

As we walked away I was thinking about the money lying there unattended on the floor, and I wondered who would benefit from the generosity of the givers. Surely, I reasoned, it was for the poor. Then I stopped in my tracks. Who in the world could be poorer than Harry and me, walking barefoot in the snow, with no home and no destination? Within minutes we were back with the Madonna, but this time not to admire but to pillage. With a piece of stick we scraped the coins back along the tiles, under the wire, and into our pockets. I must admit to feeling guilty, and I glanced up at Mary, half-expecting to find that she was frowning, but her enigmatic smile remained unchanged. Maybe she was so familiar with the sins of the world that she was prepared to overlook our little peccadillo. (That same statue of the Madonna still stands in the exact spot along the road from Monte Vedoni to Falerone. It has now been rebuilt and is much larger and grander than when we found it so many years ago. I always make a point of visiting her when I am in the district, but she pretends not to recognise me. She just smiles into the distance, leaving me to ponder whether or not she has found it in her heart to forgive me.)

It was an eventful afternoon. After leaving Falerone behind us, we came across a lady filling a pitcher from a well by the roadside. Never able to rid myself of the idea that women should be treated in a chivalrous manner, I offered to carry it for her. She was dumbfounded by such a suggestion (Italian men were not noted for their chivalry) but after some persuasion she allowed me to hoist the pitcher on to my shoulder, and we all three set off down the lonely road. As was always the case when I tried to carry pitchers of water, I only succeeded in drenching myself to the skin. I did not have the skill to walk evenly, and so the water swilled about inside the pitcher and out through the spout to land on my head. Before we had gone fifty yards I was wet through but I could see a house not too far away, and I was thankful when we drew near because two gallons of water in an earthenware pitcher is some considerable weight. To my horror and dismay the woman never paused in her stride as we passed the building I had thought to be her home, and I could see no other sign of habitation anywhere along the road. It was a very sorry creature that eventually handed the half-empty pitcher back to its owner outside her small cottage. During the entire journey of almost a mile she had never uttered a syllable; now she murmured 'Grazie', and disappeared into her home, closing the door behind her.

By now we were coming to the end of a very cold winter afternoon, and I found myself shivering inside my wet clothes. The sky was clear, promising a hard frost, and as darkness approached, the snow-covered hills took on a menacing aspect that did little to welcome two homeless wanderers. Away to our left we could see the little town of Sant Angelo in Pontano standing black against the sky, the white road snaking up the steep hill towards its huddled buildings. Maybe it was a longing to rediscover some aspects of town life that had become no more than a half-forgotten memory; maybe we were seeking shelter from a cold and hostile world, but whatever the reason we decided to follow that white road and visit the town of Sant Angelo.

It was quite dark by the time we had climbed the hill and followed the winding road under the trees that sheltered the entrance to the town. The narrow streets were deserted and the little square was just a wilderness of trampled snow. So much for the 'town life' we had hoped to find; there seemed to be no life at all in this desolate place. All the inhabitants were sensibly huddled inside their homes, glad to escape the icy wind that whistled down from the mountains and chased flakes of frozen snow along the empty paths. It was most decidedly not a night to be outside with bare feet and nothing but thin, cotton clothes as a protection from the weather, and we were eagerly searching for a place to shelter. It was then we saw a dim light over one of the doors and could just make out the words, 'Dopo Lavoro' ('After work') written on a crude sign beneath.

We pushed open the door to enter a small, smoke-filled room. An equally smoky lantern burned dimly on the bar and two or three rough, wooden tables with stools were arranged on an earthen floor. It was certainly the most primitive bar that I have ever seen. Three or four men were engaged in conversation with the barkeeper when we entered; they fell silent, and watched us warily as we made our way forwards. They barely responded to our words of greeting, and waited until we had ordered a litre of wine and carried it to one of the tables before they continued to converse in muffled voices.

Thankful to be out of the reach of the penetrating wind, we happily poured the rough, red wine and relaxed, regardless of the suspicious glances that were being thrown at us from the direction of the bar. It was a good feeling to have money in our pockets, and it was but a short time before we were replenishing the carafe with a second litre of wine. At first we spoke in Italian, keeping our voices low to conceal our accents, but we hadn't reckoned with the effects of strong local wine on empty stomachs. As the evening wore on, the carafe made several journeys to the bar; our voices grew louder and we began to speak to each other in English. By this time, more men had come into the bar and we were obviously the centre of their attention. It was all becoming very blurred and hazy, but I heard someone demanding to know why I was carrying a knife in my belt. The wine must have gone to my head, because I drew the knife and plunged it into the table top with the words, 'That is for Mussolini!' Needless to say this caused some consternation, and I think the locals were alarmed in case we attacked them. Nothing could have been less likely; in fact we were barely capable of standing.

Having spent all our money, the time came for us to leave, and we staggered to the door and out into the night. The cold air hit us like a whiplash, and we groped our way along the narrow street in search of a place to sleep. Rather to our surprise, we met a man wearing a white raincoat. This is all we ever remembered about the appearance of this man: the fact that he wore a white coat. Being so drunk as to lack any sense or caution, we called out to him that we were escaped British prisoners looking for a bed. He almost did a double somersault with surprise, and then, cautioning us to be silent, he beckoned us to follow him. He was very agitated and kept muttering about danger and Fascisti as we made our way beyond the buildings to a little dwelling under a steep bank, just outside the town.

He knocked on the door and called in confidential tones to the occupants. Within seconds we were being ushered into a dismal, poverty-stricken room that housed two old ladies. The man in the white coat was eager to be away, and after a hurried conversation with his compatriots he made a hasty exit and we never saw him again. The old ladies gave us a plate of cold potatoes each and a hunk of dry bread, all of which we devoured like hungry wolves. Then they led the way to a barn that stood across the yard, a little distance from the house. Here we were to spend the night. We were grateful to be out of the penetrating wind, and the old ladies held lanterns whilst we lost no time in burrowing into the hay. Within seconds we were both fast asleep.

At some time during the night we both awoke with raging thirsts, brought on by the wine no doubt. We had no water, and so we decided to quench our thirst with snow. There was a full moon and we could see its rays chinking through the many holes in the walls of the barn as we made our way towards the door. But this was as far as we got: the door was locked. After trying every way we could think of to get out, but all to no avail, we realised that we were trapped there for the night. At first we were concerned solely with our unquenchable thirst, but slowly the real implications of our position dawned upon us. We had been captured again, and this time by two old ladies. We were aghast, our thirst all but forgotten as we sat and considered our situation. It occurred to me that this was the result of stealing from the wayside Madonna. Without that money we would have remained sober. No wonder she had smiled so enigmatically. Looking round the barn we found that we were sharing it with two oxen and two sheep, and we had to see the funny side of it. In the barn were two cows, two sheep and two bloody idiots, who had allowed themselves to be captured by a couple of old women.

It was due more to a kindly fate than to our own intelligence that our captors had been considering nothing more than their own security when they had locked us in the barn. They came to let us out long before daylight, anxious to be rid of us whilst most good folk were still abed. We asked for water, but first they gave us each a wineglass full of a white liquid made by distilling wine. It is a deadly brew of pure alcohol, which burns the throat and gallops around the stomach like a team of horses in some fiery chariot race. We drank it down and then followed it with copious draughts of ice-cold water. The old ladies had been kind in their intentions – a drink to give us warmth on a winter morning – but the result could have been catastrophic, because when we set off into the darkness that precedes the dawn we were both as drunk as fiddlers.

The next few hours are lost forever. How far we walked I shall never know, but we must have travelled in a huge circle. It was mid-morning before our senses began to return and we found ourselves heading in the direction of Sant Angelo, and not half a mile from the point of our departure. It was an escapade that could easily have finished in disaster, and I can think of no way to excuse such stupid behaviour.

During the afternoon we passed the town of San Ginesio, resisting the temptation to walk along the tree-lined avenue that led to the gates. Instead we skirted the formidable walls that completely enclosed the town. We had been told that San Ginesio was a Fascist town and therefore extremely dangerous to us. It certainly looked very sinister behind those high walls.

By nightfall we were tired and very hungry, having eaten nothing at all since the potatoes of the previous evening. We found a lonely farm where we begged food and shelter for the night, and the good folk took us in. They gave us a plate full of dried broad beans that had been cooked in boiling water. Those brown beans must have been tasteless and unappetising, but to us they were absolutely delicious, being hot and mealy, and ever since that day I have been fond of all kinds of legumes. We were also given a piece of dry bread and several glasses of wine, and they permitted us to sleep in the cattle stall, where it was warm and cosy under the hay.

Another day's walking brought us into close proximity to the mountains, which loomed large and forbidding as we approached them. After a great deal of searching and questioning local people, we came to meet our first partisan. He looked like someone dressed for a role in a musical comedy. He carried hand grenades and magazines of ammunition. He had two pistols stuck in his belt and he walked with an exaggerated swagger. When we introduced ourselves and stated our purpose, he asked us if we had courage, and if we were prepared to fight to the death. Harry was annoyed and replied that we were British soldiers and this made such questions superfluous.

We were both immediately suspicious of this man. He neither spoke nor dressed like a battle-hardened soldier. Men who have experience of combat do not swagger about in a boastful manner, nor do they engage in such lurid conversations. Of one thing we were certain: this man had never been in battle. However, he was our only lead to the partisans we were seeking and so we followed him. He was leading a string of laden mules that were carrying supplies up to the camp in the mountains.

It was early evening when we set off up the track and soon we were climbing steeply along the edge of a valley. He told us we were making for a small mountain village by the name of Monastero. The snow was deeper here and as night fell it became bitterly cold. It was not difficult to follow the track because the whole scene was bathed in moonlight. As we trudged up the icy path he told us the story of an incident that had taken place some days previously. He related how two of the partisans had been drinking and had become involved in a fight. Both men had drawn knives and after a vicious struggle one had stabbed the other to death. A summary court-martial had followed, at which the guilty man had been condemned to death. We learned how the unfortunate man had been taken to a place below the village and made to dig two graves, one for himself and the other for his victim. He had then been shot in the head, and the two bodies had been interred side by side.

We were very sceptical about this story, which seemed far too melodramatic to be true, but after we had been climbing for what seemed to be an age our guide stopped the mules by the side of a narrow path that led off from the main track. We followed him through some trees to a little clearing and there were the two graves. It was a ghastly sight, made even more gruesome by the utter silence and the moonlight. There were no crosses to mark those shallow graves, but there was no mistaking their place, for the wolves had been at work. They had half-dragged the two corpses out of the ground and feasted on them. I had seen some terrible sights in the desert, but this turned my stomach and we both began to feel rather uneasy about these partisans we were going to join.

The little hamlet of Monastero lay sleeping at the top of the track. On our arrival there I was immediately concerned because we had entered the village without being challenged, and I found it hard to believe that there were no sentries posted. We wound our way along a narrow lane that was the only street, and eventually found ourselves being led into a smoky room to be questioned by a small group of men sitting round a table. The man in charge claimed to be a deserter from the Italian Marines; he said he had been an officer. We were accepted almost without question, but were warned that if we left carrying any of their weapons or ammunition, we would be followed and shot.

It was not a very friendly atmosphere and we were made to feel more like interlopers than allies. We said that we were hungry and after some shouting and hectoring of an unseen woman, a meal of dry bread and minestrone was produced. This was very welcome for we had not eaten for many hours. We were then escorted to our sleeping quarters, which proved to be nothing more than a three-sided barn. Our bedding consisted of two sack bags. Considering the fact that we were half-way up a mountain, and the snow was seven feet deep, it was hardly four-star accommodation. We climbed into our sacks and tried to get warm, but in order to cover our shoulders we had to bend our knees. There was only one thing left to do in such a situation: the well-tried remedy that never failed – we started to laugh. The more we thought about it, the more we laughed. Murder and lynching, graves and wolves, a very dubious band of outlaws, and finally the frozen ground for a bed and a sack bag for a coverlet – what else was there to do but laugh?

I disliked the village of Monastero from the start, and the more I saw of the so-called partisans the less I trusted them. They were a motley bunch, collected from a variety of nationalities. The majority of them were Italians, but there were Slavs, Russians and even a German deserter amongst their numbers. For the most part they were deserters, and their stated aim was the downfall of Nazi Germany, but their conversations led me to believe that this was not their true purpose.

Listening to accounts of the various raids they had made, it became fairly evident that robbery and violence played no small part and I suspected that some personal scores had been settled. They were very proud of a recent sortie when they had placed high explosives at the four corners of the house of some local Fascist dignitary. No warning had been given, and this man, together with his family, had been blasted into eternity as they slept. They had also ambushed some small German convoys from which they had been able to replenish their store of weapons and ammunition, and this caused me to prick up my ears. When we asked what had happened to the German prisoners they had taken, they just laughed and turned their thumbs down.

The knowledge of this last episode caused us much disquiet. We both had a very healthy respect for the efficiency and ruthlessness of the German Army. Under no circumstances could we imagine them allowing their convoys to be raided and their troops killed without any sort of retaliation. This group of partisans was most certainly due for a raid in the very near future.

With this in mind we began to look closely at the defences that had been prepared to fight off any attack. To our dismay we discovered that no such preparations had been made. There was a heavy machine gun, wrongly sited, at the entrance to the village. It only covered the last hundred yards of the track. I suggested that it should be moved to a position where it could be trained on a wide area of the approach road, half a mile further down the mountain, but no one would listen. I also pointed out several positions higher up the mountain upon which the enemy could site mortars and machine guns. From these vantage points the whole village would be open to a murderous fire. Again no one was prepared to take advice or to think constructively. They were relying solely upon the fact that they were in the mountains and they considered themselves to be invulnerable. It was unbelievable.

There was another incident that caused us to have second thoughts about the wisdom of remaining in this mountain lair. It started when a woman came screaming down the narrow street, obviously in great distress. She was seeking help for her husband, who had been felling a tree on one of the slopes above the village and had sustained an injury to his eye. The victim was half-carried back to the village, and I was horrified to see a piece of splintered wood protruding from his eye socket.

It was immediately evident that there was not a single person in the village with any medical knowledge at all. They all stood helplessly in groups whilst the poor man lay in the road with blood pouring down his face.

Harry immediately took charge of the situation. He called for a room where he could attend to the injured man, and for boiling water and scissors and bandages and so on. I kept well out of the way; this was Harry's domain. I went to have another look at the defences and to wonder how I could persuade these men that they were all in mortal danger.

Harry was in his element and he did a marvellous job in the most difficult circumstances. He extracted the wood, stitched up the torn flesh, and by some miracle managed to save the man's sight. Everybody in the village held Harry in very high regard after this; they thought he was a surgeon, and no small wonder. For one man at least, it was very fortunate that the medical orderly of the South Notts. Hussars happened to be in the small Apennine village of Monastero at that precise moment.

The longer I stayed, and the more I considered the situation, the more uneasy I became. There was nothing of the disciplined efficiency that I associated with warfare. There was no training, no mounting of guards, no proper system of command, and it was obvious that no thought had been given to the treatment of casualties. We were involved with a group of amateurs, who had no battle experience to guide them. I was also rather suspicious of their real motives, partly political no doubt, but there was also a strong element of thuggery. In my opinion, they were more like a band of robbers than a group of dedicated men fighting for an ideal.

They called themselves 'Patrioti' ('Patriots'), but the Germans called them terrorists. I am still not quite sure which of those two epithets was nearer to the truth. One thing was certain in my mind: it was only a matter of time before they would be facing highly skilled German troops who would show them no mercy, and I elected not to be present when that moment arrived. It was not a difficult decision to make. We had been living very meagrely, more or less on scraps, ever since our arrival, and although everybody else had a warm billet in one or another of the houses, we were still spending freezing nights in the open barn. We had been able to supplement our bedding with a few extra sacks, but it was hardly ideal accommodation during the bleak wintry weather we were experiencing.

Our excuse for leaving was that we considered them to be more than capable of carrying on without our assistance, and that our departure would mean less mouths for them to feed. What they really thought I shall never know, but they raised no objections, and so we handed back the weapons they had issued to us and set off on our return journey.

By late afternoon we were well clear of the mountain and making our way back across the foothills. Finding a lonely farm, we made our usual careful approach, and asked for something to eat because we were ravenous. They took us into the house and gave us a small loaf each. We had just started to tuck in when we realised that they had just killed a pig. This meant feasting! There were no freezers or refrigerators to preserve the food; what could not be salted down had to be eaten straight away. To fill our stomachs with bread at such a time would have been stupid, and so, bit by bit, we secreted the bread in our pockets and in our haversacks.

Sure enough they started to prepare the evening meal and soon the air was filled with the delicious aroma of pork cooking over little charcoal fires. What a meal we had that evening! No banquet has ever equalled for me the sensuous enjoyment provided by those delicious titbits of pork offal, hot from the fire and helped down with crusty bread, and an unlimited quantity of strong red wine. These good folk were pleased to share their food with us, and our appetites astounded them. They kept telling each other that we had each eaten a loaf of bread before the meal had even begun. Two very happy little ex-partisans snuggled down warmly in the hay that night. It was good to be back in the civilised world again, where guests were provided with reasonable amenities like comfortable cattle stalls, and bundles of hay. All things are relative!

Two or three days later we were back at Massa Fermana. Harry made his way along the road towards Loro Piceno and I turned down the track which led to the farm. Harry had just been involved in an escapade that had been entirely of my making. He had walked well over a hundred miles through the snow, facing unnecessary dangers and hardships on my account, but there were no recriminations. It was the old comradeship, the never failing bond of friendship that had been forged in the hot fires of conflict. Dear old Harry, he was a good and loyal friend and an excellent companion in times of danger and discomfort.

It was rather like going home on leave. I received a very warm welcome from all the family, who were relieved to see me back all in one piece. I ate a substantial meal, and after recounting my adventures to all the family, it was time for bed. Oh, those lovely white sheets, and a pillow! I fell asleep wondering how long it would be before the Germans attacked the village of Monastero, and how many of the partisans would survive.

\* \* \*

The Germans did make an attack on the partisans at Monastero and they had no difficulty in overcoming them. Some of the defenders were killed in the fighting but the majority were captured. Typically, the Germans showed no mercy to their prisoners, and hanged them all in the village street.

I visited the village of Monastero again in 1990 and talked to a local man who had been a boy during the war years. He pointed out to me the locations up in the mountains where the Germans had positioned their machine guns and mortars. They were the exact spots that I had pointed out to the leader of the group in 1943.

## Chapter 19

# One of the Family

Slowly the weeks turned into months, and having no contact with home for such a long time often made me feel quite miserable. It was now over four years since I had left and I felt that I was losing touch with my family. My life now was naturally centred on the people of San Ruffino, the area around Massa Fermana where we lived.

The relationship between Bill and I had been deteriorating steadily for several months. We had many petty quarrels; as with all arguments, there were probably faults on both sides. I was certainly resentful of the fact that whilst I was out slaving on the land, he was usually sitting comfortably back at the house with the sewing machine and never did a stroke of work on the farm. It came to a head one afternoon when we were hoeing in one of the fields. We had been out there working from the crack of dawn whilst Bill had been sitting in the sunshine doing nothing, as usual. For a long time I had realised that much of his time was spent chatting with the women, who took turns in remaining at the house to do the cooking, etc. He was certainly putting on weight whilst we were all as thin as greyhounds. Bill strolled down to the place where we were working and began making witty remarks about the quality of our work. For me this was the last straw. I told him that I was no longer prepared to work in order that he might live in idleness and, throwing my hoe to the ground, I made my way back to the house.

I was so angry that I decided to leave, throwing prudence to the winds. Collecting my few belongings, I gave my thanks and said my farewells to an astonished family, and made my way, in a thunderous rage, across the fields to say goodbye to Elena. She had been working in a field across the little valley and had heard and witnessed our altercation. Poor Elena was very upset and begged me not to leave. Igino and Nichola came after me hot-foot to try to persuade me to return, but I was in a black mood and not open to reason. Whilst they tried to talk some sense into me, Elena disappeared. I learned afterwards that she had gone running across the fields to the home of her aunt, to ask if they would give me shelter.

By the time she returned, troubled and out of breath, I was beginning to calm down, to the extent of realising that I had placed myself in a vulnerable situation. After surviving for all those months, it was ridiculous to have put myself at risk in this way. But Elena saved the day. She had persuaded Ida and Carluccio, her aunt and uncle, to give me a home. This was the second time that Elena had come to my rescue. Nichola and Igino were relieved that I was safe and only moving half a mile or so down the track.

It was the end of my stay with the Minicucci family, who had always been so kind and considerate to my needs. I had come to think of myself as part of their family, as I still do to this day. Alessandro and Paolina had always treated me as if I had been their own son, and Nichola had taken me under her wing like a loving and caring sister. I had come to feel a deep affection for each member of the family, and I was very sad when I realised that there could be no turning back. But thanks to Elena, and the generosity of Carlo and Ida, I would still be near enough to maintain a close relationship with them all. With these thoughts in mind, I set off in company with Elena and Angelina to establish myself in my new home, the cottage of Carluccio, which nestled into the bank beside the track that led to Massa Fermana.

Carlo, who now offered me the shelter of his home, was never known as anything but Carluccio, but his real name was Carlo Lattanzi. He came from the same family as Mamma. His wife, Ida, was Ida Vita in Lattanzi (Vita was the real name of the La Varese family), and Angelina was Angelina Minicucci in Vita. It was all very complicated, but it added up to the fact that the three families were all inter-related, and I had merely moved from one section of the family to another.

Whilst Alessandro was a highly respected man in the local community, there was never any doubt as to who ruled in the house. It was Mamma who had the more dominant personality, and everybody jumped at her command. Paolina made the final decisions, quietly but decisively. This does not mean that she was in any way a nagging virago; on the contrary, she was extremely kind and considerate, but she was the ruling force. Alessandro was a gentle, kindly, considerate man, always quiet and self-effacing. Together they made an excellent team.

Carluccio was the very antithesis of Alessandro. For one thing he was much younger, but he was also completely different by nature. Quick and positive in his manner, he had no time for gentleness. He had a short fuse and it took little to arouse his fiery temper. His bursts of rage were often spectacular to behold: short staccato sentences, often repeated, his voice growing louder with each utterance. Sometimes he would actually dance about in a frenzy of anger, threatening his adversary with any weapon that came easily to hand. He was also very intelligent and had a keen eye for business. Carluccio was not a man to be taken lightly. He was nobody's fool. I believe he took me into his house only because he had come to know and trust me. All this being said, it should also be recorded that beneath his harsh and rather brittle personality there was a very kind heart.

It was a short time after my arrival at their house that Carluccio and I went down to one of his fields to scythe the grass. Never very clever with the scythe, I kept digging the point into the ground. Each time this happened, Carluccio had to put down his own scythe, and come over to reset the blade on mine. After this had happened several times, he went into one of his rages, swearing and hurling insults in my direction. I stood quietly for a few moments before telling him that he could do unmentionable things with his bloody scythe. I was not a Contadino, I had no experience of scything, and I would not be improving my skills on his land because I was on the point of leaving. With that I turned and walked away. He immediately stopped shouting and came running after me. He threw his arm over my shoulder and apologised for his behaviour, promising that it would never be repeated. I must say that he kept his word. No matter how angry he became Carluccio never vented his anger on me ever again.

I came to be very fond of Carluccio, who always treated me with both respect and consideration. We were to become very good friends, and remained so for the rest of his life.

I also kept in close contact with Paola, Alessandro, Nichola and all the other members of the Minicucci family. I visited them whenever possible and little Benito still enjoyed riding around the farm on my shoulders. I was still a frequent visitor to Elena's home as well; in fact I was very much involved with all the families who lived in the area known as the 'Contrada di San Ruffino'. It had become my home, and the people who lived there were a part of my family.

There was my good friend Luciano, who lived in a house that was little better than a mud hut, just down the track. He had a younger brother named Secondo and a sister named Pia. They were a very poor family, and Luciano's father was perpetually drunk. He sat under a hayrick all day guzzling wine, and I never ever saw him sober. Nearby, in an even poorer dwelling, living with her mother and her father who was dumb, was a very pretty and vivacious girl named Sandrina. In the opposite direction, and further up the hill in a farm similar in size to our own, lived another large family, and their children, Sandi, Diego and Medina, were regular visitors to our house.

The home of Carlo and Ida (pronounced 'eeda') was tiny in comparison to the house I had left. As far as I remember, the downstairs comprised nothing more than one room and a stable. Upstairs there were three small bedrooms. Rather to my surprise I found that I was to sleep in the largest room of the three. My bedroom was used as a storeroom for sacks of grain and maize and other seeds. There were also hams and bladders of lard hanging from the beams. There were two tiny casement windows, and near them, on the far side of the room from the door, a single bed had been rigged. The floors were of stone, and there was no attempt at decoration; everything was very basic, but the bed was clean and vines grew up around the windows.

The other two bedrooms were similar but smaller, and there was a noticeable lack of furniture. The room downstairs was equally bare of any softness or luxury, containing just a crudely fashioned table with wooden chairs, and a stone bench that held a pitcher of water and a tiny charcoal burner. There was a big open fireplace and little else. Typical of all the homes in the area, there were neither curtains nor carpets, all the doors were crude and ill-fitting, and the walls were bare of pictures or decoration of any kind.

Carlo did not own very much land, just a couple of fields near the cottage and some other land down at the bottom of the valley. For most people this would have meant remaining a poor struggling peasant for the rest of their days, but Carlo was no ordinary man. He had launched out into a new venture: he had become a butcher. In a country where meat was at a premium, this could be very remunerative, but there was one huge difficulty. Where did you find the cattle to provide the meat? I never did discover the answer to that question but the cattle did arrive, singly and on the hoof, with Carlo driving them. He would go off for days at a time without us having any knowledge of his whereabouts. He went on foot, carrying neither food nor clothes, and just disappeared into the countryside. Then, without any warning, he would return, often at night, and as often as not he would be driving a young beast before him.

With Carlo being absent for most of the time, practically all of the work on the land fell to Ida. She was very glad of my help, and we spent all our time together working in the fields. She had two young children: a pretty little girl of three or four years, named Maria, and a very wayward boy named Giovane, who was about seven or eight. It was a strange situation to be sharing the cottage with this young mother and her two children. The situation did not go unnoticed by the local gossips, and this meant every woman in the vicinity!

In fact, there was never any untoward behaviour between Ida and myself. We worked very hard, and we became quite good friends. Maybe a relationship could have developed had we allowed it to do so, but we always skated around the issue. During those long summer days we had endless conversations as we worked, ate our meals together, and shared each other's company when the work was finished. I am sure that we both often climbed the stairs at night with identical thoughts, but I always turned into my room and she into hers. It would have been poor reward to Carlo's generosity in giving me a home to have made a cuckold of him in his absence.

Writing this today, it seems rather silly and naive. I can almost see the lips of a modern young person curling in scorn and derision at such behaviour. Maybe we were foolish, but I wonder if we did not gain more in the long run by trying to maintain some moral standards. At least it has stood the test of time: we are all three still good friends.

I gradually settled into yet another way of life that was quite different from what had gone before. There was the normal round of hoeing, ploughing, setting and gathering, but every so often this pattern was rudely interrupted. Carlo would arrive home with an animal for slaughter, and then, for the next few days, pandemonium reigned. As this sideline of Carluccio's was strictly illegal, we had to work quickly. The meat was destined for the black market and so it was imperative that all evidence of its existence be removed as quickly as possible. Almost invariably he returned during the hours of darkness, when we were fast asleep. He would call us up in stentorian tones, and within minutes we would all three be in the cattle stall working by the light of a single lantern.

The animal would be dragged down and poleaxed, and then its throat was cut and the blood caught in a huge metal bowl. Later, when the blood had coagulated, it was cut into cubes to be cooked and eaten. A pulley and blocks system was used to hoist up the carcass until it hung from one of the beams to be skinned. Carlo taught me how to skin a beast, and we were soon busy with our knives, working in opposite directions, starting from the belly. As there was only one lamp, held by Ida, we were continuously demanding more light and she spent her time dashing from one to the other of us.

One night whilst this was taking place, she tripped over the bowl of blood, which tipped over and the floor became awash with blood. Carluccio immediately flew into one of his rages. Brandishing the skinning knife, he flew at Ida, who shrieked and dodged away. The two of them dashed madly about, she with the lantern and he with the knife, both of them splashed to the knees with blood. It was a hair-raising episode whilst it lasted, but no harm was done. Like most Italian furores, it was quickly over and we soon settled back to work again amidst the gory mess.

The next job was to bone and quarter the carcass. The bones were bagged and hidden, and any unusable parts dumped under the manure heap. The meat was then cut into pieces. This was a long and tedious process which invariably lasted well into the next day, and it was evening before the beast that had arrived the previous night was reduced to small pieces of beef.

There was still no time for sleep. All this beef now had to be passed through a mincing machine: a small, hand-driven mincing machine! It took hours and hours and hours, turning, turning, turning. We took spells, of course, but it was a prodigious task. All through the night we continued, dozing and working in turn until every ounce had been minced. Then salt and black pepper was added, together with onion, garlic and the rind and juice of many lemons. These ingredients had to be mixed by hand, and it took some considerable time, as there was a vast quantity of meat.

Whilst all this was taking place, another job was accomplished. During spells of resting from turning the handle of the mincer, we cleaned the animal's intestines. This was a noisome and messy occupation, made all the more difficult by the fact that there was no running water. I seem to remember that we finished them off down in the stream.

Then we were faced with the soul-destroying task of passing it all through the mincer yet again. This time the meat was fed into the intestine tubes to produce salami sausages. It meant another night of dozing and mincing to produce dozens of these long, fat cylinders of raw meat. It also produced three very weary workers, but there was still more work to be done.

A log fire was lit in the wide, open fireplace, and allowed to burn until it had become a mass of red, glowing embers. Several of the long cylinders of meat were then suspended from a metal pole that was slotted into position above the fire. Wet straw was then thrown onto the embers to produce a thick, yellow, acrid smoke that immediately filled every room in the house. We had to stand well clear to escape the choking fumes.

From time to time one of us had to take a deep breath and dash into the house, either to stoke the fire or to throw on more wet straw. The salami sausages had to be removed when they had been smoked and new ones hung in their place. This went on for the whole day. There was no question of returning to the house to prepare food until the last of the sausages had been smoked, and by this time it was early evening. Ida then prepared a meal while Carluccio and I loaded all the meat into three enormous sacks.

After supper we set off, each carrying one of the sacks. It was a backbreaking task, and struggling down the steep track trying to keep one's feet in the darkness was a nightmare. But the real grind had yet to come. The long haul up the precipitous track to Mont Appone was a struggle that stretched every muscle beyond endurance. Step by step we made our way up this pitiless hill, our backs bent and our knees buckling under the weight of the heavy sacks. The load had been evenly shared, and Ida carried an equal share without complaint. There were frequent rests but no conversation; we had no breath for that.

Having reached the top of the hill, we often had to wait for several hours for a lorry to appear. First we would hear its engine labouring in the distance, and then it would lumber into sight and pull to a halt where Carluccio stood waving in the middle of the road. No words were exchanged and I never saw any money change hands. The sacks were hoisted into the back of the lorry that drew away and disappeared into the darkness. This was the signal for us to make our way back down the hill, over the stream and up again to the little cottage. Within minutes we were all wrapped in sleep, and all that was left of the animal was some food for ourselves and the hide, which was soaking in chemicals in the water trough behind the cottage.

It was the day following one of these black market episodes that I was sitting talking across the table to Carluccio. We always had an easy day after these strenuous occasions, and also plenty of good meat and red wine that put us all in a very amiable frame of mind. I thought that this might be a suitable moment to enlighten him about the prevailing gossip that was going the rounds about Ida and me. Very warily I broached the subject, but before I could get to grips with the story, he waved me aside. He said that he had known about the gossip for weeks. Then getting up from his chair, he came and put his arm across my shoulders, and said that we were friends, and he trusted me. When I thought about him chasing Ida with the knife, I was very thankful for his trust. I could imagine how easily his knife could have slipped between my shoulder blades!

I was always very apprehensive whilst these black market affairs were taking place. Had we been raided, Carlo and Ida would certainly have gone to prison. I dreaded to think what would have happened to me. An escaped prisoner engaged in black market activities would have had short shrift from the Fascists.

Whilst the life was hard and sometimes dull, there were moments that I remember with pleasure. Harry still kept in touch, and now that the summer had returned, we often went together to a favourite place in the valley that was known as the Chiusa. Here the stream tumbled over a cliff into a deep pool that was about twenty feet wide and twice as long. Here it was possible to swim and we spent some enjoyable hours there together.

Another happy memory concerns the cherry trees that grew along the track quite close to the cottage. They formed an archway over the path, and in the springtime the blossom had been something to behold, but now the trees were full of ripe fruit. It became a habit of mine to spend the afternoon siesta in the branches of these trees, gorging myself with rich juicy cherries. They hung in large clusters, shining, black and red, a joy to the eye and an enchantment to the stomach. I often think with pleasure of those beautiful and fruitful trees.

\* \* \*

From the moment I had arrived to live in the cottage with Carluccio and Ida, I had been puzzled by the fact that I had the largest bedroom in the cottage. It is a puzzle that I never properly solved. There was definitely something strange about this room, and I am sure that people with a taste for the supernatural would say that it was haunted. I make no such claim, but there were incidents that I find difficult to explain.

It was a practice of mine always to take a glass of water with me when I retired for the night. I invariably placed the glass on the stone windowsill, which was quite close to the bed. Sometimes I would awaken during the night for a drink, but not every night. One morning when I awoke, I found the glass lying on its side, but no trace of dampness on the stone sill. The first time this happened, I thought that I had been in some sort of dream state in which I had drunk the water during the night. I gave it no further thought until it happened again and again. In fact almost every morning I would find the empty glass lying on its side, but never a drop of moisture to be seen. When I mentioned these occurrences to Ida or Carlo, they just shrugged the matter aside.

One night Carlo had friends in, and they were playing cards. I have never been a card player and Italian playing cards were, and still are, a complete mystery to me. Bored with the verbal excitement that always accompanied their play, I took myself off to bed. After some time, and just as I was dropping off to sleep, I heard the latch of my door click open and became aware that someone was in the room. For a moment I thought that it was Ida, but then I heard her voice in the room below. Before I had time to investigate further I felt a heavy object fall across the bed and felt myself suffocating. In a panic I grappled with my hands against something woolly or hairy that was lying across me. I pushed and struggled and whatever it was broke free and escaped through the door, which closed with a distinct click. Springing from the bed, I leapt across the room, through the door and into the narrow passage, but there was nothing to be heard or seen except the voices of the card players below.

The following day, whilst the three of us were sitting at the table, I recounted these events to them exactly as they had happened. Ida started to tell me something, but she only got as far as saying: 'Si Raimondo, e vero ...' ('Yes Raymond, it is true ....') when Carluccio stopped her.

'Stai zitto,' he commanded. 'Non dici piu' ('Keep quiet, don't say any more').

No amount of cajoling could elicit another word on the subject from either of them, but I began to have an idea why I had the largest bedroom.

I asked around to see if anyone knew anything about the cottage that might have some bearing on these strange affairs, but there seemed to be a conspiracy of silence. Even today they refuse to discuss the matter. When Carluccio and his granddaughter Romina came to visit me at my home in Lincoln, I raised the subject yet again, enlisting the aid of Romina, who speaks fluent English. Carlo just shook his head and refused to discuss the matter. Some months later, when I was in Italy, Romina told me that even to her they were very reluctant and evasive on the subject. Her grandmother had conceded a hint about somebody being murdered there, but beyond this, she had refused to elaborate.

There it must remain, an unsolved mystery. I shall never know what happened to the water, or what, on that one single occasion, threatened to suffocate me in my bed. It never came again, and I was not particularly alarmed; in fact I rather liked my bedroom with the vines growing around the window.

We began to hear rumours that there was some movement on the battlefronts further south. Large formations of American planes were often to be seen flying at great altitude. It was thought that the Germans were suffering heavy losses. We were also told that they were stealing corn from the Italians to feed their troops. The local people became alarmed in case a raid was made on their own grain store, which was on the left of the road that led towards Mogliano.

Harry and I discussed this at some length and eventually decided that it would sabotage the German cause if we opened the grain store ourselves, and distributed the grain among the local people. My job was to open the store and arrange the distribution, and Harry was to tour the village informing everybody of our intention. He went off after dark to spread the news and I set about breaking open the store. Harry did his part very well; he went into the canteen, knocked at doors and made sure that everybody in the village knew that Raimondo had opened the grain store. I borrowed a crowbar from a nearby farm and wrenched the locks and bolts off the door, so that the grain was available.

Soon there was a procession of very apprehensive people to the store, but, as they became bolder, ox carts began to appear and the grain began to be moved more quickly. There was a moon that night which gave ample light for our needs. Unfortunately, Harry had done his job so well that the news travelled further afield until it came to the ears of the Fascist authorities. They took immediate action that was to put an end to my career as a grain distributor – in fact it very nearly put an end to me altogether.

The first knowledge I had of their arrival was when the crowd began to scatter with shouts of 'Fascisti'. Unbeknown to me, the Blackshirts had already established roadblocks and set up a machine-gun emplacement at the crossroads below the cemetery. I walked out of the grain store to see a group of men approaching, then there was a flash and the crack of a pistol, and I heard the bullet strike the wall beside my head. Having no weapon of my own, I could do nothing to retaliate, but I did have a lot of experience in self-preservation and within a split second I had dodged behind the corner of the building. I could see a round hayrick only a few yards away and scuttled towards it as a second shot was fired.

What followed was like something from a third-rate Wild West novel. I played 'catch me if you can' with the man who had the pistol. Backwards and forwards we scampered around the rick, with him taking pot-shots whenever I came into view. It was a very unhealthy situation that could only have ended in one way had I allowed it to continue. Realising this, I made a sudden break, and with a staggered run made off up the hill into an olive grove interspersed with vines. He fired several shots after me, but pistols are notoriously inaccurate weapons.

Before starting on this rather foolish mission, we had agreed to meet in the Campo Santo (cemetery) if anything went wrong. Accordingly I made my way to the top of the hill overlooking Massa Fermana and found Harry waiting just inside the gate of the Campo Santo. This was a marvellous vantage point that we often used. It gave a wonderful view of all the countryside for miles in each direction. From here we could see the machine-gun post at the crossroads, and groups of uniformed men walking about or standing in huddles at various points along the road.

The only sensible thing for us to do at this stage was to melt away into the night. It was too dangerous for me to make my way back to Carluccio's cottage, and so we went in the opposite direction. Skirting the hill, we eventually came down on the Loro Piceno road and followed it, very stealthily, back towards Massa Fermana.

We reached the house of Antonio Terrabasso, one of Harry's friends, and we slept that night in his hayloft. Before we went to sleep Harry regaled me with what he said was the latest hit song back in England. I do not know from where he got this information, or the words and music, but he was in good voice. It seemed rather incongruous to me at the time, but looking back it appears even more inexpedient. There we were, having been chased at gunpoint, and with men still searching for us in the nearby village, and Harry was singing. I can still remember the words: 'Moonlight becomes you, it goes with your hair.' Well, it was one way of forgetting that most of the grain was still in the grain store and available to the German Army.

It should not be imagined that we had remained all those months in Ascoli Piceno because we enjoyed living as peasants. The fact of the matter was that in the autumn of 1943 the front had become static. The Germans maintained a strong line across southern Italy and on the eastern side, in the vicinity of Pescara. We had no clear knowledge of the enemy dispositions, but we were experienced enough to know the impossibility of walking through such a fortified region. Even if such a feat could have been achieved, there would still have been the problem of entering the Allied zone. One does not casually stroll across no-man's-land. The only thing that we could do under the circumstances was to wait for the front to become fluid. Only when there was movement would we stand even a remote chance of breaking through.

For this reason we were eager to hear any scraps of gossip regarding the situation at the front. From what we were able to gather there was some bitter fighting taking place and the general opinion was that it was only a matter of time before the Germans would be forced into retreat. One day Carluccio took me into his confidence to the extent of revealing the contents of a large chest that he kept in his bedroom. I was astounded when he threw back the lid to see the chest was crammed full of paper money. It would be impossible to estimate how much there was; to me it seemed like the riches of Croesus. Certainly there must have been the equivalent of several thousand pounds. It occurred to me that when the Allied armies broke through and came to occupy this part of Italy, there would most certainly be a change of currency. I explained to Carluccio that he stood to lose a great deal if the old currency was devalued. I did not know much about such things, as banking had never figured very largely in my education or mode of living. It was merely a matter of common sense. Carluccio listened, and became very disturbed to think that he could so easily lose all his money. I did not know if the money would have been safer in a bank, but in any case he dared not take it to a bank in case his black market activities came to light. In the end I advised him to turn all the money into goods that could be resold when the new currency had been established.

Never a man to dither, he went off the following day with a satchel full of money and came back two days later driving a car. His next expedition produced a couple of horses. It went on day after day until his material possessions started to become something of an embarrassment. Dinner services and other expensive crockery, silver cutlery and ornaments were easily hidden, but two cars and a string of horses were bound to arouse interest and suspicion. It became necessary to remove the cars from the notice of any casual passer-by, and so I set to work on this project as a matter of priority.

It was not a difficult task and it only took me a few days with Ida's help. I merely built a hayrick around each of the vehicles. What could have looked more natural? The horses we staked out among the olive trees and things began to look natural again, although it was like living in Ali Baba's cave.

There was a white horse called Pipo that was kept in the stable. He was a bad-tempered creature and very difficult to groom. He once kicked the currycomb out of my hand and on many occasions he turned to snap at me whilst I was brushing his flanks. He did not get sufficient exercise and was just bursting with energy. One day the young people had come down from the farm and we had Pipo out standing on the track. They dared me to ride him and so I jumped onto his back. The next second I was flying in the air over his head. This happened four times, to the onlookers' merriment but to my chagrin. The fifth time I managed to get a grip with my knees and he failed to unseat me. Then, without warning, he set off up the track at a full gallop. As I was riding bareback and with only a head halter rope, I was completely powerless to control him.

Up the track we went, then left across a field of growing crops, with me hanging on for dear life. To my horror he turned into an olive grove that had wires stretched from tree to tree to support the vines. I could only put my head down on his neck and pray as we charged down the steep field with the wires just inches above my head. At the bottom of the hill were the steep banks of the stream. Pipo stopped dead in his tracks at their very edge, propelling me in a graceful arc to land squarely on my back among the reeds.

\* \* \*

Despite the lack of official news, the signs of a German withdrawal were unmistakable. Whereas previously their troops had, for the most part, been evident only on the main lines of supply, they were now seen in larger concentrations in the country districts of this region. They were also confiscating everything they could lay their hands on, particularly those things that were of immediate help to them. It was a very worrying time for the local people who stood a good chance of losing their possessions and, as the war passed by, their homes and probably their lives as well.

Carluccio was concerned about his valuable horses. He had heard that the Germans were short on transport facilities and were using horses for this purpose whenever they could find them. Then we got news across the valley that a contingent of German troops with horse-drawn transport was approaching. We quickly rushed around the olive groves where our horses were tethered, gathered them together, and took them down the valley bottom. Some way along the track we turned off along the foot of a sheer rock face which was about fifty feet high. Along the bottom of this cliff was a fringe of trees, mainly silver birch. As the trees were in full leaf, this made a good hiding place for the horses.

It fell to my lot to stand guard over them, and so I settled myself comfortably in the shade and prepared myself for a lazy day. It was not to be. Within half an hour I became aware of considerable activity above me at the top of the cliff: guttural voices shouting commands, and other noises which left me in no doubt of the fact that fifty feet above me German troops were bivouacking. Sitting there under the trees trying to hide a string of horses with the enemy almost within touching distance was not a happy situation. I wished that I had some sort of weapon with which to defend myself but I was completely unarmed. Then, to complete my discomfort, it started to rain. Some time later I heard someone approaching and stiffened with apprehension as I waited for a group of German soldiers to appear, but it was only Ida. She had brought me an umbrella! What I needed was an automatic rifle, but all I had was an umbrella. At least it defended me from the rain.

We took turns in guarding the horses, carrying food down to them and taking them singly to the stream to drink. Walking back up the track to the cottage we were in full view of the troops, but they were well disciplined and left us in peace. They did not find the horses that were concealed so close to their camp, and three days later we breathed a sigh of relief when they moved off.

Distant rumblings told us that the advancing Allies were getting nearer, and for some people this was a moment to be dreaded. One such person was the local Fascist official, an ugly little man whose name I have forgotten. He had been a big noise in the village for many years, throwing his weight about and strutting about in his black-shirted uniform with the strength of the ruling Junta behind him. Now that was all to be peeled away and he was in fear of retribution. I had known of this man for many months and had taken great care to keep clear of him. Now he actually sought me out, and invited me to dinner. Knowing full well what he was about, I accepted and ate everything he put before me, drinking deeply of his best wine as the meal progressed. After dinner, the ingratiating little rat asked me if I would write a letter for him to show the British troops when they arrived. He wanted me to clear him of any connection with the Fascist party, and to say that he had always been a true democrat and a supporter of the Allied cause.

I agreed to his suggestion without hesitation, and he hurried to get me pen and paper. I enjoyed writing that letter. Naturally, I cannot remember it word for word, but it ran something like the following:

Dear Winston Churchill,

I would like to bring your attention to the bearer of this letter, *******
*******. He is a native of Massa Fermana and for many years he has been a keen supporter of the fat, over-decorated leader of the black-shirt legions that have ruled this country for far too long.

He has always been anti–British in his attitude and has done everything in his power to denigrate our nation. He has been a scourge to the local people who have lived in fear of him. He is also a snivelling little wretch and completely beyond redemption.

I recommend that he be placed against the nearest wall and shot, or better still, hanged from some nearby tree.

Yours faithfully
R.K. Ellis
Sergeant, 107th RHA, South Notts. Hussars

He thanked me most profusely, folded the letter carefully and put it in a drawer. I have had many laughs to myself imagining the situation when he handed that letter to some British officer of the occupying force. It says much for the tolerance of the folk at Massa Fermana that he lived to be a ripe old age. I have seen him several times when visiting Massa Fermana, but I have never sought his company, and he has never recognised me as the man who wrote the letter for him.

It was during this period that I met a German soldier on one of the country roads. We sat together on a grassy bank that was ablaze with flowering dandelions. He thought I was an Italian of course and we spent the best part of an hour together. I always think of him as 'the sad German soldier'. He told me that he had become separated from his unit and was trying to find some way of getting back to it. (It reminded me of the time when I had been similarly stranded in Mersa Matruh two years previously.) He knew they were losing the war but he was past caring. He came from Cologne, where his wife and two children had all perished in an air raid. He was heartbroken, and sick and tired of fighting and all the horrors and privations of war. I felt very sorry for this dejected man, who seemed to have lost everything, including hope. He was one of the many pieces of flotsam and jetsam which warfare casts carelessly aside.

During the summer of 1944 we all knew that my time in Massa Fermana was rapidly coming to an end. The next few weeks would either see me dead, a prisoner or safely back behind Allied lines. Of course my main concern, as ever, was self-preservation, but there were other considerations that even in these dangerous times could not be overlooked. First of all there was a girl who had become very fond of me, and had twice saved my life during the previous months. What was I to do about her? Then there was the thought of leaving behind me a family of people I had grown to love.

It was a paradoxical situation; I should have been overjoyed at the prospect of returning home to England, and indeed I was, but any anticipatory pleasure was overshadowed by the sadness of leaving the little part of Italy which had been my home. I had built a new life and become part of another family and it was only now, when our parting was imminent, that I realised the depth of the affiliation that had been formed.

Paramount among these was my relationship with Elena. There was no doubt at all about her feelings: she was just waiting for me to discuss our future together. Had things been normal I would certainly have considered the possibility, but things were far from normal – there were many factors to be taken into consideration. I wrestled with these thoughts for hours on end, trying to come to the right decision. Someone said to me recently, 'Obviously you were not in love with her, otherwise you would have married the girl.' It is surprising how easily people can analyse the problems of others. They just reduce human anxieties to a few basic facts, and, hey presto, the answer is simple. Would that it worked out so facilely in real life. There were many imponderables, not least among them another girl named Binkie, who also laid claim to my thoughts. For over four years she had faithfully corresponded with me, and for a long time I had taken it for granted that she would one day be my wife. In normal times situations such as these work themselves out naturally, but I was forced into making an immediate decision.

Rightly or wrongly, I decided that if I married Elena, I would only bring her unhappiness, and so the question was never asked. A few days before I left, she joined me on the track as she had done many times before and we walked up the hill to Massa Fermana together. It was a painful journey that ended sadly. Nothing was said directly, there was no quarrel or bitter words, just a mutual understanding of what was not to be, and when we parted we both had tears in our eyes.

The following day I went again to Massa Fermana, where I met Harry. We made our weary way up the steep hill to the Campo Santo, our vantage point, and as we climbed our ears were beset by the old familiar noise of battle. From the top we could see large columns of smoke in the near distance, and the sky was criss-crossed with the vapour trails of high-altitude bombers. The war had arrived. It was a depressing sight, as the ominous sound of aircraft engines and bombardment grew nearer by the hour. We stayed there for several hours, leaning with our elbows on the wall, watching and wondering as we tried to decide on a plan of action. It was a Monday; I can remember that because we christened it 'Black Monday'.

There was no point in delaying any longer and so we made the decision to leave the following day, and make an attempt to break through the lines. Harry returned to his adopted family to say his goodbyes, and I made my way for the last time down the steep track that I had come to know so well to bid farewell to my second family.

I remember so many sad and disturbed faces. Parting, they say, is such sweet sorrow, and there was the added misery of the passing destruction of war. Yet there was also hope for a brighter future for all of us, though no longer together. We would never again share the hardships and simple pleasures of that pastoral life among the foothills of Ascoli Piceno. I have a recollection of brown, sometimes bristly faces, with moist eyes and escaping tears, of hugs and husky voices trying to utter words that could not escape from choking tears. In the house of La Varese, Daniello, Umberto and their wives. Dearest Elena, and Nerina, and Argentina and all the other children. Angelina, a true and loyal friend, and her pretty little daughter, Marianina. In the house of Medina, Sandi and Diego and their families. In the house of the Priori family that was the home of Luciano and Secondo, Sandrina and Pia – the list seemed endless. Then I made my final visit to the farm, as I had come to call it, the place that had been my home for so many months. This was the most difficult of all.

Saying goodbye to Paola and Alessandro was a huge sadness. Poor Nicolina hugged me and refused to let go. Igino, Giuseppe and Maria, Nonna Giacinta, Constantina and my good friend Pierino were all weeping, and so were the children, who did not properly understand, but were just weeping in sympathy with everybody else. At last I sadly returned to the cottage to spend my last night with dear old Carluccio and Ida and their two children. I was never to see their pretty little daughter again. Poor little Maria had but a short time to live.

For the last time I put my glass of water on the windowsill and crept into my bed in the room where I had slept for the past three months. Sleep did not come easily that night; my mind was full of memories. It had been a hard time in many respects, a continual grind of labour and a minimum of comfort. A life without books or music or poetry or art of any kind; no theatre or cinema or concerts. Only the bare necessities of clothing and not even a pair of boots for my feet. A repetition of boring often-tasteless food and never a cup of hot, sweet tea, or a glass of beer. Just a continual round of unremitting toil for little reward. Why then was I so sad to leave? Maybe I had found the secret of true happiness: that it lies not with material things, but with people. It matters little where you are, or what you are doing, so long as you are sharing what you have with those you love.

The following morning Carluccio said he would accompany us for part of the way, and we harnessed one of the horses to a light cart. Harry arrived in good time as arranged and, after a last hug from Ida and the children, I set off on my homeward journey. There were more last hugs as we passed the farm and a final wave as we topped the hill. Going down the other side I caught sight of two lonely figures half-way down the sloping field. It was Angelina and Elena cutting the corn with their sickles. I slid from the cart and asked Carluccio to wait whilst I went to say my last goodbye. Angelina looked sad and troubled, and Elena's eyes were red with weeping. I don't think a word was spoken. I gave her a last hug and she threw herself down on the stubble and sobbed, her whole body shaking.

I walked slowly back up the hill, and without a word Carluccio jerked the reins and the horse moved forwards. We slowly climbed to the top of the next hill, from where I was able to look back and see the part of Italy that had been my home for almost a year. Dear old Massa Fermana away on the hill, the white oxen toiling in the fields, the vineyards and the olive groves, the familiar homes of so many friends, and a girl still lying among the stubble with Angelina kneeling beside her. Then it all dissolved in a mist of tears, and my life as a Contadino had come to an end.

\* \* \*

Many years later Elena was to tell me that she had run back to their house and packed a few things in a kerchief with the intention of following me, but her father had restrained her. He kept her locked in her bedroom for three days, by which time there was no hope of her ever finding me. We are still very good friends and will always remain so.

# Chapter 20

# Repatriation

It was fortunate for us that there was no pitched battle in the area of Ascoli Piceno. The retreating Germans were content to fall back in this region through a series of running battles and harrying tactics. This meant that there was no evacuation of the civilian population. As there was now no static front, we had the opportunity to try to make contact with the Allied forces. There were some moments of anxiety, naturally, and we lost a great deal of sleep for a few days, but for the most part we were fortunate enough to get through without mishap.

We were lying in a ditch somewhere in the region of Fermo one bright morning when we heard the sound of engines approaching. They were scout cars of a design I had never previously seen, but I had a strong feeling that they were British. With nothing more than this to recommend them, I jumped from the ditch and ran into the road waving for them to stop. They did so, and we rushed towards them calling out that we were English. Then, to our horror, the man in the forward car called back to us in a foreign, guttural language, and we saw that his cap badge was in the form of an eagle. For an awful moment we thought he was German, and that after all this time we had given ourselves up again, just as we were on the point of regaining our own lines. But it was not the case. These men were Poles, part of the Polish Brigade fighting with the British Eighth Army. We had made it!

They directed us to a nearby Castello that was being used as forward headquarters by the advancing troops. We came to the gates of the Castello and walked down a sweeping drive to find a group of British officers in consultation over their maps. We quelled the urge to rush forward to greet them and instead stood politely some distance away and waited for them to finish their deliberations. After a few moments the senior officer looked across at us in a puzzled and rather hostile way. We must have looked rather strange: dirty and unshaven, walking barefoot, and dressed in rags. I in particular must have looked very inelegant, wearing a straw hat that had long since lost its brim.

'Who are those people?' he asked no one in particular. I replied proudly, 'Sergeant Ellis and Bombardier Day of the South Notts. Hussars, Royal Horse Artillery. Escaped prisoners reporting back for duty, Sir.'

He was astounded. Then there was a great deal of hand-shaking and we were given cigarettes as they questioned us about our experiences. It also occurred to them that we must have a very good knowledge of the locality, and as they were a reconnaissance unit they were not slow to ask for our assistance. We were quite willing to offer our help and within a short space of time we found ourselves riding as passengers on their vehicles. These were the same models as those we had seen earlier, and we now learned that they were Daimler Armoured Cars, a type that had only recently come into service.

It is one thing being in a reconnaissance unit when one is properly clothed and fed and probing forward in an armoured car. It is a totally different proposition to be sitting on the top of the vehicle dressed in rags and with no protection at all. In such a case, bursts of machine-gun fire and splinters from shells bursting nearby take on a far more sinister aspect. Our hosts, though keen to seek our advice about the local topography, showed themselves completely disinterested in our personal welfare. When we asked to be provided with boots and uniforms, they replied that they were unable to give us anything because we were not really members of their regiment. When the rations came up there was nothing at all for us. Again they explained that we were not on their ration strength. It was beyond belief. Here we were, back with our own countrymen, exposing ourselves to danger on their behalf – and they were refusing to clothe and feed us. In order to find food we had to revert to begging from the local people.

Needless to say, we did not allow this state of affairs to continue for very long. After a few days we just slipped away and left them to consume the rations that they were reluctant to share with us, and to find their own way through the foothills of Ascoli Piceno. I have not the slightest doubt that they were adequately equipped to do so.

It took some time for us to properly appreciate that we had at last found the security of our own lines. We had never really thought about what would happen to us once we had met up with our own troops again. I think we had assumed that we would be congratulated on our escape, and the fact that we had survived for almost a year in enemy-occupied territory. Certainly we had expected to be equipped with uniforms and boots, to be properly fed, and given transport to some base camp to await repatriation. All such assumptions proved to be completely spurious. We were in fact left entirely to our own devices. We received no help at all: no clothes, no boots and no food, apart from what we could scrounge from individual soldiers. As for transport, we had to rely on begging for lifts, jumping trains and sometimes just walking as we made our way towards Naples three hundred miles away.

This may be difficult for the reader to believe, but it is true; we received no help at all. However, we were well used to looking after ourselves, and we gloried in the knowledge that we were on the way home. Some miles south of Chieti a group of soldiers helped us on our way with a loaf of bread and a tin of corned beef, and we were also able to scrounge a blanket each from the same men.

That night we boarded a train of freight wagons travelling south and carrying a mixed load of goods and civilian refugees. These people had lost their homes in the fighting and, like us, had nothing but what they were able to carry with them. The wagon in which we travelled was full of these unfortunates, and amongst them was a young mother with a small child. These two in particular caught our attention because they had neither food nor luggage. They were a pitiful little pair, looking pinched and cold as they lay without protection on the steel plates of the wagon. Harry and I looked at each other for a moment, and then grinned as if to excuse a weakness. It was worth the sacrifice to see them snuggling under our newly acquired blankets and to watch as they hungrily consumed our bread and bully. It mattered little; we were well accustomed to hard beds and empty stomachs.

We spent about twenty-four hours on this train, but for most of the time it was stationary and we did not get very far. Among the refugees was a young Italian, who told us that he had served in North Africa in the Italian Air Force. He had been a bomber pilot, and in 1940 he had taken part in many air raids on Mersa Matruh. We remembered the dronc of those planes shining silver in the blue skies over Matruh. We recalled the screaming of the falling bombs and the way we had flattened ourselves on the ground or crouched in narrow slit trenches to escape their blast. It seemed strange that this pleasant young man should have been trying to kill us in this way. As the train rolled slowly southwards, we exchanged memories of those early days of war. I cannot remember our immediate destination, but before we parted company he gave me his address and told us to call and see him if ever we found ourselves in a place called Torre Annunziata.

One sight I shall never forget was the wasteland that had once been the marshalling yards of Foggia. This town had been pattern-bombed by the combined Allied air forces and it had been reduced to a black wilderness. Not a building remained, not a wall, not a tower, not a tree; everything had been flattened. It was a scene of complete devastation.

I cannot truly recollect how long that journey lasted, but it must have been something like a fortnight or three weeks before we arrived in the vicinity of Naples. In fact it was almost like a trick of fate that we should arrive one evening at the station in Capua to spend the night aboard the train in a cattle wagon. It was almost the identical spot where I had spent that miserable night packed suffocatingly in a similar truck full of starving prisoners. Now we had the whole wagon to ourselves.

I went in search of food and found a British sergeant. When I asked for something to eat, he replied that he did not have the authority to give us anything. He promised to ask his officer if we might be given some rations. Whilst waiting, we walked to the other side of the station where we found some American troops. When we explained that we were escaped prisoners, and that we were hungry, they gave us a royal welcome. Within minutes we were sitting down to a huge meal of bacon and beans, with plenty of bread and huge mugs of hot black coffee. They offered us chocolate and cigarettes in abundance, and more friendliness than we had found since leaving our Italian friends in Massa Fermana.

As we were preparing to sleep in our cattle truck, the British sergeant arrived to tell us that his officer had given him permission to supply us with a tin of bully beef and two packets of biscuits. Our response to this bountiful outpouring of generosity can probably best be imagined.

We arrived in Naples the following day and reported our presence to the railway transport officer (RTO), but he had no idea what to do with us. Eventually we were put on a truck and taken to an army camp. They did not want us either and so, after a long wait, we were directed to another unit, where the same thing happened. This went on for the whole day; from one camp to another we traversed the streets of Naples, but no one knew what to do with two escaped prisoners dressed in rags. It was not until nightfall that a general service unit of British Intelligence accepted us. They were occupying a large villa in the town of Torre del Greco. We were given a place to sleep in a tent that had been erected in the grounds.

During the next few days we were interrogated several times and when they were satisfied with our credentials, we were at last fitted out with uniforms and boots, and issued with some basic equipment. It was good to be back in uniform and to feel part of the British Army once more.

Eventually I received orders to prepare for embarkation. A convoy was about to leave for the United Kingdom and we were to travel on one of the transports. Harry and I arrived at the docks to find the usual chaos. As we did not belong to any particular unit, we were left sitting on our kit outside an office for the whole day. It was not until the boat was about to sail that we were taken aboard.

The following morning the convoy set sail. Our ship was *The Queen of Bermuda*, a huge vessel with three funnels. Before the war it had been a cruise liner and despite its conversion to a troopship, it still carried evidence of its former glory. With the sun-drenched white buildings of Naples falling astern, we passed the isle of Capri and out to sea. It was a wonderful sight to see all the ships of the convoy steaming into position, with the attendant destroyers taking up their protective stations. Then the coast of Italy disappeared over the skyline, and we were on the way home.

I had been abroad and in almost constant danger for five long years, and by some miracle I had survived to tell the tale. That part of my life was now over, but I was merely steaming towards further disasters, disappointments and sometimes delights and success. That is how it is on this terrifying, exhilarating, roller-coaster journey through life. But that is another story, best left for another time.

\* \* \*

On that first day of sailing the captain of the ship made an inspection of the vessel with the usual retinue in tow. When they opened the bulkhead door of our mess deck the whole party came to an abrupt halt. It was supposed to be an empty deck, but we were there, established near the door. The captain turned to one of his attendant officers to ask the reason for our presence, but I forestalled the answer. I explained who we were and why we were not attached to any particular unit. Then I sought his permission to remain, promising to keep everything in ship-shape order. He gave it a moment's thought, and then, to my complete surprise, he accepted my proposal. It was a stroke of good fortune for no one could gainsay the captain, and it meant we would be able to enjoy a quiet and peaceful voyage in the privacy of our own quarters.

We settled back in comfort. To avoid the U-boats, the convoy sailed far out into the Atlantic. Even so, we did come under attack and it was a frightening experience. I remember standing for hours at lifeboat stations on the deck listening to the awesome thump of exploding depth charges. We could see the escort vessels steaming at great speed around the convoy as they sought to destroy the hidden enemy. There were also columns of smoke rising from stricken vessels that had been hit by torpedoes. Sadly we watched as they fell astern and were left to the mercy of the unforgiving sea. We suffered no damage at all and there were no further attacks on our convoy.

Sailing down the Irish Sea in the driving rain, we made our way into Liverpool Docks, and tied up beside the Liver Building. I looked out across the blue-slated roofs, wet with rain, and the drab buildings and narrow streets of the dockland area, and I had a mental picture of the Bay of Naples and the isle of Capri. What a contrast!

This was the moment I had been awaiting for so many years, and now that it had arrived, I could not help but feel a momentary disillusionment. Then I dismissed such thoughts from my mind and concentrated on collecting my kitbag and making my way down the gangway. As I once more set foot on English soil, I realised that I was a very lucky man, and I silently thanked God for bringing me safely home.

Most of the men who had been aboard our ship went straight home on leave, but Harry and I were sent to a camp near Birkenhead, where we had to wait a further three frustrating days. During this time we visited a cinema, without bothering to find out was film was showing. It turned out to be a film called *The Desert Song*! We also discovered that there was a shortage of beer and the pubs only opened for short periods each day. We were refused admittance to one public house until we told the landlady that we had been abroad for five years and had only just returned. She looked at us for a moment before saying, 'I believe you,' and then she let us in and pulled us a pint each: our first pint of beer for several years.

At last we were given twenty-eight days' leave and we set off in high spirits. We arrived in Crewe station late at night and waited there until the early hours of the morning before catching another train to Derby. Here we caught the Nottingham train, which left about eight o'clock. It was carrying people who were on their way to work. Harry and I climbed into an empty compartment, and as the train pulled out we started to sing at the tops of our voices. When we stopped at the next station lots of people came from other parts of the train to see what all the noise was about.

Our happiness seemed to be contagious: the people filled our compartment to overflowing and joined in with our singing, and soon everybody on the train was taking part. All these strangers were suddenly happy and full of laughter and goodwill; it was amazing. When we arrived at the Midland station in Nottingham, they all waved to us and wished us well. I could not help glancing down the platform to see if my old friend was still there. The old clock was still ticking away serenely and his minute hand moved in friendly salute to welcome me back.

I shook Harry's hand before we parted and then I made my way to the city centre. There on Long Row, in its customary place, stood the number twenty bus for Arnold, just as if nothing had happened during my five-year absence. I climbed aboard and began the journey I had made so many times before: along Mansfield Road, through Carrington, and Sherwood, and Woodthorpe, to Daybrook Square, and then along Nottingham Road to Front Street. I alighted at the same old bus stop to walk the last few yards to home.

I went through the iron gate to the front door, and gave three rings on the bell – the signal that it was one of the family. The door opened and there stood my mother. As I walked into the hall, she threw her arms around me and I knew that I was safely home after an absence of five long years.